Fresh Eyes to READ the BIBLE

Book 3

Fresh Eyes to READ the BIBLE

Book 3

Good, Evil, and the Resurrection

Chung DuckYoung

HAGGAI BOOKS

Copyright © 2012 by Chung, DuckYoung. All rights reserved.

Unless otherwise indicated, Scripture is taken from the King James Version of the Bible (American).

Scripture marked NIV is taken from the Holy Bible, New International Version®, NIV® Copyright © 1973, 1978, 1984 by International Bible Society. Used by permission of Zondervan. All rights reserved.

Haggai Books

Printed in the United States of America

ISBN: 978-89-953885-6-3

To those who hope for a beautiful life on account of Jesus Christ

I find then a law, that, when I would do good, evil is present with me. [22]For I delight in the law of God after the inward man: [23]But I see another law in my members, warring against the law of my mind, and bringing me into captivity to the law of sin which is in my members. [24]O wretched man that I am! who shall deliver me from the body of this death? [25]I thank God through Jesus Christ our Lord. So then with the mind I myself serve the law of God; but with the flesh the law of sin.
_____ Romans 7:21-25

CONTENTS

PREFACE — 11

PART ONE
WHEN I WOULD DO GOOD

1 COMMUNICATION WITH GOD

Hearing God	20
Communication with God by Stages	28
The Tragedy of Eli's Family	39
Who Shall Persuade Ahab, that He May Fall?	50
It Repents Me That I Have Set Up Saul to Be King	61
The Widow Woman at Zarephath	72

2 OFFERINGS AND TITHES

What Are Offerings?	81
He Who Sows Sparingly Shall Reap Also Sparingly	84
The Tithe That Always Abides, Part I – Two Types of Tithe	90
The Tithe That Always Abides, Part II – Is the Tithe of the Law Taken Away?	103
Two Mites of A Certain Poor Widow	112
I Pray You, Give Whatever Comes to Your Hand, to David	122

PART TWO
EVIL IS PRESENT WITH ME

3   THE ORIGIN OF EVIL; DEVIL, SATAN AND DEMONS

The Origin of Evil	137
The Devil	147
The Devil Having Tempted Jesus I – Man shall Not Live By Bread Alone	155
The Devil Having Tempted Jesus II – Do Not Tempt God	170
Satan	180
Satan Mentioned in the Scripture	183
Demons	193
A Man With An Unclean Spirit, Legion, Part I – Come Out of the Man	200
A Man With An Unclean Spirit, Legion, Part II – Unclean Spirits Having Entered the Swine	209

4   ANTICHRIST AND EVIL SPIRITS

Antichrist	217
Evil Spirits	228

PART THREE
I Thank God Through Jesus Christ

5   Jesus As the Word

Jesus Is the Christ	239
Who Is My Mother?	244
An Ax That Was Borrowed	251
O You Dry Bones, Hear the Word!	258
The Dead Son of the Widow Revived	266

6   The Resurrection

What Is Resurrection?	279
I Am the Resurrection and the Life	282
Rapture	
– Those Who Are Asleep and Those Who Are Alive	292
The Rich Man and Lazarus, Part I	
– Resurrection of the Just and Unjust	309
The Rich Man and Lazarus, Part II	
– Crafty Old Self	328
Sadducees Say, No Resurrection!	335

Finishing the Book…   348

Preface

Many people say they believe in Jesus, but very few actually believe in Him in the real sense. When we believe in Jesus and are then glorified, we will be one with God Almighty. However, in spite of this precious promise that is in Jesus, no power and glory of God comes out of us. On the contrary, we disgrace the name of Almighty God and Jesus, His Son, by behavior that is no different than that of nonbelievers.

God entrusts the word of truth to us, but we fail to appropriate the power and glory given in the Word and preach it to other people. All these things happen because we neither understand who Jesus is nor correctly believe in Him. You may think that you are sincere Christians and that you know Him very well. If so, where are the power, glory, life, and love He has given you? Our Jesus is alive, but in our thoughts only. He is dead in our actual lives. All Christian tragedies begin from here.

Ever since we believed in Jesus, God has blessed us so much and we are happy to be Christians. But our belief has reached a limit that traditional church teaching cannot move us beyond. Over a long period of time, in churches all over the world, Christians have tried every possible endeavor such as prayer, fasting, giving alms, soul healing, Bible study, charismatic movements, spiritual gifts, church growth, repentance, discipleship, and so on.

However, we achieve no satisfaction, no peace in faith. What is even more depressing, we have no other new initiatives to try since we have tried everything that we know. Indeed, it will only be a waste of time if we try to correct our current stagnated faith by adopting new initiatives.

Why? Because, fundamentally, it is not a problem that can be solved by man-initiated programs and efforts. Up until now, we have believed in a "legalistic Jesus," thinking him to be the real, living, Jesus. The legalistic Jesus is the wrong one, created by us according to our superficial understanding of Scripture. This created concept of Jesus is not alive in our real lives, but is confined and we think of him only as a dead person who once lived long ago and who will come in the future on cloud. All our current problems are caused by this legalistic Jesus.

Primarily, Scripture, if we read it correctly, introduces us to Jesus, a man whom we should meet for salvation. We may think we meet Him because we are reading and studying Scripture and go to church. But the real Jesus is *not* mere understanding or knowledge about Him in our thoughts; He is "a man" whom we should meet.

Jesus will come to us as "a man who has Christ in him," such as Peter, Paul, and John, the apostles. He will save us with the power of Christ in him. Meeting a man who has Christ in him is the way we meet Jesus to be saved in this age.

And if we meet "a man Jesus," all of our current problems will be resolved. We will be saved, as well as the church, and everyone who meets and follows Him.

Of course, God allows, so far, the blessings and prosperity of this world even through the legalistic Jesus. However, God would not give us such *milk* all the time, which is for an infant, but wishes now to give *solid food*, which is for the mature. The time past may suffice us to search for the worldly blessings, *milk*, in Jesus' name. Now we should look for the salvation of our spirits, *solid food*, in our lifetime (I Corinthians 3:1-2).

This book testifies *freshly* about Jesus through reading Scripture correctly. We will speak of the following:

In Part One, "Communication with God" and "Offerings and Tithes" are explained. We cannot believe and understand Jesus correctly because we have had no spiritual communication with God. You will learn through Part One what this spiritual communication is and what are true offerings and tithes offered to God.

In Part Two, the "Origin of Evil: the Devil, Satan, and Demons," "Evil Spirits" are explained. They are the ones that interrupt communication between God and us and make us think the living Jesus is dead; a Jesus who remains in our thoughts only. Evil's true colors have been hidden throughout Christian history, but now their shocking natures will be disclosed.

In Part Three, "Jesus as the Word" and "Resurrection" are touched on. Jesus will lead us (who are taken by the devil) to resurrection and we will be freed and able to communicate perfectly with God.

The above arrangement has followed the thrust of some last verses of Romans 7 and the first two verses of Romans 8; that is, paraphrased, when I want to do good, evil is always present with me in my heart. I am a wretched man because I cannot destroy this evil. But, I can defeat the evil through Jesus, reach the world of resurrection, become one with God, and do good.

Now, we should hear humbly what the Scripture, the testifier of Jesus Christ, the Savior, really speaks about, rather than trying to interpret it according to the doctrines and the traditions of men.

I hope through this book you would meet Jesus as a living, breathing man and begin to believe in Him in the real sense, and live the glorious life of Jesus for the rest of your days.

Chung DuckYoung
November 2012

PART ONE
When I Would Do Good

As Paul the apostle wanted to do good, so we all hope to live a good life. In fact, we believe in Jesus so as to finally lead a good life. Yes, we can live a good life by believing in Jesus. However, while sincerely hoping for a good life and making every effort over a long time, we cannot live as such.

Why do we fail? Because we believed in Him but miss something: Spiritual communication with God. We fail since we attempt to do good without communing with God. God is *good* itself. When we communicate with Him, we do good in this world as it originates from Him. Yes, we can do good only when we receive it. However, we reverse the concept: We think we would be received into the good kingdom of God when we do good in this world by ourselves. However, nothing we do of our own accord in this world is acceptable—good—to God.

Consequently, if we desire to do good in believing Jesus, we must communicate with God to know His good and do the same. This way then, we can live a good life in this world.

In Part One, I will touch on "Communication with God," which is essential to do good, and the "Offerings and Tithes" we offer to Him according to the communication.

1. Communication with God
2. Offerings and Tithes

1

COMMUNICATION WITH GOD

The body and its members communicate with each other organically. Each member receives the intention of the body and works according to it. This communication system of the body and its members represents the perfect relationship of oneness of life.

Originally, we were one with God, the *life* and *good* itself, and we were His body members in Eden. However, we became depraved and were separated from God. Such separation is obvious when we realize that we had no communication with Him at all while living in this world. Being separated from *life*, quite naturally, we are now dying little by little every moment.

As long as we are separate from Him, we can never glorify Him ever, even if we trust in Jesus, do good works, build churches, or preach the gospel. We will be able to do these good things in His glory only after we have restored communication with Him and have become one with Him. Salvation through Jesus means that we who were separated from God become one with Him by virtue of Jesus and, consequently, restored to life with and through God.

Many people try to define what this life is and what this life is for, but this life is only given to us as a process to become one with God again through Jesus. And when we become one with God, we will then have perfect communication with Him, as in the case of the body and its members. We can live the rest of our lives doing *good* with the life of God, which is eternal. The perfect communication with God is the only way that we can glorify Him.

Hearing God

As I have already explained, if we wish to do good and hope for eternal life, we ought to communicate with God, the *good* itself, which is spiritual.

Jesus is the Son of *God*, and at the same time He is son of *man*. This means that Jesus has man's nature and God's too. We might expect to know Him as man because we are men also. However, we cannot expect Him as God because we do not know God. If we claim that we believe in Jesus, we should have communication with God to believe Jesus correctly.

Let us not be confused by the notion that we communicate with God because we keep the commandments of God in the Scripture. But that is not the living communication that God wants. In fact, to keep the commandments that are stipulated in Scripture, you do not need to hear the voice of the living God who is present, but you just obey the commands. In this case, the commandments will serve something like God's Last Will and Testament to you. In this case, God who appears to you as the commandments on the stone tablets is not living, but dead. The Scripture says those who serve that God are under the law. We, as the believers, do not wish to be like those who are under the law, so we should communicate with the living God.

God Who Says to All of Us

The important starting point for communicating with God is to hear what He says. I will now focus on this.

First, before you hope to hear His voice, please know that He already speaks to you. He speaks to everyone. But only a few will hear. For example, God brought Abram forth out of Ur of the Chaldees, the city of idolatry. He did not call Abram only. He called every person in there, but only Abram was ready to hear and respond to Him. Abram was chosen amongst all the men of Ur.

Therefore, it is improper to say that the chosen, or special people, such as prophets, servants of God, or charismatic persons, are the only ones blessed to hear Him. He has already been speaking to you! Nevertheless, you cannot hear Him because you do not pay attention.

Hearing His voice is a matter of whether you want to hear His voice or not. If you desire to listen to Him, you can hear a very small voice; and if you do not wish to listen, you will hear nothing at all even if he speaks in a very loud voice. Those who hear and obey Him are "Abrahams," prophets and friends of God in these days.

If you wish to hear and obey God, it means that you want to leave the world of death and join the world of life in God. It is natural for Him to be much pleased with such persons who have their mind on eternal life. They will hear Him.

"Hearing God" is the first step to believe correctly in Jesus.

What is Communication?

Communication with God refers to the communication between God and *me*, not others. Therefore, we should not only understand what communication should be but also have actual communication with Him.

To communicate, we should remember two steps: The first step is to *understand* His will, and the second step is to *execute* His will.

We will first *understand* His will through hearing His voice in our mind through the voice of preachers, ordinary people, or adversaries, as the case may be; and in dreams, visions, or understanding circumstances, and so on. Then, we are to *execute* His will without changing it. Only when we complete these two steps have we communicated correctly with God. Therefore, if a man misunderstands His will, or if he has understood it correctly but has failed to execute it for any reason whatever, in both cases the communication with Him failed.

We aim at perfect communication with God in life and that will be accomplished through Jesus when we become one with God. Under this oneness, we can communicate with Him without any misunderstanding and disobedience. Perfect communication with Him is the synonym of salvation, being born again and going into the kingdom of God.

This is not something we can finish in a single stroke by making up our mind, as it is a life-growing process. Perfect communication will be finally achieved once we have passed through the cross being united with Jesus. It took three and a half years for the disciples. If you believe in Jesus correctly, you will come to communicate with God; and furthermore, communicate perfectly.

How to Hear God's Message

I will now explain the first step of how to hear God. You do not need to sit up all night praying hard in the prayer house or have a fasting timetable in order to hear His voice. You are not required to hope for special Spiritual gifts to hear, either. You do need to have a sincere heart to listen for His voice. Then, you will hear.

If you are expecting some advance information about which stock will rise suddenly in the market tomorrow or to learn a secret method of promotion to a higher rank through hearing His voice, you are mistaken. You need to seek His voice for the purpose of knowing and loving God Himself, and living the rest of life as a born-again man.

📁 Pizza or Pasta?

If you want to hear Him, you start by asking Him to speak to you. He answers all our prayers because He really wants to be sought, like a father wants to be sought by his son. If you want Him to reply to you, you should ask Him in all sincerity and with a humble heart. If you ask carelessly or lightheartedly, it shows that you do not revere or respect Him, and you will receive no response.

The steps for hearing Him can be summarized below.

Step 1: "Clear your mind and start with a small issue."

It is simpler to hear God's voice than you may think. With small issues, clear your mind, pray to Him, and hear His voice that comes into your heart.

Regarding the small issues, for example, you can pray about what food to eat at the restaurant, either a pizza or pasta, or you can pray about direction while driving down the road, whether you should go this way or that way to avoid a traffic jam.

Why should you pray with small things, then? It is because you are unable to follow the answer if it is a very big issue. For example, if you pray concerning the purchase of a house which costs several tens of thousands of dollars, you may not be able to decide it only with a small voice coming into your heart. However, since you will not suffer a great loss if you go wrong with the little thing, you can obey and do it in either way.

It is wrong if you think He will not answer small matters. God never ignores the sincere prayer of His children, whether it is big or small. He only wants you to speak to Him.

Clearing your mind means that you must not have any prejudice or preference when you ask for either *this* or *that*. If you get *this* as answer, then you leave *that* without regret, and vice versa. During the earlier days when I met the Lord, I used to pray what I should order in the restaurant, for example: pizza or pasta. It would be more appropriate to say that I instantly asked Him within myself, instead of through an elaborate formal prayer. When He answered me, I would surrender the other one without hesitation and would obey Him. This is the clearing of mind. Also, I had no difficulty in following through with His answer because it was a small issue to choose food.

If you pray to God with a full of desire for pasta, you will receive pasta as an answer to your prayer in most cases, which will be an example of praying without clearing your mind in advance. In such cases, you had better order pasta without asking Him.

In conclusion: clear your mind, then pray and hope for a reply from Him.

Step 2: "Pray when the time draws near."
Pray just before you start to do something if you want to hear a message from Him. When you prayed in advance but the situation changed, the previous answer you received could be unavailable. For instance, you should pray for ordering piazza or pasta not while you are in the office but when you are at a restaurant table. The response of pasta that you had in the office will be ineffective if the restaurant does not serve it or it is closed on that day.

So pray at the site.

Step 3: "Do with faith."
God speaks in your spirit. His voice comes to you through your spirit as an intuition. The intuition has the characteristic of sensing something without delay before you begin reasoning or analyzing. As soon as you ask Him, He answers you as if the answer was already ready there. However, you may feel it is very hard to sense His voice in the early stages, but when you pray for "pizza or pasta?" you will feel sure in your mind that one of them is superior to the other. Choose it. The voice of God is not like the sound we can hear through our ears. It comes as we feel it.

However, when we try to decide one from the other, a doubt will follow immediately. "Isn't this coming from my own thoughts? It can't originate from God." But, once you have cleared your mind in advance and prayed sincerely to receive an answer, it is given by Him. His answer will come to you always with vague and doubtful feelings. You must not give up at this point.

Once you have reached the conclusion that what you have received is His answer, proceed to follow Him. The doubt that you might have a wrong answer will follow, but you should ignore it and carry on. Even if you received the answer incorrectly, there will be no problem because He will turn it into good because you prayed to Him with all your heart.

I have explained about praying for small issues to hear God. If you want to try, you may wish to pray when you decide whether to refer to either NIV or KJV, or whether to fork right or left at the crossroad where you do not know the direction. Or you can pray that you will not wait for a taxi or a bus long or you will find one hidden parking space at the fully-occupied parking lot.

You may not see the necessity of prayer for such issues which are unimportant. However, this prayer will make it possible for you to open your heart to hear God and gain spiritual sense. He answers these little things as well as significant things in the same way. You will be able to know how to receive answers about important matters through the prayer for insignificant things. And you will gradually be able to pray to Him and rely on Him about matters, big and small. This is the life of those who depend on Him and acknowledge Him in all their ways.

When you have grown spiritually, furthermore, you do not need to try to hear Him in this way. He will lead you to a higher level of communication.

📁 Testimony of Prayer

One church member used to take a bus from office to home. The buses on this route came at thirty minute intervals. After work, if he missed the bus in sight, he had to wait thirty minutes. He always hoped to catch the bus as soon as he arrived at the bus stop in order to get home as soon as possible.

Having been advised he should pray for the little things so that he could develop communication with God, he prayed within himself each time as he waited for the bus.

"Lord, please send the bus quickly."

When he finished praying, the bus always came earlier than he expected, which he thought was marvelous. Each day he prayed, the bus came there within ten minutes. He enjoyed the happiness of praying to God in this way.

One day, however, he prayed that the bus would come early while approaching the bus stop after work, but found there that the bus had just left the bus stop.

"Oh no, I prayed, but it was useless. I have to stand here and wait for the next thirty minutes. The Lord did not hear my prayer."

Disappointed, he was about to turn around, but he raised his head and saw that the next bus was coming near. He was so happy that he could get home that day without waiting long.

When I heard his testimony, I felt that his prayer to Him pleased Him very much. In fun, He gladly allowed the bus to leave the bus stop just before he arrived there, and He also sent him the next bus when he was discouraged. Even though he could not feel the depth of God's love at that time, God was pleased with him who is eager to hear Him that much.

Yes. God hears every prayer and answers it. He is well pleased with us who seek Him in this way. God has a personality. Therefore, during communication with Him, we meet a person. Please meet the God who tells a joke, scorns, teases, and sometimes rebukes you severely. Above all these, He is love itself who loves you without end.

I am not simply saying that it will be good to rely on God for everything, but I am saying this because it is the essential first step to meet our God of salvation. It is not an empty trial, but the starting point of your salvation, which will eventually be everything for you. If you want to know more about the way to hear what God says, please find some books in the bookstores with themes of "How to hear Him" or "The presence of God." They will be of great help.

Epilogue

We believe in Jesus for the purpose of knowing God. And knowing God is eternal life. Nobody can know God without communicating with Him no matter how hard he may study the Bible and live a sincere Christian life. Until now, we have believed without hearing God's voice and communicating with Him. Have we known the truth and enjoyed the satisfaction and peace that He gives us in our heart? I do not think so. And that is the result of our believing the legalistic Jesus so far.

Unfortunately, we cannot hear and know God in any way by ourselves. Therefore, we need to meet Jesus as a man who will show us the way to communicate with God, and take us to Him.

Now, have hope to hear His voice and open your heart to Him. He responds to you who seek Him and will not disappoint you in this respect. Hearing His voice is the beginning of the perfect communication to come, which is to be one with Him.

In the next chapter, I will explain the process of perfect communication with Him. It matches the process in which we are saved and born again in Jesus.

Communication with God by Stages

I will now explain the process of perfecting our communication with God. During this process God will appear to us in three different aspects. In this respect, we call him the triune God.

Triune God

God is called the God of the Trinity in theology, the union of Father, Son, and Holy Spirit as three persons in one Godhead. Yes, the Scripture speaks of the triune God, such as, "Baptize in the name of the Father, and of the Son, and of the Holy Spirit" (Matthew 28:19), and "I am the God of Abraham, and the God of Isaac, and the God of Jacob" (Matthew 22:32).

One God; but according to the growth stage we are in, God will appear progressively to us first as *God*, then *Jesus*, and finally as the *Holy Spirit*.

God is the God who appears to those who have sinned, are spiritually separated from Him, and are under the law; *Jesus* is the God who appears as "a man" to those who have truly repented and He forgives them their sins through the cross; and the *Holy Spirit* is the God who appears to those who have had their old self destroyed on the cross and are thus born again.

To understand this triune God, we should consider the relationship with God and *us* together and bilaterally, by which God makes *us* grow and *we* are grown by Him.

For example, a father will treat his son differently to fit his growth level; i.e., Baby–Youngster–Adult. On the other hand, to the son himself, the father will look differently depending on what level of growth he is in, as the father of Baby, and the father of Youngster, and the father of Adult respectively; but he is meeting one same father.

And if a son undergoes these three stages led by the father, at the stage of the father of Adult, he will become an Adult who knows the heart of his father.

Likewise, led by God, if we go through three growing stages of God–Jesus–Holy Spirit, at the stage of Holy Spirit we will be grown up, born again and saved, having the perfect communication with God. Therefore, the triune God implies the God who saves us through the sacrifice of Jesus.

At each stage of our seeing the triune God, we will have corresponding communication with God. We will have communication of the Stage of God, the Stage of Jesus, and the Stage of the Holy Spirit. The faith of a person can be identified according to his Stage of communication with God. And the communication that we will have in the Stage of the Holy Spirit is the perfect one.

We will now discuss communication with God by each stage.

Stage of God

Everybody will perceive God as *God* first. This God who abides in the highest heaven created heaven, earth, and everything on earth, and controls life and death and misery and prosperity of people and all things in the universe.

In this stage our communication with God is, in fact, nil. Even believers mostly have no communication with God. We only hear and learn about Him through the Bible, pastors' sermons, prophesy through brothers or sisters with spiritual gifts, visions and dreams, or books that introduce knowledge about God. Quite frankly, we are not sure whether God really lives or whether the spiritual world really exists. We are dead to God at this stage, so cannot have communication with Him.

📂 Communication of Prophets

Nevertheless, some of us hear Him directly and communicate with Him through dreams, visions, or spiritual gifts. Naturally, their confidence and faith in Him is extraordinary. Their neighbors envy them their strong faith, and pray and fast in order to have similar spiritual gifts and communication with God.

However, although they hear His voice and see visions directly, they still stay in the "Stage of God," not in the "Stage of Jesus/Holy Spirit." This will be clear if you read the following verse in Numbers 12.

Moses has married an Ethiopian woman, and Miriam and Aaron who were leaders of the Israelites together with him, spoke against him: "Has the Lord indeed spoken only by Moses? Has He not spoken also by us?" and "How can the leader offend the law and marry a Gentile wife? I don't think he is decent."

We would probably be of the same opinion as them. Yes, Moses was surely wrong. However, strangely enough, God showed unhappiness towards Miriam and she became leprous.

In this regard, God says in Numbers 12:6-8, "Hear now my words: If there be a prophet among you, I the LORD will make myself known to him in a vision, and will speak to him in a dream. My servant Moses is not so, who is faithful in all my house. With him will I speak mouth to mouth, even apparently, and not in dark speeches; and the similitude of the LORD shall he behold: why then were you not afraid to speak against my servant Moses?"

God speaks about how He communicates with a prophet and how He does with Moses. He says He communicates with the prophet in visions or dreams, but He does with Moses mouth to mouth, which is often translated "face to face," and apparently and he will see the form of the LORD. His communication with the prophet corresponds to the "Stage of God," and that with Moses corresponds to the "Stage of the Holy Spirit" following the "Stage of Jesus."

Moses, in this case, is the symbol of the one who has been perfectly healed by Jesus on the cross and has received the Holy Spirit to dwell within him. Thus he can communicate with God perfectly.

This is mouth-to-mouth communication which is referred to by God in the passage. He is born again in the image of God and has communication in the stage of the Holy Spirit.

📂 Lack Point of Prophetic Communication

If we can hear Him, or receive revelation through visions or dreams like the prophets, we cannot fully understand the heart of God because we have not yet spiritually grown to know God's intention and heart. I am not saying that we shouldn't trust that sound because we can't know God's intentions, but there is another deeper stage for us to consider and proceed to in receiving God's word and visions. Just think about the case of Miriam and Aaron above. They were receiving God's voice all right, but that turned out not to be the final and perfect stage in terms of communication with God.

Communication at Miriam's level can be likened to the case in which a blind man hears what God says, he moves to the left if he hears God say "Left!" and he moves to the right if he hears "Right!" mechanically without knowing why God says "Left" or "Right." He would be regarded as being far better off than the other blind men who cannot hear God at all; nevertheless he is still blind.

Moses is the symbol of man who has his eyes opened by Jesus, and Miriam is a symbol of one who hears God while being blind, without yet having her eyes opened by Jesus. God wants us to have open eyes; He does not want us to work with blind eyes.

Now you will know why God is pleased with Moses in spite of his unlawful marriage and is displeased with the lawful-looking accusation of Miriam. In fact, Miriam is accusing God based on her self-righteousness, which is the act of the spiritual leper, the sinner.

I say that our current faith level of the Christianity does not go beyond that of Miriam's, which is a faith based on what is legalistic — the maximum point the law can bring us. At this point, as the leaders and scholars of the Christianity do not know and fail to provide us with what's next, many believers are hungry for the true Word and stagger from here to there. Many of them try to find the teachings from other religions, forsaking the Scripture.

All of these unfortunate problems arise because we have not yet met Jesus, the real One, in Scripture. We should meet this Jesus, who will be tested in the next section, "Stage of Jesus."

In summary, communication with God when we are in the Stage of God" is blocked; it is indirect, fragmentary, temporary, and limited. Most of all, all these communications are done in the sinful state, so such communications have innate flaws which we cannot handle at all. Those who have communication in this stage are under the law, and are dead. We need Jesus to make us alive.

Stage of Jesus

Those who communicate at the Stage of God will feel empty because they have not yet become one with Him, the Truth.

While living such an empty life for a long time, they will become desolate and used up. In this book, I will often describe this situation as the "experience of the prodigal son" in Luke 15, whereas the Scripture says "When he came to his senses, he said, 'How many of my father's hired men have food to spare, and here I am starving to death! I will set out and go back to my father and say to him: Father, I have sinned against heaven and against you. I am no longer worthy to be called your son; make me like one of your hired men'" (Luke 15:17-19 NIV). And I will say such experience as the "true repentance."

If you eagerly pray to God under this situation, God will send you Jesus, the Savior. When you meet Him, you meet God as *Jesus*. From this time on, you begin communication with God in the Stage of Jesus. When you are in this stage, you will realize that you are meeting Jesus as "a man." Jesus is "a man who has Christ in him for us to meet." I will explain about this Jesus now.

📂 Jesus, A Man to Meet

In order for Jesus to save us He must come as a man to meet, not as the understanding of the Scriptures, not as the Scripture itself, not as visions, thoughts; not as sermons or any forms other than human being. Now, if we believe in Him without meeting Him as a man, we are not on the correct course of salvation, but are under the law.

Read the following passage from John.

> Search the scriptures; for in them you think you have eternal life: and they are they which testify of me. ^{40}And you will not come to me, that you might have life. _____ John 5:39-40

The Jews diligently studied the Scriptures to possess eternal life. However, Jesus said to them, standing in front of them, "These are the Scriptures that testify about me."

Likewise, we also diligently study the Bible, for in it we think we will have eternal life and enter the Kingdom of Heaven. We learn by heart the important verses, have QT, study the Bible, see the visions, and feel the Lord stir us up in our heart sometimes. Excellent.

However, eternal life will not pop up from the Scripture, but it will give us a man to meet, one who is testified to in the Scriptures. Expect to meet Jesus if you want eternal life. As food is to eat, not to study, Jesus is a man to meet, not to study.

Why Should We Meet Jesus As A Man?

In order to save us, Jesus should come to us as a man in the flesh. It is because Jesus needs to lead sinful men to the cross to destroy their old self, and have them resurrected thereafter. If He does not come to us as a man, we, the sinners, will attempt to do all things which relate to salvation by ourselves. That is, being born sin-possessed, we will read and interpret the Bible, pray, worship, love, donate, go to church and believe in Jesus for salvation. All these works will be just sinful, because they are done by the sinners.

Think about the Jews. They were given the book of salvation, all Scripture, but none of them were saved until a man, Jesus in the flesh, came to them. When the sin-possessed Jews read the Scriptures, they interpret it according to their spirit seized by sin. And sin, their lord, will not ever destroy sons of sin. It is quite natural for them to interpret and understand all the Scriptures and any and all types of input from God so their sin needs to survive in this world. Thus, sin in them remains safe all the time. It is no wonder that they are not saved in spite of the word of salvation given to them.

Therefore, each of us should meet a man Jesus, who is other than sinful *me*. However, the believers do not want to meet Jesus because we misunderstand the legalistic Jesus that we currently have as the real Jesus. But we will realize later that the legalistic Jesus is an idol created by thoughts of the sin-possessed.

📂 The Christ Gene

You may wonder how we can meet Jesus as a man while we are living in a different time period. We can meet Him through a man who has Christ in him by being born again. As for the relationship of *Jesus* and *Christ*, you may wish to refer to Part Three of this book, the section titled "Jesus is the Christ."

Paul says in Galatians 2:20, "I am crucified with Christ: nevertheless I live; yet not I, but Christ lives in me: and the life which I now live in the flesh I live by the faith of the Son of God, who loved me, and gave himself for me."

Paul is a man who has Christ in him. If you meet Paul in person, you are meeting Jesus and will be saved by the Christ who abides in Paul. A man is a vessel in which to carry Christ, so he can be any ordinary man. He could be Jesus, Paul, Peter, John, Apollos or Barnabas of the Scripture and any other human, including you, who are correctly born again, around us.

The Disciples who have Christ in them are the second generation of Jesus, and the Christ, the gene, will be inherited in us, the believers, generation to generation.

Read the following passage from Romans.

> But you are not in the flesh, but in the Spirit, if so be that the Spirit of God dwell in you. Now if any man have not the Spirit of Christ, he is none of his. ───── Romans 8:9

To inherit the Christ gene, we need to meet Jesus Christ first. In the Old Testament age before Jesus came, there were the *figures of*

Jesus, like Samuel, Elijah and so forth, and in Jesus' age, He was *Jesus*, and after Jesus' ascension, there were *many Jesuses*, those who have Christ in them. We can meet "a Jesus" in our days and come to have Christ in us. Thus, we are saved. As for us, we will meet Jesus by meeting "a Jesus."

Jesus, therefore, is not only He who remained on earth for thirty-three years two millennia ago, but also, he is a man who has Christ in him at the present time. It is prudent for us to have the definition of Jesus as "a man who has Christ in him" particularly with reference to our real salvation.

Let me sum up what was explained about Jesus so far: Jesus is "a man who has Christ in him for us to meet." In short, I will use the term "a man Jesus" or "Jesus, a man to meet" in this book to express such Jesus. When I say "meet Jesus," "follow Jesus," "obey Jesus," "united with Jesus" etc., with reference to our real salvation, I mean especially Jesus whom we need to meet in person.

Then you might say, "How am I going to know whether "Jesus, a man to meet" is coming from God or on his own?" We need to search the Scriptures and see whether they testify to him. In fact, we, the sinners, basically, will have no eyes to search the spiritual Scripture. Therefore, when we meet Jesus, He will teach us how to read the Scripture freshly and correctly. And He himself will be testified to in it.

📂 What Jesus Will Do to You

When you meet Jesus, you begin to communicate in the Stage of Jesus. He will lead you to perfect communication, the Stage of the Holy Spirit.

We cannot hear God because we are spiritually deaf, and Jesus will make us hear. Read Mark 7:37, "And were beyond measure astonished, saying, He has done all things well: he makes both the deaf to hear, and the dumb to speak."

He, as the Savior, will only heal us in order to hear, because when we can hear God perfectly at the Stage of the Holy Spirit, we will be saved and born again.

We normally expect that Jesus will comfort us when we come to church because we have spent a hard time in this world. Yes, we will be comforted at the initial stage, but sooner or later, He will start to heal our sins to give us the ultimate comfort, the Holy Spirit. And the healing process is to take us to the cross to destroy our old self who is sin-possessed, who prevents our perfect communication with God.

During his process, you will experience tough spiritual wars. This is what is described in Revelation as "judgments" and the thing that will happen before the end times as described in Matthew 24, and elsewhere in Scripture.

When you have communication in the Stage of Jesus, you will be led to a new world that you have never experienced before. Therefore, you cannot walk this way if you do not completely obey Jesus in all things. Many people wish to follow this path but they often assert their own self-righteousness and unwittingly disobey Jesus and fall apart. And many people withstand Jesus because they are deceived by their own avarice or self-pity. All of these things happen because they are deceived by their old self who does not wish to die on the cross by following Jesus.

However, you cannot have new life if you operate in agreement with your old self. You must remember that you believe in Jesus so that you may receive new life, and the new life only comes after your old self is crucified by following Jesus. No death, no new life! Jesus will have this thing fulfilled in you, finally, on the cross. In this way, you can have your spiritual eyes opened and now you are different from the you who, before, was under the law, blind.

In summary, through communication in the Stage of Jesus, we are healed so that we may not distort the will of God, but obey Him and do His will. In fact, all the Scripture testifies to these works of Jesus. It took three and a half years in the case of the Disciples.

When we are healed finally on the cross while in communication with Jesus, we will be resurrected and will have communication in the stage of the Holy Spirit.

Stage of Holy Spirit

Those who are healed by Jesus will receive the Holy Spirit in them. Thus, they become one with God and will communicate perfectly with God. This is communication in the Stage of the Holy Spirit.

Receiving the Holy Spirit through the healing of Jesus is totally different from receiving the spiritual gifts whereby a person prophesies, sees visions, shows healing power, and performs other spiritual acts through the help of the Holy Spirit. The latter is prophet-level communication, and the former is Moses-level, as explained in the earlier section.

The Stage of the Holy Spirit represents perfect communion between God and man. The man who has such communication has Christ in him and is born again as His son. So, the perfect communication means the relationship that exists between a father and son who have the same life.

The next passage, generally quoted as a benediction, reveals the process of perfect communication.

Read the following passage from 2 Corinthians.

> The grace of the Lord Jesus Christ, and the love of God, and the communion of the Holy Spirit, be with you all. Amen.
> _____ 2 Corinthians 13:14

Salvation is planned by God, who is love, even before we came into this world. When we became desolate after having lived a life without God in this world, we meet Jesus Christ and receive His grace. Receiving His grace refers to the process of the forgiveness of sin, our receiving the love of God and becoming one with God by His healing us. This healing period matches the communication of the Stage of Jesus. As a result of the Stage of Jesus, we can receive the Holy Spirit in us, so we have communion (fellowship, communication; *koinonia* in Greek) with Him.

Therefore, communion in the above verse does not merely mean linguistic communication but it refers to oneness. We can find the same term, *koinonia*, in the book of First John.

> That which we have seen and heard declare we to you, that you also may have fellowship with us: and truly our fellowship is with the Father, and with his Son Jesus Christ. _____ 1 John 1:3

Here, "fellowship" is translated from the Greek *koinonia*. When the Holy Spirit comes on us, we will be one with God and Jesus Christ, and have *fellowship* with Him. We will also be like-minded with such people as John, Peter, and Paul, who have become one with God through the process.

We try to hear God's voice and obey it for the purpose of finally fulfilling communication in the Stage of the Holy Spirit through Jesus. This is what it means to have truth and life; it is salvation and being born again.

In the next chapters, I will explain communication with God through the Scripture. I will explain the case of four characters, that is, Eli the priest, Ahab the king, Saul the king, and the widow woman in Zarephath, progressively in terms of their faith.

Tragedy of the Eli Family

1 Samuel 2:22-26
Now Eli was very old, and heard all that his sons did to all Israel; and how they lay with the women that assembled at the door of the tabernacle of the congregation. ²³And he said to them, Why do you such things? for I hear of your evil dealings by all this people. ²⁴No, my sons; for it is no good report that I hear: you make the LORD's people to transgress. ²⁵If one man sin against another, the judge shall judge him: but if a man sin against the LORD, who shall entreat for him? Notwithstanding they listened not to the voice of their father, because the LORD would slay them. ²⁶And the child Samuel grew on, and was in favor both with the LORD, and also with men.

Eli the priest believed in God, but he had no communication with Him and could not follow His will, and he naturally fell.

The background to this story is that Hannah, having no children, prayed to God with her whole heart and she was finally in great favor with Him and gave birth to Samuel. She lent him to the Lord so that he lived and learned in the house of the Lord where Eli the priest lived.

Eli had two sons, and they behaved badly. They lay with the women who assembled at the door of the tabernacle of the congregation. Eli called his sons and scolded their evil dealings but they did not hearken to their father's voice.

As a result of this behavior, a man of God prophesied that a tragic curse would come on the family of Eli. He said Eli's two sons would die before Eli died, and that there would not be an old man in his house because all the people of his house would die in the flower of their youth (1Samuel 2:31-34). After this prophecy, the sons were slain in one day by the Philistines in battle, and upon hearing this message, Eli fell over backwards, his neck broke, and he died (1Samuel 4:17-18).

When we read of this kind of tragedy, we tend to make resolutions like, "I will raise my kids and educate them properly so that I do not suffer the tragic end that Eli did." If we have reached this conclusion, we will also unavoidably judge Eli's indecision and believe that he had not raised them well by ignoring their immoral conduct. But was this really a problem of his children's up-bringing? No, indecision and hesitancy may be one of his characteristics, but it would not cause him to be destroyed before God. Eli's problem is spiritual.

Then, what was his spiritual problem? Eli had no idea of God's heart and he believed in God without communicating with Him.

How do we prove this? Let's get started.

He Loved His Sons More Than God

As I explained, Eli also wanted his kids to walk with God. When they fell into error, he did not let them do as they liked, but he rebuked them. He tried to correct them, because he feared God and knew He was austere. We learn this from the following passage:

"If you sin against another man, I will entreat God for you, but if you sin against Him, who shall I beg for you? Don't do it (v. 25)."

In addition, he mentioned God when rebuking his sons, which implies that he prayed to Him and fasted about the problems he was having with them.

In this way Eli's attitude reveals ours. We believe in Jesus and leave our children in the care of the Lord so that they may succeed in life. We think it will then be a good example to unbelievers and their lives will glorify God. We keep on giving offerings to Him for our children even if we are badly off, and we rebuke them if they miss the Sunday service. We believers are Eli.

📁 God Being Dismissed

However, such faith has its own inevitable limitations although it is wise and right for us to lend our children to God. In this way, we show our trust in Him, but frequently we are not sure if we can still believe in Him and depend on Him when something happens to them. For example, if our kids whom we have given Him, fail to enter university or an accident happens, we will immediately break faith and blame Him in our mind: "I have prayed to God for so many years…" or "I have committed my kid to His care, but she had her leg broken in an accident. How can He leave her unprotected in this way? It's no use committing my children to His care."

And then we may take back our children from Him and we take all necessary measures to protect them in our own power. In such a case, we did not believe in God but hired Him as a bodyguard for our children. Whom do we honor more—the children or their bodyguard? The children, of course. We honor our children above God, the bodyguard. In this case, God was not found to be a good bodyguard and we dismissed Him.

This is not only in the matter of children. We pray to God for a cure for a disease, making fortune, success in the world, church revival, and spiritual gifts. And when we do not receive what we want we are downhearted and murmur against Him. This grumbling signifies the confession of faith that we value these things above God. Therefore, God rebukes Eli who has this kind of faith.

Read the following passages from 1 Samuel.

> Why kick you at my sacrifice and at my offering, which I have commanded in my habitation; and honor your sons above me, to make yourselves fat with the most chief of all the offerings of Israel my people? _____ 1 Samuel 2:29

> For I have told him that I will judge his house for ever for the in-

> iquity which he knows; because his sons made themselves vile, and he restrained them not. _____ 1 Samuel 3:13

When He rebukes Eli by saying, "...and honors your sons above me," He points out the essential limit of Eli's legalistic faith. Such faith has a restriction that we love our kids more than God and we prefer the things of the world to Him. There is no reason for Him to be pleased with such faith. Can Eli save his sons, who make themselves vile, even if he prays day and night, while at the same time he does not please God? It is not at all possible.

When God says He will judge Eli's house, He does not display His temper but gives the natural subsequence. That is, since Eli does not have faith in God, everything belonging to him, that is, his house, is judged.

Absence of Spiritual Communication

What is the fundamental reason Eli honored his sons above God? Eli, by his own effort, believed in God. Eli did not pay attention to and grab the spiritual communication with God. However, true faith comes from God when He makes us believe. We have to hear from God in order to believe.

God is *life* and Eli is *death*, as he was separated from God who is life itself. In this situation, even if he believes in Him and serves Him in all eagerness and sincerity, it will only result in death. Therefore, if a person hopes to believe, he must first communicate with God. Then, he can believe in Him correctly and receive life. However, Eli believed according to his own effort and self-righteousness, so his sons and all his things of the world bore fruit he did not want. In fact, Eli believed in God without knowing God.

We will now check whether all the problems of Eli were caused by his non-communication with Him.

Read the following passage from 1 Samuel.

> And the child Samuel ministered to the LORD before Eli. And the word of the LORD was precious in those days; there was no

> open vision. ²And it came to pass at that time, when Eli was laid down in his place, and his eyes began to wax dim, that he could not see; _____ 1 Samuel 3:1-2

When Samuel was a child, Eli was a priest. At that time, Eli's eyes began to deteriorate. This passage shows Eli's physical state, but it is also written to symbolize that his spiritual eyes were dim. He could not receive the Word of God, who is Spirit, and he could see no open vision because his spiritual eyes were weakened. The fact that "the word of the LORD was precious and there was no open vision" means that there was an absence of communication with God and this will be confirmed in the following passages.

> That the LORD called Samuel: and he answered, Here am I. ⁵And he ran to Eli, and said, Here am I; for you called me. And he said, I called not; lie down again. And he went and lay down. _____ 1 Samuel 3:4-5

> Now Samuel did not yet know the LORD, neither was the word of the LORD yet revealed to him. ⁸And the LORD called Samuel again the third time. And he arose and went to Eli, and said, Here am I; for you did call me. And Eli perceived that the LORD had called the child. _____ 1 Samuel 3:7-8

The Word of the Lord was precious to Eli but it came to Samuel. This signifies that overall Eli had no spiritual communication with the living God. He thought he knew God but he did not know the living God. This means he followed and believed according to the written will of God, neglecting the living God who spoke to him in his life. Therefore, it is natural that he had to believe in Him by himself and behave according to the common sense of man, which is no more than deeds of dead faith. If he had actually communicated with Him, he could have saved his sons and house.

A lot of people around us believe in Jesus, but most of them know nothing about communication with the living God. If they know, they only know a dead version of God that is locked in their thoughts. If we believe in Jesus in this way, we are Eli. Eli, who has no communication, is the symbol of legalistic faith, and Samuel, who has communication, is symbolic of the gospel.

Meet "A Man Jesus" To Know Mind of God

Even if you understand the necessity of communication with God after reading this message, you will not know the way by yourself. Sooner or later you will go back to your previous faith, that is, of Eli. You need to meet "a man Jesus" in your life, who knows the mind of God. He will take you to the way through which you communicate perfectly with God.

📁 Testimony of a Lady and Her Child

We have had the following case in church. A lady, one of our church members, had a very cute and cherished son. Since her kid was so young, he sometimes went in and out of the service on Sunday. The church members were distracted by him, so she felt sorry for them and told him, "Don't come in when I'm in the service"; but she told him in her heart, "Come to me anytime you want to see me, my little baby," unwittingly. The son, having understood what was in her heart, went in and out constantly while the service was in progress.

In one case, he came in and called to her that he was going for a pee, and in other cases, he sat or slept on her lap when it was her turn to take up the offering so another member had to replace her duty temporarily. Such cases happened many times, but the pastor did not say anything specific on this matter.

She thought in her mind, "My pastor, as well as God, accepts my son's behavior."

One day when the Sunday service was in progress, the child came in again. This time, however, the pastor paused preaching, looking annoyed. Everybody knew that he meant she had to take prompt action on the boy who was interrupting the service. She instantly got angry, and complained to the pastor in her heart, "Why did the pastor pause the sermon because of this boy? He is only a child."

From the viewpoint of the flesh, her complaint can simply be an unjust thought of the moment merely, flitting through her mind. But this thought shows her spiritual status. That is, she confessed from the bottom of heart that she valued her son much more than God because the service towards God and the sermon by the pastor are expressions of God Himself, and she revealed her heart by thinking she cherished her kid above them.

She had prayed and gave offerings to God for her son. In a word, she had *hired* Him in such manner. And at this moment, He was *fired* by her. Am I employing violent language? No, never. We have no idea what God feels because our spiritual sense is dead, but as a matter of fact, He is hurt very much by such acts of unbelief. Many believers do not know God is being hurt like this case, and we hurt God this way almost every day without feeling guilty or feeling we've unwittingly done something wrong. How can we expect something good from God in this situation? No wonder our lives end in full of sorrow and woe.

Eli believed in the Lord, and quite naturally, he wanted his sons to succeed him by His grace. However, Eli did not know the heart of God as the lady in our church did not Most believers believe under such situation without anyone around who would enlighten them. However, she had the pastor.

Let us continue with the story. Such thoughts in her heart and murmurings were reported to the pastor by her leader. Upon hearing this, the pastor was very upset and conveyed His message to her. "You honor your son above God, as Eli the priest did."

Upon hearing this message, she became sober. She repented that she had considered God so lightly because she loved her son, and that she hurt Him because of her idle thinking. She could not allow her son to go the same way as the sons of Eli.

From that time on, she strictly prevented her son's coming in and out of the worship hall during the service. At first, he blubbered and knocked on the door of the hall. She felt sorry for him but she would not open the door until the service was finished. After several repetitions, this child no longer called his mom during the service. He, though young, completely knew that he was not allowed to come in when the service was in progress.

Even during the Friday night service, knowing what he should and should not do, he used to play alone at the back of the hall while his mother approached the pulpit at the front to pray to God. Is not this the work of God? Man cannot do so.

This testimony does not focus on any apparent severity on her part towards her son since children are not always obedient to their parents who display severity towards them. The key point is that she has communicated with God, in this event, after all.

The factors that enabled communication are:

First, she obeyed the pastor who knew the heart of God. He knew that carnal people see some things as trivial which are not and he was able to convey God's heart in that matter to her.

Second, she was obedient to His will. She correctly knew His mind through the pastor, obeyed it, and worked so that her communication with Him about this case was made perfect. It was fruitful. She was ready to communicate with God, and did so.

Now, if you want to see something you cannot see in relation to your salvation, try to meet Jesus in your life. If you meet Him in person, you are entering the communication Stage of Jesus. He will heal you and forgive you your sin on the cross to give you the Holy Spirit. Then, you have perfect communication with God.

In short, Eli was in the communication Stage of God which is no practical communication. He needed to meet Jesus to reach the perfect communication stage. But he was the sign of the man who lacks the communication, Eli, and was ruined.

If we also stay at the same Stage of God in terms of communication like Eli, we will follow his path of ruination.

Because the LORD Would Slay Them

"...Notwithstanding they listened not to the voice of their father, because the LORD would slay them" (v. 25).

This verse looks as if God slays him and his sons willfully because Eli cherished his sons more than Him, but, in fact, their destruction shows the natural law. If there is no communication with God, the dead receive no life and they remain dead. That they are dead already will be revealed naturally when the time comes. "Let the dead be dead and let the alive be alive." This is the natural law and His will at the same time.

The sons of Eli had, of their own volition, left God, who is *life*. Their father told them to repent but they did not listen to him. The result was death. This is the law as declared by God. Therefore, the Scripture expresses that God intends to slay those who have left Him, *the life*.

Samuel was in favor with Him, but the family of Eli was gradually reduced to ruin. Those who win His favor are not appointed. Samuel was in favor with Him not because he was Samuel but because he communicated with Him who lives. If we also open our hearts and communicate with Him, we, each of us, is Samuel, who is in favor with Him.

"A Man Jesus" To Eli

We believe in Jesus and read the Scripture to possess the perfect communication with God in the long run. And perfect communication can only be achieved in us through Jesus. To achieve that, we, each of us, need to meet Jesus and follow Him to the cross. Especially here, Jesus, whom we are to meet and follow, is "a man who has Christ in him." As explained in the earlier section, we cannot meet Jesus who came to earth in the past, but we will meet Him as the Christ who abides in the bodies of the born again apostles, like Paul.

In Eli's case, he did not meet Jesus as a figure, who would show and lead him to the way of perfect communication; he had to believe "on his own way." This is made clear when the man of God came and said to Eli, "And I will raise me up a faithful priest, that shall do according to that which is in my heart and in my mind: and I will build him a sure house; and he shall walk before my anointed for ever" (1Samuel 2:35). This proves that Eli believed God on his way without knowing His heart and mind.

Having believed God alone, Eli did not know what to do when the man of God came to him and prophesied woe to his family. Read the following verses from 1 Samuel.

> Behold, the days come, that I will cut off your arm, and the arm of your father's house, that there shall not be an old man in your house. ³²And you shall see an enemy in my habitation, in all the wealth which God shall give Israel: and there shall not be an old man in your house for ever. ³³And the man of yours, whom I shall not cut off from my altar, shall be to consume your eyes, and to grieve your heart: and all the increase of your house shall die in the flower of their age. ³⁴And this shall be a sign to you, that shall come on your two sons, on Hophni and Phinehas; in one day they shall die both of them.   _____ 1 Samuel 2:31-34

This woe signifies the inherent curse of the people under the law. Therefore, at that time of impending woe, what Eli really needed was not some works on his own way like strictness to his sons, praying for them, etc., but "a man Jesus" who would lead him to the perfect communication and save him. Unfortunately, in the absence of such Jesus, he had to face the woe, as it was, by himself.

In fact, in Eli's time, there was "a man Jesus" who would save him. This "a man Jesus" was Samuel. But at that time Samuel was too little, or young, to do the work. This signifies that Eli's faith was too little to be saved. That is, he was not much concerned about his salvation.

Eli symbolizes we who believe in Jesus based on our own thoughts and own reading of the Scripture. Such Jesus Christ who is formed in us is too little to save us who are to receive condemnation due to our sin (Romans 6:23). Therefore, if we do not meet Jesus and follow him now, we have to remain as sinners and face death, as Eli did.

We should advance to the perfect communication Stage of the Holy Spirit without remaining in the communication level of Eli. Compare Eli in terms of meeting "a man Jesus" for the perfect communication to those who will be explained next, that is, Ahab, and Saul, who failed, and the widow at Zarephath who succeeded.

Epilogue

As already explained, the family of Eli was cursed because he could not communicate with God. If we, like Eli, believe in Him in our own way without communication, we can only have the self-righteousness of sinners. Such faith, no matter how sincere it may be, is not acceptable to Him.

If you want your children to succeed in life, hope for revival in the church, seek true faith, long for correct preaching of the word of life, and desire to be in favor with Him like Samuel and David were, and you should meet Jesus in your life now to have perfect communication with Him. Then, all the difficult problems you have in this world will be cleared through it. And most of all, you will become one with God and be saved.

Next I will touch on the case of Ahab the king, who shows some development compared to Eli in terms of the communication with God, but yet lacks.

Who shall Persuade Ahab, that He may Fall?

1 Kings 22:19-29

And he said, Hear you therefore the word of the LORD: I saw the LORD sitting on his throne, and all the host of heaven standing by him on his right hand and on his left. [20]And the LORD said, Who shall persuade Ahab, that he may go up and fall at Ramoth-gilead? And one said on this manner, and another said on that manner. [21]And there came forth a spirit, and stood before the LORD, and said, I will persuade him. [22]And the LORD said to him, With which? And he said, I will go forth, and I will be a lying spirit in the mouth of all his prophets. And he said, You shall persuade him, and prevail also: go forth, and do so. [23]Now therefore, behold, the LORD has put a lying spirit in the mouth of all these your prophets, and the LORD has spoken evil concerning you. [24]But Zedekiah the son of Chenaanah went near, and smote Micaiah on the cheek, and said, Which way went the Spirit of the LORD from me to speak to you? [25]And Micaiah said, Behold, you shall see in that day, when you shall go into an inner chamber to hide yourself. [26]And the king of Israel said, Take Micaiah, and carry him back to Amon the governor of the city, and to Joash the king's son; [27]And say, Thus said the king, Put this fellow in the prison, and feed him with bread of affliction and with water of affliction, until I come in peace. [28]And Micaiah said, If you return at all in peace, the LORD has not spoken by me. And he said, Listen, O people, every one of you. [29]So the king of Israel and Jehoshaphat the king of Judah went up to Ramoth-gilead.

You should keep one thing in mind during communion with God: Receive the message after you have cleared your mind of greed and desire. Otherwise, you will receive the wrong answer. For instance, if you pray with the full intention of going to New York, you will finally receive a self-fulfilling answer from God to go to New York, and you will stumble.

The passage concerning King Ahab corresponds to this situation. The relevant passages are 1 Kings 22:1-38, but I have quoted only a part of it because the story is very long.

To sum up, Israel was divided into two countries after the death of Solomon the king; Israel in the north and Judah in the south. The two countries frequently fought with Syria in the north. There was no war between them and Syria for three years, and in the third year, Ahab the king of Israel suggested to Jehoshaphat, the king of Judah that Israel should enter into an alliance with Judah and attack Syria in order to take back Ramoth in Gilead from Syria. Jehoshaphat was pleased to agree to this but he said that he first wished to ask the prophets before giving his final consent.

Ahab gathered about 400 prophets of Israel and asked them if God consented to fight with Syria. Representing the 400 prophets, Zedekiah made horns of iron, displayed them, and said the Israelites would push the Syrians until they had consumed them; the other prophets advised the kings to go up to Ramoth-gilead and prosper.

However, Jehoshaphat asked if there was another prophet besides them. Ahab said there was one man but he rejected him because he prophesied evil. Finally, an officer was sent to summon the prophet who was named Micaiah. The messenger who went to call him told him to speak favorably as the other prophets had. However, Micaiah spoke as the LORD instructed him: "He will smite the shepherd and the sheep of the flock shall be scattered abroad."

In verse 19 cited above, Micaiah continued to speak out the vision from heaven. "The LORD sitting on His throne said 'Who shall persuade Ahab that he may go up and fall at Ramoth-gilead?' and a spirit came forth and said he would go forth and would be a lying spirit in the mouth of all the prophets, and He told him to do so."

But, Ahab listened to Zedekiah rather than Micaiah, and put

Micaiah in prison. Ahab then went up to Ramoth-gilead with Jehoshapaht to fight with the Syrians, as in verse 29 cited above. In the battle, Ahab was struck with an arrow from the bow of a Syrian soldier and died bleeding in his chariot. As a result, the prophecy by Micaiah proved to be the word of God.

The readers will probably question this story because God had a meeting in heaven (1Kings 22:20) and spoke of enticing Ahab to go up to Ramoth-gilead and have him killed there, and his death came about as He intended. It is not easy to understand that God who is neither Satan nor an evil man who forms a plot to murder another.

God has one thing to tell us through this story: We ought to eliminate the evil desire that is in our heart before receiving His answer. And this is God's way to make us grow in "good" of God.

I will now explain what this story is intended to teach us.

Two Kings Hoping to Know the Will of God.

Ahab the king of Israel proposed to Jehoshaphat the king of Judah that they join forces to retake Ramoth-gilead from Syria. Jehoshaphat assented to it with pleasure, but recommended that they inquire of the Lord. We can understand from their dialogue that they knew God as the ruler of all things in this world as well as war and they tried to depend on Him. Before they started out on an important venture they approached God for His word on the subject, which they ought to do.

The kings of Israel appearing in the Scripture are examples of we who believe in God. So are the two kings in this story. But, what can we say about the reality of our lives? If we do not know the will of God even though we sincerely believe in God, we are not walking in faith. We should pray to Him to know His will at all times if we are not doing so.

It is important to try to hear the message, and it is equally important to receive it correctly. The present passages reveal the trap those who want to receive the Word of God are apt to fall into. If caught in such a trap, we get the wrong answer despite having tried to seek His will.

Answers We Want to Hear

Ahab intended to receive the Word of God but he had already made up his mind to go against the Syrians. He asked 400 prophets who prophesied favorably concerning him at all times, and he left out Micaiah who would prophesy evil. As was expected, the 400 men gave the message Ahab hoped for. However, Jehoshaphat called Micaiah because he wanted to hear what the other prophet would say.

It is wise of you to inquire of God. The essential reason for this is to ensure that we are in obedience to Him. But if you ask Him having already decided on your course of action, you are simply trying to co-opt God into your plan. You must be faithful and sincere when seeking His word, and once having received it, you must obey it whether it is positive or negative, advantageous or disadvantageous, and then you will not stumble and fall.

I knew a thirty-eight year old bachelor who was in anguish because he had not yet met a good woman whom he could marry. Then, finally, he met a woman who had graduated from a famous university and was thirty-two years old. Even though he had not seen her for a long time, he decided to marry her because she was to his liking. One thing to worry about was her character. She was not meek. But he thought he could accept her with a broad mind because he was much older than her. He thought he could lead a smooth and happy married life with her.

Over the phone he told me that he would marry her. Knowing that he used to pray to God for every matter before his decision, I asked him:

"Did you pray to God concerning your proposed marriage?"

He gave an evasive answer. "God will accept her, I think."

I guessed that he would have prayed about this important matter of marriage. He said he would send me a wedding invitation shortly, and I said I would gladly come to his wedding ceremony, and hung up.

A few days before marriage, he called me again and said the wedding was postponed indefinitely. I asked him what had happened, and he said he had decided to break off the betrothal because she was too impolite to his parents and family. He was deeply hurt and heartbroken.

Afterwards he gave me more details. He said, "I really wanted to marry her. But if somebody asked me if I had prayed to God concerning her, I really hated hearing from Him since I was afraid He was against this marriage. So I never prayed to Him concerning this marriage. But I went ahead with it, saying within myself 'God, You know I'm too old. Please help me.'"

He finally realized that the Lord did not support the marriage.

When Ahab did not want to hear the word of the Lord, it was like this case in which this brother did not want to hear from Him. Ahab's attitude is very typical of how we behave towards God in such situations.

When, like Ahab, we only hear the word supporting us and conclude we hear the word of God, we will often hear the voice of Jehoshaphat in our heart, which contradicts it. We must pay attention to it. And Ahab paid attention. So far, so good.

Micaiah, having come to Ahab at the request of Jehoshaphat, prophesied as follows.

Micaiah Who Sounds Ahab Out

Micaiah gave an unexpected message: "Go against Ramoth-gilead to battle, and He shall deliver it into the hand of the king." But, Ahab told him to tell the truth. When Micaiah said that God would give Ahab the victory, Ahab could have simply celebrated and gone on to do battle with the Syrians, but he wanted confirmation so he asked Micaiah again. Good for Ahab! In fact, God tempted the thought Ahab had in his heart through Micaiah. Ahab had done an excellent job up until then.

Regardless of the reason why Ahab asked Micaiah again, we must also check our hearts over and over again as Ahab did when we receive word from Him; even in the case of the positive answer. This is what I mean: we must try to read the heart of God, not the superficial answer itself. If not, we will be enticed by our own ideas and lusts, and then die.

Who Shall Persuade Ahab, that He May Fall?

When Ahab presses Micaiah to tell the truth, he responds that God puts a lying spirit in the mouth of all these prophets of Ahab as in Kings 22:19-23 above.

The title of this section is "Who shall persuade Ahab that he may fall?" It sounds as if God tries to have him killed. But, it is the other way round. God wanted to save Ahab. If He had determined to have Ahab killed, He would not have let Ahab hear this prophecy through Micaiah. God stopped him because Ahab would die if he went up to Ramoth-gilead.

The message that "He has put a lying spirit in the mouth of 400 prophets as well as Zedekiah" also tells Ahab in advance that they are flattering him and will not correctly convey God's word to him. In the spiritual sense, the number *four* represents the number related to man. The prophets who prophesied man's message, not God's, were *four* hundred.

What else can God do in order to save Ahab? Some people may raise a question by saying "Can God let him escape from death if he went up to Ramoth-gilead?" In such a case, Ahab will be God, and God will be nothing but his servant. God has His own plan to rule the universe and everything on earth. He cannot modify His predetermined plan for the purpose of satisfying Ahab's avarice. The way to save Ahab is to let him know the plan in advance and provide him an opportunity to escape from it.

Like being willing to go to the death to regain captured territory, we are willing to go to hell ignoring God's word in order to grab the earthly things. Hell is there. God prepares the way for us to stay away from it through Jesus. We will not go to hell if we obey and follow God's way through Jesus, but if not, we will go there due to our sin. It is impossible to transform hell into heaven for those who have gone to hell. It would have been better if they had listened to the word of God and obeyed it, but they did not. Therefore they reaped what they had sown.

Now I will explain the response of Zedekiah and Ahab the king to the prophecy of Micaiah.

Final Decision By Ahab

When Micaiah prophesied that Ahab would fall if he went to battle, Zedekiah struck him on the cheek and said that his prophecy was incorrect. Ahab, trusting Zedekiah, put Micaiah into prison. Ahab went up to Ramoth-gilead. He could not return alive.

In fact, Ahab felt worried by the precise prophesying of Micaiah. However, he did not wish to hear that prophesy, and choose to believe prophesies of 400 prophets which suited him as the will of God. And he justified himself, secured by thinking that many prophets express the same prophesy. Maybe Ahab's decision was natural from the standpoint of the natural man, but it was to self-deceptive.

Ahab wanted to know what God would say to him. But he was blinded by his own preconceptions and his desire to go to battle. As a result, when he heard the true Word of God, he had to disregard it. Thus he brought tragedy on himself.

In fact, we frequently feel quite relieved about the fact that many other people also trust and follow the same traditional doctrines we believe and follow. We may say, "I quoted from the famous theologian. Is he wrong? Further, did all the many well-known theologians and pastors in Christian history go wrong? They devoted their whole lives to the Scripture and prayer. I'm repeating what they said."

If we speak in this manner, it shows that we depend on the greatness of many men, not God. We may persecute a speaker of truth unwittingly as Ahab did to Micaiah. We should not be tempted or swayed by the number of men who declare same doctrines or viewpoints.

It is important for you to hear the word of God, but it is more important that you are ready to hear it and obey it. God speaks *already* to all of us who want to hear Him. If you wish to receive the Word of God correctly, you must first clear your mind.

Ahab is not unique in this case. He is the prototype of all believers at present.

📁 Testimony of Church Member

The following is the testimony of one of our church members, and illustrates a common train of thought amongst believers. One of our church members found that after offering her tithe, the Lord blessed her in every respect in her life. She tried to make her tithe the first priority of living expenditures every month, and gave ear to His leading.

Quite recently, however, her finances came under pressure and she could not manage her monthly household expenses. As a result she got behind with the payment of utility bills and school expenses for her children. Naturally, she felt overwhelmed by the pressure of tithing, and she could not tithe in the last month because she had to pay for other urgent expenses.

She felt that the Lord was not pleased with her failure to tithe. In this situation, when she heard sermons, she could hear the voice of the Lord telling her to tithe, and she could hear the same voice during conversations with other church members. Time passed while she was in this mental conflict concerning her desire to tithe and her difficult financial circumstances.

One day, at a gathering in the church, the pastor preached a message to the members to tithe regularly, and she began to come to herself. "Yes, knowing that the Lord is not pleased with me, I will begin again to tithe no matter how difficult my circumstances are." Making this resolution, she wanted to reconfirm the will of God by seeing the pastor in this respect.

She met with the pastor. During counseling, she told the pastor everything she had been thinking up until then. Having heard what she said, the pastor told her that her first priority in life is the Lord. He then said that she should not spend money for all she needed first, and give tithes from what was left over. The Lord would not be pleased by this kind of faith. He said that she must give the first priority to the tithe. Tithing was not a simple matter of money, but it was her confession of her love of God and a celebration of His provision in her life.

At the end of the counseling, however, the pastor recommended that she should pray and ask for God's guidance in this matter. If the Lord advised her not to tithe in her particular situation, she could skip tithing, and if not, she needed to tithe in spite of her difficulties.

After meeting with the pastor, she was very glad to find such a marvelous way to skip tithing. She was quite confident that the Lord, knowing her condition, would surely allow her to skip tithing in those months of trouble. She had met with the pastor with a resolution that she would tithe for sure, but when she had finished meeting with the pastor, she thought that he had shown her a way to avoid tithing. She prayed to Him eagerly to confirm the waiver of tithes. And she finally got the answer from Him to skip tithing. And she could reduce her burden of tithes and she felt relieved.

However, for some reason, she felt uneasy in her heart. As time went by she felt that she was on pins and needles. And she met with the pastor again to ask why she felt so uncomfortable in her heart. She said to him that she had stopped tithing as a result of the response she had received from the Lord.

The pastor, immediately knowing that she was deceiving herself said, "Try to know His mind other than the literal meaning of the response itself. When I told you that you could skip tithing if the Lord permitted, do you think that the Lord really meant that you should stop? The Lord wished to test your heart and see whether the Lord really was your first priority even in times of hunger. If you claim that you are obedient to the Lord when you have a full stomach, this is not obedience. Even sinners would do that. If you stop giving tithes because of a lack of money, you are confessing that money is more valuable and powerful than the Lord in your life. How can He be pleased with such faith? Please think again about how you can please Him."

She realized that she had failed to understand the real meaning of the response from the Lord, being overwhelmed by her financial situation. This test revealed to her that she was giving her financial situation priority over her relationship with the Lord. She was very ashamed, repented and prayed for forgiveness.

Meanwhile God moved her to offer more money than the original tithe. She did not know why He wanted her to offer more, and she accordingly had difficulty with this new instruction from God.

"Do I have to give the tithes that I used to offer or do I have to give more as I was moved by the Lord?"

But, she immediately realized that she was in fact altering the word of the Lord this way and disobeying Him. Therefore, she gave as much as He had said to her, and realized later that the excess was the penalty imposed by Him.

She understood once again that giving tithes was not just offering money but the pathway through which she could know God better.

By contrast, Ahab the king did not repent at the message of Micaiah, the messenger of God, and was ruined.

"A Man Jesus" to Ahab

Now I will explain about Ahab's meeting with "a man Jesus." Differently from Eli who had no "a man Jesus," Ahab had many prophets who would advise him of the mind of God. Moreover, amongst them, he had "a man Jesus" who told him the way to live. He was Micaiah. However, Ahab did not hear and follow him, the true one, but followed those who gave him the prophesy he wanted, and then he died. This was the faith level of Ahab.

This Ahab signifies the believers nowadays who have many pastors and instructors in Christ whose words are sweet because they are saying that Jesus would give us food, health, power, and prosperity in this world and the next because of His name's sake. Moreover, many of them say there is no hell because God loves us so much, so you sit back and relax and enjoy your life. How sweet!

This means we want go to Ramoth-gilead, and these leaders say to us, "Go up; for the LORD shall deliver them all into your hand," with the voice of 400 prophets who prophesied good concerning Ahab.

However, Micaiah in the present age, as in the text, will not speak good concerning us, but evil. "You have to take up your own cross to come after me, denying yourself and forsaking all," as Jesus said to the disciples.

If you hear only a sugar-coated gospel from instructors you will surely die, but you will live if you hear Micaiah who speaks evil concerning you. Like Ahab, we have many men around us who teach of Christ. Who then should we follow? Follow him who is testified to by Scripture, regardless of what he says is evil concerning you.

Remember, Eli did not have "a man Jesus" around, and he died. But Ahab showed some development. That is, he had "a man Jesus," Micaiah in this case, around him. However, he forsook Micaiah and chose the false prophets, and also he died. To have "a man Jesus" around us is a blessing, but we, like Ahab, tend to kick him out, and if we do so we will die.

As a next development in relation to "a man Jesus," we will discuss Saul, who also failed.

Epilogue

When trying to receive the Word of God, you will stumble and fall if you miss the following points.

First, it is meaningless to ask the will of God after you have already decided what to do in your mind. You should cast aside your thoughts and inquire of Him with a humble heart.

Second, when you have received the word of God, you must think deep and long. Instead of rejoicing over the fact that you have received what you wanted, you must consider every possible condition, and try to know the heart of God who said it.

Third, you must not be tempted by numbers. Even if a huge number of people say the same thing, it may not be of God. You should bear in mind that the will of God can be conveyed through the mouth of one man opposing four hundred men.

If you start to communicate with the living Lord, He will guide you into truth through tests as I have illustrated above. If you repent whenever you fail, you will become a person who can gradually overcome evil. In this course, you will need "a man Jesus" who will enlighten you and take you to the cross where your old self, the evil in you, will be destroyed. This way the Lord enables you to have perfect communication with Him.

Let's be the followers of Micaiah.

It Repents Me That I Have Set Up Saul to Be King

1 Samuel 15:1-11

Samuel also said to Saul, The LORD sent me to anoint you to be king over his people, over Israel: now therefore listen you to the voice of the words of the LORD. ²Thus said the LORD of hosts, I remember that which Amalek did to Israel, how he laid wait for him in the way, when he came up from Egypt. ³Now go and smite Amalek, and utterly destroy all that they have, and spare them not; but slay both man and woman, infant and suckling, ox and sheep, camel and ass. ⁴And Saul gathered the people together, and numbered them in Telaim, two hundred thousand footmen, and ten thousand men of Judah. ⁵And Saul came to a city of Amalek, and laid wait in the valley. ⁶And Saul said to the Kenites, Go, depart, get you down from among the Amalekites, lest I destroy you with them: for you showed kindness to all the children of Israel, when they came up out of Egypt. So the Kenites departed from among the Amalekites. ⁷And Saul smote the Amalekites from Havilah until you come to Shur, that is over against Egypt. ⁸And he took Agag the king of the Amalekites alive, and utterly destroyed all the people with the edge of the sword. ⁹But Saul and the people spared Agag, and the best of the sheep, and of the oxen, and of the fatted calves, and the lambs, and all that was good, and would not utterly destroy them: but every thing that was vile and refuse, that they destroyed utterly. ¹⁰Then came the word of the LORD to Samuel, saying, ¹¹It repents me that I have set up Saul to be king: for he is turned back from following me, and has not performed my commandments. And it grieved Samuel; and he cried to the LORD all night.

I will now describe the example of Saul the king who heard God's message many times but disobeyed each time and finally walked the way of destruction.

By order of God, Samuel the prophet anointed Saul to be the first king of Israel. In 1 Samuel 9:2 we get an insight into Saul. "There was not among the children of Israel a goodlier person than he: from his shoulders and upward he was higher than any of the people." In spite of this, he was humble.

When Samuel told Saul, "On you is all the desire of Israel," Saul answered to Samuel, "Am not I a Benjamite, of the smallest of the tribes of Israel? and my family the least of all the families of the tribe of Benjamin? why then speak you so to me?" (1Samuel 9:21). And when he was elected as king, he hid himself among the equipment because he felt ashamed (1Samuel 10:22). This shows his humbleness as a natural man.

After he was anointed as king, God gave him the Holy Spirit to support him so the people of Israel would accept him as their king. However, after he became king, he gradually began to behave according to his own desire of the world, forsaking the will of God.

In 1 Samuel 13, when Saul was besieged by the Philistines, he felt very fearful and he transgressed God's commandment and offered the burnt offering in the place of Samuel. After this, again Saul disobeyed the word of God to utterly destroy Amalek. Saul followed God's commandment, but not completely. He destroyed them but spared what he thought should be spared. And he lied to Samuel that the people spared them to sacrifice to God.

Until he died on Mount Gilboa, Saul had many opportunities to repent, but he failed and died a miserable death as king.

We normally accuse Saul on account of such behaviors, but you will realize that you also cannot make any better decision if you are in his shoes. He is a prototype of all of us who are born as sin-possessed.

We may be good people in this world, but in the course of doing the work of God, our sin-possessed real nature will be disclosed. And that is the time for us to repent. If we do so, we will live; if not, we will remain in sin and die.

From the viewpoint of communication, God wanted to communicate with Saul till the end, but Saul rejected it to the last.

Now I will explain Saul's real problem so we do not to follow his trail.

Smite Amalek

"Now go and smite Amalek, and utterly destroy all that they have, and spare them not; but slay both man and woman, infant and suckling, ox and sheep, camel and ass" (I Samuel 13:3).

When reading this, we generally think: "Isn't it cruel to kill even the enemy's infant and suckling, and cattle?" or "Do they have to go that far?" But we should not look upon this story as merely an historical event. All records in the Scripture have spiritual meanings, which we should focus on when reading the Scripture.

The people of Israel symbolize us, the believers in Jesus, and one Israelite indicates *me*; i.e., each believer. Amalek is the symbol of the desire of the world in *me*. The reason is that Amalek was the son of Eliphaz who in turn was the son of Esau (Genesis 36:12). As is well known, Esau sold his birthright for a pottage of lentils. He gave up the glory of being born again as a son of God for food. So he and his descendant Amalek are a symbol of the desire of this world in us and those who are living possessed by such desire.

The desire of the world represents the lust of the flesh, the lust of the eyes, and the pride of life (1John 2:16). If you want to enter the Kingdom of God, you must utterly destroy this Amalek in you, even the smallest seed. This is why God instructed Saul to eradicate the Amalekites so completely.

Selective Obedience of Saul the King

Saul smote the Amalekites according to the commandment of

God but he did not obey God's commandment. Saul spared Agag the king and the best of the sheep and oxen, and destroyed everything that was refuse. When Saul later gave his reasons for not obeying God, he said he had done so in order to sacrifice to God.

However, Saul's lie can be likened to a servant, when instructed by his master to dump the refuse, keeps some of it so as to give it to the master. By changing God's command, Saul was in effect placing himself in a superior position to God. Whether he knew it or not he was claiming so. As long as he held onto this kind of thinking, he could never be a king that God would use.

The basic reason for Saul's disobedience was that he succumbed to greed (1Samuel 15:19). While he loved the things of the world, he could not seriously consider God's commandment to destroy everything about the Amalekites. The fact that Saul did not destroy them all means he has worldly avarice left in his mind, so for following the avarice he disobeyed God. To see Saul's action of the disobedience is to see worldly avarice in his mind.

Can we do any better than Saul? We cannot. For example, when God moves us to give a certain amount of offering to church, we will object in our mind that "I only live from hand to mouth, such big amount I cannot bear. It cannot be the voice of God. I may give one tenth of the sum later."

This is our case of Saul, that we obeyed, but selectively, with our own righteousness and reasoning. We all will be like Saul when we are in front of the commandment of God. Why are we so? It is because we are born sin-possessed, having left God. Under the sin-possessed status, we cannot keep the commandment of God in nature. If we keep His commandment, we do it superficially and selectively as hypocrites.

We must understand that this disobedience of Saul is not a one-time mistake, but innate disobedience caused by being sinful. We cannot keep the commandments unless we are born again as sinless through Jesus. Therefore, this commandment, including all the commandments of Scripture, is, in other words, "You should follow Jesus to the cross to be born again." When we are born again we can keep the commandment of God.

Therefore, Saul died not because of disobedience concerning the smiting of the Amalekites, but died of sin as he did not repent at each occasion of disobedience to God.

It Repents Me That I Have Set up Saul to Be King

God says it repents Him that He set up Saul to be king. Some people may wonder that He did not know in advance that Saul would disobey Him. In fact, He did. God's plan would not be thwarted simply because Saul changed. In spite of this, the Scripture said God repented. This is to express His feeling sorry for us. We should not be like Saul who was disobedient and made God feel sorry.

Now that He said it repented Him that He had set Saul up to be king, was He giving up on Saul? No, He was not. On the contrary, He was trying to awaken Saul to his situation because He loved him. The fact that Saul did not utterly destroy the Amalekites was not a problem to God, because it could have been rectified by any other means. What was more important was that God was revealing to Saul his spirit of disobedience by this event to give him an opportunity to repent. However, to our sorrow, Saul was still tempted and blinded by the things of the world, so he did not realize how serious this case was. And he thought, "What kind of big mistake did I make? Am I so wrong?"

Saul did not know the heart of God. And he did not want to repent of the fact that he disobeyed Him concerning the battle against the Amalekites, but he defended his incorrect decision. In addition, he only thought about how to be accepted by the people. This is how blindness worked in Saul.

Read the following passage from 1 Samuel.

> And Samuel said to him, The LORD has rent the kingdom of Israel from you this day, and has given it to a neighbor of yours, that is better than you. [29]And also the Strength of Israel will not lie nor repent: for he is not a man, that he should repent. [30]Then he said, I have sinned: yet honor me now, I pray you, before the elders of my people, and before Israel, and turn again with me,

that I may worship the LORD your God. _____ 1 Samuel 15:28-30

Saul said this after he had heard a very serious warning from Samuel who had said, "God has rent the kingdom of Israel from you this day, and has given it to your neighbor, that is better than you. God will not repent this decision." If Saul had been contrite and humbled himself in repentance at this word, he would have been used as a great king of God. But he was only interested in being honored before the elders and the people of Israel. He deserved to be ruined.

We are talking about spiritual communication with God, but we can know from this story that communication is not limited to hearing His voice. While we clearly know His will and understand what He wants, we still need to obey. If we know His will but ignore it due to our self-righteousness as Saul did, it would be better not to have known His will. We should take his case as a lesson of how not to reach perfect communication with God.

📂 A Church Staff Who Would Not Repent

I will share a case that occurred in our church. One day, one of the church staff went to Seoul to inspect land without the permission of the pastor. At that time, every church member was super busy preparing for the church summer school. Knowing that the staff member was out of town, the pastor called him over the phone and asked him to return, cutting the journey outright. After the call, the pastor did not feel him to be back immediately. Surely enough, the staff member did not return immediately in spite of the instruction of the pastor. Not because he had a disobedient heart, but he simply thought that he could inspect the property in a short time because he had almost arrived there. But the road was jammed with traffic and the whole trip took him much longer than expected.

When he came back to church after his excursion, those who were working at the church had already finished their various jobs. Upon seeing him, the pastor was displeased. If we think carefully, when he disobeyed the pastor's instruction, he considered that his thinking was superior to the pastor's and that he could do better than the pastor. If we fail to look such a thing through and correct it, we cannot be united as one with the pastor and cannot work together at the same church.

God prepared this case and He said to the staff worker, "You disobey your pastor without being aware of it. Look deeply at your attitude of mind." It was not an accident that his trip was further delayed when he had almost arrived there, taking much longer than expected. It was God's purpose for him to repent of his disobedience by making the matter worse.

Unfortunately, however, he did not realize this, and thought, "I don't think it's a big problem. What's the fuss?" as if he was in a dream. He could not take this opportunity for repentance as God wished by this precious occasion. We tend to disobey the will of God so easily like this. We say later, "When and in what way did I disobey God?" We disobey Him but have no idea of it. It is the typical symptom of the spiritually blind that they do not know they are blind.

📂 God Who Loved Saul to the End

The Scriptures repeatedly say God has rejected Saul but all of these situations show the love of God. He wanted to make Saul repent to maintain his kingship. God truly gave Saul opportunities to repent and turn to Him up until the time of his death. The story about smiting Amalekites was one of the ways in which God sought to show and correct the disobedience of Saul, and the story concerning the burnt offering in 1 Samuel chapter 13 was another example.

I will now briefly explain the story of Saul's burnt offering. At that time Philistines gathered to fight with Israel.

Read the following verses from 1 Samuel.

> And some of the Hebrews went over Jordan to the land of Gad and Gilead. As for Saul, he was yet in Gilgal, and all the people followed him trembling. ⁸And he tarried seven days, according to the set time that Samuel had appointed: but Samuel came

not to Gilgal; and the people were scattered from him. ⁹And Saul said, Bring here a burnt offering to me, and peace offerings. And he offered the burnt offering. ¹⁰And it came to pass, that as soon as he had made an end of offering the burnt offering, behold, Samuel came; and Saul went out to meet him, that he might salute him. ¹¹And Samuel said, What have you done? And Saul said, Because I saw that the people were scattered from me, and that you came not within the days appointed, and that the Philistines gathered themselves together at Michmash; ¹²Therefore said I, The Philistines will come down now on me to Gilgal, and I have not made supplication to the LORD: I forced myself therefore, and offered a burnt offering. ¹³And Samuel said to Saul, You have done foolishly: you have not kept the commandment of the LORD your God, which he commanded you: for now would the LORD have established your kingdom on Israel for ever. ¹⁴But now your kingdom shall not continue: the LORD has sought him a man after his own heart, and the LORD has commanded him to be captain over his people, because you have not kept that which the LORD commanded you.
_____ 1 Samuel 13:7-14

Saul offered the burnt offering on his own without Samuel. Due to this single act, he was told by God to be removed from the throne (1Samuel 13:14). Is making an offering to God a blunder that deserves dethroning? Moreover, Saul did it because his people were scattering out of fear of the Philistines, and that Samuel did not come within the days appointed. Saul felt that Philistines would come down now upon him, and he was worried because he had not made his supplication to God. Saul forcibly offered a burnt offering. We do not see any mistake from Saul's behavior. And we would do the same thing if we were in his shoes.

Nevertheless, we guess that God was angry because Saul did the work the priest should have done. Some people say that Saul did not offer a burnt offering but he did so through Ahimelech the priest (1Samuel 21:1) and his offering was poor. But here the issue is not about "Who offered it, the king or the priest?" or "Was that offering full or not?" God does not say that He will remove him from the position of king for such reasons.

What then was the true nature of Saul's disobedience? Saul had no mind to obey the will of God. Saul obeyed when he had a reason to, according to his own carnal judgment, but he neglected God's will if he had an irresistible reason of his own. By acting in this manner, Saul set himself above God.

Actually, God had made the army of the Philistines look terrifying and He delayed Samuel's coming within the set time on purpose to test Saul. It was not a coincidence that Samuel came as soon as Saul finished offering (v. 10). It was God's plan.

Under the terrifying situation, Saul made his own decision without asking God. If he was in a real emergency, he should have prayed to God to seek His will as that was the commandment of God originally. If there was no answer from God he had to wait until God responded, even in the situation that Samuel was delayed. But Saul did not have such communication with God. Saul, who did not have communication with God and did not know the heart of God, cannot be used as a king for God's people, of course. This is the valid and natural reason of dethroning.

God knew it. God tempted Saul to perform the offering by himself in order to reveal his poor faith by which he might repent and be healed accordingly. But, he did not repent at that occasion and he did not repent in the later case of smiting the Amalekites either, giving excuses.

Nevertheless, God gave him a further chance to repent, as is shown in the Scripture. The day before Saul died, Samuel, who was dead, appeared to him and said, "And tomorrow shall you and your sons be with me" (1Samuel 28:19), which was the last opportunity to repent God gave to him. But he did not repent and turn to God. This is evidenced by the fact that he ate the food provided by the woman who had a familiar spirit. This shows that he depended on the teachings and comfort, which are symbolized by food, of man. As foretold, he died a miserable death the next day.

God wanted to save Saul to the end, but Saul relied on the means of the world to the last instead of repenting and turning to Him. That is, he refused to communicate with Him and was destroyed.

God makes us grow in faith in this way: *first*, God makes ground for repentance by disclosing our poor faith; *second*, we truly repent to God; *third*, our faith grows. This represents our sin-forgiveness process while we are led by Jesus to the cross.

Like Saul, God loves us as much. God set us up as the kings and priests for the people. Differently from Saul, if we repent at each occasion of disobediences and establish communication with God, we will be the real glorious kings and priests of God.

"A Man Jesus" To Saul

Eli had no "a man Jesus," and Ahab had many "a man Jesus," come to him, as well as false ones. Both failed due to "no man" and "many men." Differently from them, however, Saul had one "a man Jesus," who was Samuel. Saul shows the development in communication with God.

Eli did not know what to do to receive eternal life; Ahab might have difficulty selecting the true one amongst 401 prophets (400 false prophets + 1 Micaiah), but Saul had one Samuel, "a man Jesus." All he had to do was to follow Samuel, but he refused to live by disobedience.

We may think that we love Jesus so much that we can go to prison and to the death for Him. However, I bet if we meet Jesus in person, in the course of following Him we would deny three times that we know Him. We do not know who we are, actually. In fact, Saul reveals what we, the believers, are going to do when we meet Jesus for whom we have waited a really long time.

Anyhow, we have to meet Jesus to live one way or the other. When you meet "a man Jesus," follow Him to the end, and you will receive eternal life, like the widow woman at Zarephath, whom we will discuss next.

Epilogue

Saul the king failed. He blocked communication with God and

disobeyed Him until he died. In Saul's case, Samuel was taking the role of Jesus Christ, and he in collaboration with God was leading Saul to the cross to destroy his old self. But being deceived by the demon in him, Saul refused to follow and died in sin.

Spiritually speaking, each of us is a king set up by God. However, in order to be the real king set up by God, we need to go through the cross following Jesus. During the course of following Jesus, we will think of the things of the world as Saul did, and we may follow His will selectively. That is, to disobey Him like Saul. Therefore, it is wise to think deeply and eliminate the factors of disobedience from us. However, being sin-possessed, we cannot do so and will succumb to sin after all.

That's why we need "Jesus, a man to meet" around us. Follow Him and obey Him fully. In the course of following, if your disobedience is revealed, repent and obey Him to death on the cross. If we do so, unlike Saul, we will be set up as a true king whom God loves amongst the believers.

Now, two things to consider;

First, have you met a "Samuel" in person who points out your unseen sin in everyday life?

Second, if yes, do you obey this "Samuel" in person's word to the end, fully, unlike Saul?

If you are in the second stage, you are not far from the Kingdom of God. You will receive the Holy Spirit, achieving perfect communication with God.

Do not ever go to Saul's way in the course of following Jesus.

The Widow Woman at Zarephath

1 Kings 17:8-16

And the word of the LORD came to him, saying, ⁹Arise, get you to Zarephath, which belongs to Zidon, and dwell there: behold, I have commanded a widow woman there to sustain you. ¹⁰So he arose and went to Zarephath. And when he came to the gate of the city, behold, the widow woman was there gathering of sticks: and he called to her, and said, Fetch me, I pray you, a little water in a vessel, that I may drink. ¹¹And as she was going to fetch it, he called to her, and said, Bring me, I pray you, a morsel of bread in your hand. ¹²And she said, As the LORD your God lives, I have not a cake, but an handful of meal in a barrel, and a little oil in a cruse: and, behold, I am gathering two sticks, that I may go in and dress it for me and my son, that we may eat it, and die. ¹³And Elijah said to her, Fear not; go and do as you have said: but make me thereof a little cake first, and bring it to me, and after make for you and for your son. ¹⁴For thus said the LORD God of Israel, The barrel of meal shall not waste, neither shall the cruse of oil fail, until the day that the LORD sends rain on the earth. ¹⁵And she went and did according to the saying of Elijah: and she, and he, and her house, did eat many days. ¹⁶And the barrel of meal wasted not, neither did the cruse of oil fail, according to the word of the LORD, which he spoke by Elijah.

So far we have discussed the cases of the kings who failed communication with God for various reasons. Now, we will see the case of one widow who shows the perfect communication with God.

Elijah the prophet lived and worked during the reign of Ahab and Ahaziah the kings of Israel. Ahab was influenced by Jezebel his wife and worshipped Baal. God's wrath waxed hot against him, and Elijah prophesied that there would be no rain for several years since the Israelites had left the Lord. As he prophesied, the drought lasted for three and a half years.

The story of the widow woman at Zarephath begins at this time. When this long period of drought started, Elijah stayed by the brook Cherith as God led him. He ate bread and flesh that the ravens brought there, and when the brook dried up, he was commanded by Him to go to Zarephath, belonging to Zidon, and stay and eat at a widow woman's house.

Therefore, Elijah went there. He met a widow woman and told her to fetch him water and a morsel of bread. In fact, she had no cake, but she made the last one and gave it to Elijah, giving him priority over herself and her son. Then, God blessed her so that the barrel of meal did not waste away, neither did the cruse of oil fail until it rained again, and they ate their fill.

I would like you to think about following points:

First, Elijah met the widow. They did not know each other but God prepared for their meeting, and they were blessed by it. Our lives are like this. The meeting in which we had no intention includes the hidden blessed hand of God.

Second, Elijah asked the poor widow for the last little food that she had; a very difficult request. I will explain what this unreasonable demand by the man of God means.

Third, what is the secret of the faith of the widow woman? How could she give him her last meal? She must be a woman of great faith.

Elijah Meets the Widow Woman – Divine Providence

Everything that happens in this world may appear to be the result of our decisions and actions, but the will of God is behind events. As we read, neither Elijah nor the widow had reason to meet at all.

However, by the leading of God they did meet and were blessed.

Elijah received the Word of God and found her. When he met her, he knew why he had come to her. He came to her according to His will, with blessing. However, she did not know who he was when she first met him, but she followed what he told her to do. And she survived the famine.

The relationship between you and me is like this. I am visiting you, the readers of this book, as He leads me. As Elijah did to the widow, I preach to you the readers about the Word of God I received from Him. I clearly know what I write and what I say. I proclaim the life of Jesus to you to bless you all. But now, you may not know this. However, if you go on reading, you will soon find that these messages originate with God, and you will be able to follow them. I want you to welcome this book as it will bless you.

The widow solved the problem of food after having met Elijah, but now you will have the solution concerning the food which endures unto everlasting life. In this sense, the fact that you meet me through this book will be a greater blessing than the widow woman's blessing through meeting Elijah. In addition, I hope to see you, the readers, face to face by expanding this indirect communication someday. Then, you will not only understand this book but also you will see that the Word will be written upon your heart and the Holy Spirit will come upon you as a result. And this we will do, if God permits.

Widow Woman Living in Poverty

Now, Elijah and the widow meet. Elijah told her to fetch him water and also to bring him bread. She seemed to have no difficulty in giving him water, but she only had a handful of meal and a little oil, which were her last morsels of food. And she would starve to death after it was eaten. She told Elijah about her pitiful circumstance.

Here, the widow woman represents us, the believers. And she is *me*. In believing in Jesus, like this widow, we have our own difficult circumstances too. We barely manage to live from hand to mouth every month. We have to worry about what to eat tomorrow and have no money to buy tomorrow's school supplies for our children. We truly hope to give offerings to the church and buy a present for the pastor if only we could earn money. We are as poor as this widow. But our reaction will be different from this widow woman.

Inordinate Demand by Elijah

Elijah says to her to make him a little cake first and bring it to him after having heard her miserable condition. We already know that Elijah is the prophet of God, and we are on his side. However, if you are not in possession of such knowledge, Elijah seems completely unreasonable.

"How could he ask her for it? She only has one last meal, that's all!" We would never request food from such a poor person but would rather go without. With this kind of thinking, we deem it quite natural in the church that the rich give much and the poor give less in offering. And we should not devour the households of the widows and the fatherless. Naturally, we consider that Elijah was completely selfish and unreasonable here in the story.

Was Elijah really so thoughtless that he asked for the poor widow's final food? No, he was not. Then why did he act that way? He knew that God would not let the barrel of meal waste, neither the cruse of oil fail, if she first gave to him.

What if he had been overwhelmed with human pity and he had decided not to ask her for food and left? People in this world who do not know God would have applauded him, saying that he was a real prophet and a man of God. However, if he had done so he would have killed her. Because she was down to her last meal and she said, "We may eat it, and die." We can see here that we can kill the widow unwittingly out of human pity if we do not communicate with God.

Do you communicate with God like Elijah and walk with Him, and do you know the very God who works this way? If you have not yet known Him, you can do nothing but believe in your homemade idol that is based on the morality and ethics of this sinful world that is completely different from the real God. Many people volunteer to be the men of God through studies of theologies in the seminary, but without communication with God they cannot be used by God. We should have the eyes of Elijah.

Faith of the Widow Woman

Elijah came to her and said, "Bring the last meal you have to me, and God will let you be carefree with food until it rains again." She followed what he told her, and survived during the famine. How could she do so? It is not because she was more compassionate than others, but because the living God walked with her.

Of course Elijah knew that he was sent by God to the widow woman. But how could she know that he was sent to her by God? We read the Bible to know that God sent Elijah. But if we, as the widow, meet him in our daily life, will it be possible for us to accept him as he whom God has sent? This is a difficult question to answer. Moreover, if he further asks us to give him our last morsel of food, how will we treat him? We may *try* to believe in him as he whom God sent, but we will finally stone him and turn our back.

She is the figure of the person who has truly repented to God, and is waiting for the Savior who will save her from her sin. So Elijah, the shadow of Jesus, was sent to her. In order to save her, Elijah had to take her to the cross to have her old self destroyed.

She, unlike Saul, had followed and obeyed Elijah to the extent of "if I perish, I perish," which means her death at her cross. Such obedience was envisaged by the sign of her saying, "Behold, I am gathering two sticks, that I may go in and dress it for me and my son, that we may eat it, and die" (v. 12). In here, "two sticks" signify the cross and "die" the death of her old self on the cross. That is, she was obeying God, forsaking her self-righteousness if it was against God's, in her everyday life. Therefore, she could obey "a man Elijah" to the cross.

And as a result of the cross, she was resurrected into eternal life, which also is signified by "she did eat many days and the meal did not waste or fail" (v. 15, 16).

She is the figure of the born again, being one with God and having the perfect communication with God.

To sum up, realistically, the widow who can give her last food in obedience to Elijah, the figure of Jesus, can also follow "a man Jesus" to the cross to destroy old self, and be born again. Also, symbolically, to give her last food in obedience to Elijah means she is ready to give up her old self on the cross and she is resurrected.

Therefore, Jesus, when He came, spoke very highly of her.
Read the following passage of Luke.

> But I tell you of a truth, many widows were in Israel in the days of Elias, when the heaven was shut up three years and six months, when great famine was throughout all the land; [26]But to none of them was Elias sent, save to Sarepta, a city of Sidon, to a woman that was a widow. _____ Luke 4:25-26

Jesus said that Elijah was sent to the widow in Zarephath, the land of the Gentiles, because there was no one like her among the many widows in Israel. If there had been some in Israel, he would have been sent to one of them. This means that the people of Israel and the ancestors believed in God but in vain, and because of this, all of them who were in the synagogue tried to throw Him off the cliff outside the town (Luke 4:29).

📂 Elijah, the Channel of Blessing

Outwardly, the widow woman seemed to be a help to Elijah by giving food. However, what she gave to him is what she planted in God, and what she received abundantly was what she reaped. Precisely, she was not a help to him but she planted and reaped a harvest of great benefit to herself.

If we think further, God did not have to use the last handful of meal and the little oil that the widow had to feed Elijah. He could have told him to go to a certain place, and filled empty barrels with meal and oil to make cakes. But, He sent Elijah to the widow and told him to request her last food because He wanted to bless her.

If we offer something to God first, it does not mean that we give it. It means that we sow it, and will reap more because of what we sowed. God gives us opportunities to plant, such as, tithes, offerings, serving table, prayer, and helping the poor in Him. If we plant with these, we will harvest abundantly.

"A Man Jesus" to the Widow

This widow can be compared to Saul. Saul is the example of destruction, and this widow is the example of eternal life. As Saul had "a man Samuel" (a shadow; Jesus), who is true, the widow had "a man Elijah" (a shadow; Jesus), who is also true.

However, contrary to Saul, the widow followed Elijah to the cross and received the blessing, which was eternal life and salvation. Saul did not truly repent in his life so he could not obey "a man Samuel," but the widow woman did so she could obey "a man Elijah" to the end, the cross.

Our communication and relationship with God, which is actually salvation and faith, will increase progressively: Eli–Ahab–Saul–Zarephath widow. Eli, Ahab and Saul could not follow "a man Jesus," due to non-repentance. Therefore, they went back to their original place of death because they could not follow up to the salvation point, the cross. But the widow woman repented and she could obey and be saved.

In our salvation steps, as the final stage, we will get to meet "a man Jesus." Now, if we follow Him to the cross we will be saved. If not, we will be like Saul.

Epilogue

The widow woman valued the voice of God more than the lives of herself and her son, and obeyed it. Therefore, she could follow His voice and obeyed Elijah to give her last meal. This means that anyone who loves God and honors Him in this way will surely follow a man Jesus to the cross and be resurrected. And he becomes one with God and has communication in the Stage of the Holy Spirit.

As for "a man Jesus" to you, who is your a man Jesus now? Are you following him, forsaking all behind? Or have you met a man Jesus yet? If you want to increase your faith to the stage of this widow, you must meet a man Jesus and obey Him. Then you will achieve the

perfect communication, having the same faith with her.
    Let the faith of the widow woman at Zarephath be yours.

2

OFFERINGS AND TITHES

What are Offerings?

When we give offerings and tithes to God, it does not simply mean that we give money to Him. We should communicate with Him when we give offerings just as His Word commands us. Therefore, the offerings shall include our faith and obedience to Him. As the offerings express our faith, a person can be known whether he has faith or not by his offerings. We can give real offerings when we offer in communication with Him.

The offerings and the tithes I mentioned above are of God, which is the major premise. Therefore, if anyone who wishes to object my sayings here, he should first consult with the living God. Let him not object based on his common sense of men, because what I am saying is of God's mind. Any objections, judgments, and accusations regarding this message will not be valid if they are not of God.

Offerings Belong to God

The church is a building and an organization we can see and

consider, but it is managed and led by God who is unseen, doing good in the society. Therefore, if someone wishes to understand the works done by the church, he should first know God. But the people of the world see the church without God, and accordingly they regard the church as one of the many religious and secular charitable institutions of the world. This is the limit of their viewpoints towards the church, and this causes them to misjudge and misunderstand the church.

God has established the commandment that we make offerings to Him in the church. And the members offer their money to God. But those who do not know God misunderstand such offerings. They say, "If I pay offerings to the church, will God use it? No, I don't think so. The pastors will use it. God needs no money."

That sounds right. Really, when we give offerings, it does not go up to heaven for God to use. God does not need our money; he is the source of all provision. But they think in such a way because they do not know Him at all. None of us will offer that valuable money to Him if we have no faith in Him. We give to Him as a token of our faith in Him. Therefore, the offerings are given to Him with the faith of the giver being included. And offerings represent the faith of the giver.

If we meet people who have no idea of God, we should not talk with them about offerings. Will they know about offerings to God, who does not know God? No way. If they do not know offerings in the church, it simply means that they do not know Him.

Offerings in the church have the following meanings:

First, the offerings are used by the church of God to maintain its physical existence in this world. The church is the place where heaven (unseen) and earth (seen) meet. And the church, as the body of God, in this world, is offering opportunities for the unbelievers to meet God.

Second, it is the way in which we can receive the blessing of the spirit and the blessing of material riches from Him. Offerings, which are commanded by God, are different from the donations of this world. He increases our faith through our offerings and returns the given offerings to us after having blessed it many times over.

To sum up, the offerings we give to the church are an essential factor enabling us to preach the gospel to the world, increasing our faith and giving us abundant wealth.

Church That Has No Offerings?

Those who do not know the facts about offerings try to build a church that requires no offerings from its members. They think they will not trouble the church members and build a really good biblical church. They advertise themselves and say:

"You don't need to pay any tithes in our church," or

"No offerings in our group."

This kind of message may sound seductive to those who are reluctant to give offerings. They will allege that such a church is a true church of God, not focused on money.

Is this true? Even if the church gathers no offerings from you, you will not be a person who has risen above money. On the contrary, when you say, "I give up the importance of money," it confirms that you are cherishing it. Furthermore, those who have been tempted by the message and change from church to church, fall under the same group to whom the money is more important than God. Therefore, they are tempted by the message and they waver.

God Almighty does not intend to take our monies by the offerings in the church, but it is the means to give us manifold blessings. We should consider the church offerings with the mind of God.

Now I will now explain the basic principle of giving offerings to God, and how God works when we give offerings.

He who Sows Sparingly shall Reap Also Sparingly

2 Corinthians 9:6-7
But this I say, He which sows sparingly shall reap also sparingly; and he which sows bountifully shall reap also bountifully. ⁷Every man according as he purposes in his heart, so let him give; not grudgingly, or of necessity: for God loves a cheerful giver.

Paul the apostle wrote the above passage after he had received a generous offering from the church members of Corinth for the purpose of helping the church of Jerusalem which was in trouble. It is of no meaning to discuss offerings in the church without God in the picture. God and the offerings given to Him are one; inseparable.

Many believers think that offerings in the church are a kind of donation. Superficially, this may appear to be the case, but the offerings in the church are basically different from that the donations solicited by charitable organizations around the world. Offerings in the church are of God, and donations in the world are of man.

Here, in this passage, please pay keen attention to the fact that Paul does not appeal to human compassion and emotion as people do in a charitable donation in the world, but he mentions that offerings constitute sowing and reaping before God. He clearly says that when we give offerings, we sow money before God, and we will therefore reap blessings. The difference between offerings in church and donations in the world can be defined as whether God is involved, or not.

Offerings are Sowing to God

To give offerings in the church is to sow, according to the law of life. We sow in order to reap. When we have given to God, He will let us gather what we have sowed. This is one of the characteristics of God, who is life.

When we give offerings to God and hope for a harvest, we do not need to feel ashamed of hoping for worldly blessings. How can it be a bad or shameful thing to expect a harvest according to the law of life? God tells us to give offerings to Him not to take what we have away from us, but to return to us abundantly based on what we have sown. We give offerings to the church, such as tithes, offerings for building a church, offerings for an urgent benefaction, and offerings for evangelism. God gives us opportunities to sow through such cases and blesses us with a rich harvest through sowing.

I remember a pastor saying in a revival gathering, "Church members will not get blessed if the church does not build a new church building." He meant that if they would build a new church building, they would do their best in giving offerings for the building and God would accordingly allow them to reap abundantly for what they had sown. It was a very convincing message. As I explained in the previous section, the widow woman in Zarephath gave her last meal to Elijah and received a blessing that no other widow in Israel could get.

Those who know the way God blesses believers through sowing and reaping will sow on every occasion. He is well pleased with all kinds of offerings because He is pleased with the faith of those who believe in Him and give their valuable offerings to the church because of Him. If we sow much, we will reap much.

On the contrary, if we sow nothing, we will reap nothing. Read Galatians 6:7, "Be not deceived; God is not mocked: for whatever a man sows, that shall he also reap."

They who know nothing of God sow nothing and also try to prevent others from sowing. They study the Scripture very hard to justify avoiding offerings. As expected, they say:

"The tithe has passed away since it originates in the law," or

"It is to blaspheme God if we give offerings to Him, because it means we think He loves money."

God does not receive the offerings, but sees the faith of the giver; thus, this argument is flawed from the very beginning. Please do not be deceived by such vain statements and do not be short of money during your life.

God wishes to allow us money as a blessing. But He blesses us according to the law of life. That is, He has us sow and, as a result, makes us reap. Therefore, if we pray for money, He tells us without exception to sow first. This is the only way.

Let me share the testimonies regarding sowing of the offering. The pastor recommended a member of the church sow the offerings of God without grudging. On hearing what he said, the church member said within herself, "The pastor does not know me. Now I don't have money to give as offerings to the church, but I offered much when I had enough in the past. I will surely increase my offerings when I get enough."

She could not sow because she thought, "I had no money." Even though she spared the offerings, her household income remained miserable. One day, God moved her by saying, "You are eating the seed because you are hungry now." His word hurt her so much. She could not sow because she had no money but He rebuked her about not having sown in place of consolation. She realized it was the word of God when the pastor admonished her previously.

Also, I know a man who was an unbeliever. He could not run his business well and finally he went bankrupt, and was chased by the money lenders. At this difficult situation, his wife advised him to come to church to pray God to revive them. Therefore, he took her advice and attended the church regularly. While hearing sermons he felt the pastor was preaching the truth wonderfully and he was impressed very much. However, one day, it seemed to him that the pastor was stressing offerings to God at the end of the sermons almost all the time. After realizing this, he was pained to hear such admonishment, for the reason he had come to church was because he was broke. Naturally he then cursed and swore at the pastor's message about the offerings.

However, the businessman did not realize the fact that the voice of the pastor was God's. That is, God was saying through the pastor to him, "If you want to be blessed and reap, you must sow first. So sow!" Not knowing this, unfortunately, the businessman grew angry with the pastor who conveyed the good news and truth.

Yes, you will reap when you sow. If you do not sow, you will not gather and you will only envy your brother's richness. Your life is up to you. It will be regrettable to sow seed because you feel compelled. But, if you understand the principle of "no sowing, no reaping," you have to do so no matter how difficult it may be.

God also sowed Jesus, His precious Son, on this earth so that He may have many sons (John 12:24). He sowed in tears and He is now reaping many sons in joy. You should give offerings not because you are rich but because you are not rich. You will be blessed when you sow even if when you think you have nothing to sow.

Give Offerings Through God

What does it mean that "according as he purposes in his heart" (2 Corinthians 9:7)? Does it mean we decide to give a certain amount already in mind? This can't be true since what is important in this passage is what the Lord is telling us to do. To give "according as he purposes in his heart" means to give as He stirs our spirit. An offering is something given to Him. Therefore, He stirs up our heart on every occasion in which we give offerings to Him. When we give offerings as much as we are moved to (not more or less than), we give as we purpose in our heart.

In fact, it is very difficult to give offerings as we purpose in our heart. When God has moved our spirit, we ignore it with our own thinking such as, "What? Five thousand dollars? That's nonsense. How can I give that big sum? I am really badly off now."

When He tells us something like that in our mind, we generally beat it down to fifty dollars with a lot of reasons and internal rationalizing. This is not giving as we purpose in our heart, but following our own carnal inclinations.

On the contrary, if we give six thousand dollars or ten thousand dollars as an offering when He has moved us with five thousand dollars, it also does not mean that we give according as we purpose in our heart. He calls people arrogant because they override the will of God. When we give just as He said, we can give according as we purpose in our heart, and then we are called cheerful givers.

If we give grudgingly or out of a feeling of necessity, it proves that we give with our own thoughts and without God. Since we do not give through Him, we have no faith that we will reap more later. Consequently, we will display discontent or stinginess while giving. We will feel joyful when we give offerings through God, but we will show regret and pressure when we give on our own.

What is Sown Decomposes

Consider the following passage.

Truly, truly, I say to you, Except a corn of wheat fall into the ground and die, it stays alone: but if it die, it brings forth much fruit. _____ John 12:24

According to the principle of life, what is sown first decays or decomposes. That is, the seed that is sown initially decomposes in the ground and it never returns to the person who has sown it. But the person will reap an abundance of new seed from what has been sown.

This is applicable to the case of sowing offerings. God receives the offering and blesses the giver with another, similar seed. He has already accepted it instantly when we gave it. Once it is given, the giver does not need to try to find for what purpose He has used it. This has to be clear in our mind because He will have it used in the most appropriate manner by the church. When we understand that once the offering is given it first decomposes, and then it will bear much fruit.

Not many believers understand this principle of life. Most believers, after having offered it, unwittingly try to control and meddle in how and where the offering is used. This is how they used to operate when investing money in a company or project. If they had given offerings in that way, they did not give them to Him, but they invested only for their own certain profit; for example, taking pride over others, or seeking respect from others in the church. God does not guarantee a harvest for such investments (Matthew 6:2) since what they sowed did not first decompose in the ground.

If you want to be wise, give offerings and entrust the church of God with how they are used, then your offerings will bear much fruit.

Epilogue

Whatever offerings we give in the church should be through the prompting of God in our hearts. We give them to Him and they first decompose before they return to us as manifold blessings.

You reap nothing at present because you have sown nothing in the past or you have sown erroneously. If you start to sow correctly from now on, the time to reap much will come to you. God receives the offerings from us not because He wants to take our money but because He wants to bless us with increased faith and wealth.

Only they who sow will reap. I hope that all of you experience the joy of walking with Him and find greater faith through giving offerings.

The Tithe That Always Abides, Part I
– Two Types of Tithe

Hebrews 7:1-10
For this Melchisedec, king of Salem, priest of the most high God, who met Abraham returning from the slaughter of the kings, and blessed him; ²To whom also Abraham gave a tenth part of all; first being by interpretation King of righteousness, and after that also King of Salem, which is, King of peace; ³Without father, without mother, without descent, having neither beginning of days, nor end of life; but made like to the Son of God; stays a priest continually. ⁴Now consider how great this man was, to whom even the patriarch Abraham gave the tenth of the spoils. ⁵And truly they that are of the sons of Levi, who receive the office of the priesthood, have a commandment to take tithes of the people according to the law, that is, of their brothers, though they come out of the loins of Abraham: ⁶But he whose descent is not counted from them received tithes of Abraham, and blessed him that had the promises. ⁷And without all contradiction the less is blessed of the better. ⁸And here men that die receive tithes; but there he receives them, of whom it is witnessed that he lives. ⁹And as I may so say, Levi also, who receives tithes, paid tithes in Abraham. ¹⁰For he was yet in the loins of his father, when Melchisedec met him.

Some people say that a man's faith is known by whether he gives tithes to God in the church. He will be regarded as a man of good faith if he tithes, and if he does not, he will be considered a man of poor faith. We cannot arbitrarily say this is correct. However, it is in a way correct because it is not easy to give ten percent of one's gross income as offerings. Those experiencing God and loving Him with a true heart give the tithe. Therefore, it is reasonable to say that those who tithe have good faith.

The tithe is a tenth part of personal income set apart as offerings to God. However, in addition to this simple meaning, the tithe has a profound spiritual meaning. I will divide this sharing about the tithing into the following four sub-sections because I have much to tell.

- ✓ Two types of tithe
- ✓ Two types of priests
- ✓ From the tithe of the law to that of Abraham
- ✓ Jesus' view to the Tithe

Two Types of Tithe

This passage relates to the priest, and the tithe is connected to the priest. The Scripture mentions two kinds of tithes: The first one is given to the priests of the tribe of Levi by the Israelites, and the second one is given to Melchisedec by Abraham.

For ease of description, the tithe offered to the priests of the tribe of Levi will be called the "tithe of the law" since its requirements are set by the law, and the tithe given to Melchisedec by Abraham will be referred to as the "tithe of Abraham," considering that Abraham offered it for the first time in the Scripture.

The writer of Hebrews compares the priests who receive these tithes. He says how *great* Melchisedec was while drawing a comparison between Melchisedec who received a tithe from Abraham and the priests of the tribe of Levi who received the same from the people of Israel (Hebrews 7:4). Melchisedec is the sign of the priest of the gospel and Levi is that of the priest of the law. Therefore, *great* means that when the law, a *shadow* is compared to the gospel, the *reality*, the latter is expressed to be greater than the former.

The system of giving the tithe of the law and that of Abraham is shown in the following table.

Name	Giver	Priest	Role	Word
Tithe of the law	People	Levi	Shadow	Law
Tithe of Abraham	Abraham	Melchisedec	Reality	Gospel

📁 Tithe of the Law

The writer of Hebrews is talking about the tithe of the law below.

> And truly they that are of the sons of Levi, who receive the office of the priesthood, have a commandment to take tithes of the people according to the law, that is, of their brothers, though they come out of the loins of Abraham: _____ Hebrews 7:5

This tithe is given to the tribe of Levi and its priests by the people according to the law. Read the following passage.

> And the LORD spoke to Aaron, You shall have no inheritance in their land, neither shall you have any part among them: I am your part and your inheritance among the children of Israel. [21]And, behold, I have given the children of Levi all the tenth in Israel for an inheritance, for their service which they serve, even the service of the tabernacle of the congregation. [22]Neither must the children of Israel from now on come near the tabernacle of the congregation, lest they bear sin, and die. _____ Numbers 18:20-22

The tribe of Levi among the twelve tribes of Israel had no other inheritance than to serve the Lord in the tabernacle, besides certain towns to live in within the borders of their brothers' territory (Numbers 35:1-6). Therefore, the other eleven tribes gave a tenth of their income to the Levites for their living. Also, the Levites should offer a tenth part to the priests (Numbers 18:26). This is a general meaning of the tithe.

This tithe is mentioned in various ways in the Old Testament, such as, "the tithe of the seed of the land or the fruit of the tree given to the Levites and the priests" (Leviticus 27:30-32), "the tithe shared in the habitation of the LORD" (Deuteronomy 12:5-9, Deuteronomy 14:22-23), and "the tithe eaten by the Levite, the fatherless, and the widow" (Deuteronomy 14:28-29, Deuteronomy 26:12-13).

Some people say that the tithe of the law is classified as several kinds of tithes based on the above-quoted verses. However, the writer of Hebrews generally calls all these tithes as one kind and says that the priests of the Levites had a commandment to take the tithes of the people (Hebrews 7:5). Also the Jews in Jesus' time have understood various tithes that are found in the Old Testament as the tithes of all that they possess in a lump (Luke 18:12). We can draw a conclusion from this that the tithe of the law is the tithe of all that the people possess and given to the priests of the Levites by them. This tithe of the law is the tithe of income.

I will now explain the tithe of Abraham.

📂 The Tithe of Abraham

The writer of Hebrews speaks of a tithe that is different from the tithe of the law.

> For this Melchisedec, king of Salem, priest of the most high God, who met Abraham returning from the slaughter of the kings, and blessed him; ²To whom also Abraham gave a tenth part of all; first being by interpretation King of righteousness, and after that also King of Salem, which is, King of peace; ³Without father, without mother, without descent, having neither beginning of days, nor end of life; but made like to the Son of God; stays a priest continually. ⁴Now consider how great this man was, to whom even the patriarch Abraham gave the tenth of the spoils.
> _____ Hebrews 7:1-4

It is the tithe offered to Melchisedec by Abraham. It was introduced before the people of Israel received the law through Moses on

Mount Sinai in Exodus 20. Therefore, apart from the law, Abraham offered a tithe to Melchisedec after having received bread and wine from him. The tithe that is given "after receiving bread and wine" is the key point to understand the spiritual meaning of the tithe of Abraham.

The background of the above passages is found in Genesis14:1-20. When Abraham heard that his nephew Lot was taken captive, he armed his trained servants to rescue his nephew and brought back all the goods after they won. At this moment, Melchisedec king of Salem, brought forth bread and wine to bless Abraham, and Abraham gave him tithes of all.

Literally, this is just one historical scene; however there is a greater significance in this meeting. It reveals to us that we are to be saved by receiving the Word of Jesus Christ, and be born again as new men to give ourselves to God as a living sacrifice.

I will enlarge on this.

First, Melchisedec is a symbol of Jesus Christ. The writer of Hebrews portrays him in the above passage as follows: "King of righteousness, and after that also King of Salem, which is, King of peace; Without father, without mother, without descent, having neither beginning of days, nor end of life; but made like to the Son of God; stays a priest continually (v. 3)."

Isaiah describes Jesus Christ as follows:

> For to us a child is born, to us a son is given: and the government shall be on his shoulder: and his name shall be called Wonderful, Counselor, The mighty God, The everlasting Father, The Prince of Peace. _____ Isaiah 9:6

Both verses indicate Jesus Christ who is the author of eternal life. Therefore, Melchisedec is a sign of Jesus Christ. He brought forth bread and wine and gave them to Abraham.

What do the bread and wine mean spiritually? They indicate the flesh and blood of Jesus, which means the word of life of Jesus.

Read John below.

> Then Jesus said to them, Truly, truly, I say to you, Except you eat the flesh of the Son of man, and drink his blood, you have no life in you. ⁵⁴Whoever eats my flesh, and drinks my blood, has eternal life; and I will raise him up at the last day. ⁵⁵For my flesh is meat indeed, and my blood is drink indeed.
> John 6:53-55

In the night in which He was betrayed, Jesus took bread, gave thanks, broke it, gave it to His disciples, and He also shared wine. This signifies that He gives the Word of life to them. In the same manner, when Melchisedec gave bread and wine to Abraham, it symbolizes that Jesus Christ gives the Word of life to Abraham.

What did Abraham do after receiving bread and wine? He gave a tithe to Melchisedec. This is the sign for the disciples, who, after receiving the word of Jesus, offered tithes to Jesus. They offered Him their re-born selves as tithes. Therefore if someone receives the bread and wine of Jesus, he will be born again as a man in whom Christ is formed, and he will present himself a living sacrifice of tithe to God (Romans 12:1), just as the disciples did. This is the true meaning of the scene in which Abraham gave a tithe to Melchisedec. The "tithe of Abraham" means "oneself who is born again by and through the Word of Jesus."

Abraham gave a tenth of the spoil. This means our souls that were taken by Satan are restored as those of God by the Word, bread and wine, of Jesus Christ and are then offered to Him. The tithe of Abraham was literally the spoils taken from the kings he defeated, but its spiritual reality is the born again man himself.

The following tithes in the Scriptures are considered to refer to the tithe of Abraham: Jacob swears the tithe on Genesis 28:22, "And this stone, which I have set for a pillar, shall be God's house: and of all that you shall give me I will surely give the tenth to you."

This signifies that this stone (Jesus Christ) will be the pillar of the house (church), and I will make the members who are drawn by You be born again to be Yours (give tithe). That is, Jacob says that he will obey and follow Jesus to the cross to be a church member (to be His) first: and he will lead others that God brings to him to be His also.

When I Would Do Good

Likewise, the tithe which is mentioned in Malachi is basically referred to the tithe of Abraham. "Will a man rob God? Yet you have robbed me. But you say, Wherein have we robbed you? In tithes and offerings" (Malachi 3:8). This means that the priests failed to have the people be born again (give to God as tithes of Abraham), so they robbed God of the spirits of the people.

In conclusion, the tithe of Abraham is the "tithe of oneself," and it is also the "spiritual tithe" according to its spiritual meaning.

📂 Reality of the Tithe of the Law is the Tithe of Abraham

God made provision for the support and everyday living of the priests of the tribe of Levi through the tithe of the law. Did he then set up the tithe of the law purely for the Levites' living? No, He did not. He reveals the truth of the spiritual world through the law. Hence, the tithe of the law has spiritual reality in it.

What spiritual reality is this? It is the tithe of Abraham. That the people gave tithes to the priests of the Levites is the *shadow* of the reality that Abraham himself tithed to Melchisedec, the priest.

When God set up the tithe of the law, He wanted to pay for the service of the sons of Levi in the tabernacle at first place. And also by doing so, He wanted the Israelites to see the reality to which it points. That is, He intended that each time the people gave tithes to the priests of the Levites, they would remember that "I have to give myself to God as a tithe by being born again by the word!"

This is the meaning of "But in those sacrifices there is a remembrance again made of sins every year" (Hebrews 10:3), which is translated in NIV as "But those sacrifices are an annual reminder of sins." Israelites were reminded of their sins by annual sacrifices. Likewise, by the tithe of income, we are reminded we are born again as the tithe of Abraham, which is our new self. In fact, the role of all laws, including the tithe, is to show us the way to be born again as new men through Jesus.

Earlier I mentioned various tithes covered in the law, such as the tithe shared in the habitation of the Lord and the tithe eaten by the Levite, the fatherless, and the widow. All these mean helping the poor or making a donation; however they are not the only intended meanings of the Scriptures, because the Scriptures testify about Jesus, the Savior. Apparently, helping poor or making a donation are not the testimonies of Jesus Himself.

The tithe mentioned above is expressed as food to eat. That is, to reveal the fact that to the born again man, the tithe itself becomes spiritual food. He can give the spiritual food, the Word, to neighbors, as Jesus did to them. That is, they give the Word of life to the fatherless and the widow who are hungry for eternal life so that they may eat it, and have God and Christ in them as their father and husband. Therefore, the tithe of the law is written as the food to eat since its reality is the tithe of Abraham, which serves as spiritual food.

In conclusion, the reality of the tithe of the law is that it means the tithe of Abraham.

Now we will see two types of priests.

Two Types of Priests

There are two types of priests who receive the tithes: *first*, the priest of the Levites and *second*, Melchisedec the priest. Read verses 5-7 from the main text.

> And truly they that are of the sons of Levi, who receive the office of the priesthood, have a commandment to take tithes of the people according to the law, that is, of their brothers, though they come out of the loins of Abraham: ⁶But he whose descent is not counted from them received tithes of Abraham, and blessed him that had the promises. ⁷And without all contradiction the less is blessed of the better. _____ Hebrews 7:5-7

The priests of the Levites represent the priests of the law, and Melchisedec the priest of the gospel

📂 Levi, the Priest of the Law

The priests of the law represent those who only know the legalistic and literal meanings of the Scriptures. No gospel of life can come out of the mouths of such priests because they are not one with Christ. They can preach nothing but the law of death, and the people hearing what they teach cannot be born again as those who have a new life. For instance, they only know the tithe of income, but do not know its hidden meaning, which is the tithe of Abraham. Under them, therefore, people can be diligent to tithe their income, but do not know at all that they also have to be given as the tithe itself. Ultimately, they are holding up the spirits of the people which must go back to God by being born again.

The preachers of the present day are the same. They do not know the tithe of Abraham, so they focus on the only tithe they know—that of income. They speculate whether it is right to gather the tithe from the poor widows or not, according to human pity. They may get approval from the men of this world, but God is very much displeased because their spirits remain dead regardless of their tithe of income.

Accordingly, such preachers cannot but rob the spirits of the church members to be given to God. If they are born again and know the tithe of Abraham, they would have shown people the way to become the tithe of Abraham without neglecting the tithe of income walking with God.

The priests who were rebuked because of their robbery of the tithes and offerings (of Abraham) in Malachi 3 represent those preachers who do not know the tithe of Abraham in the present age. They, altogether, are the priests of the law, the Levites.

God wants such priests to be born again as the priests of the gospel, Melchisedec.

Melchisedec, the Priest of the Gospel

If the priests of the law receive the Word of life and are born again to be priests of the gospel, they can guide people to be born again by the Christ. They have already offered themselves to God as spiritual tithes and they can give people to Him as tithes also. They are the priests belonging to Melchisedec, the figure of Jesus Christ.

God said, as follows, in consideration of the tithes of such priests,

"You can return to me by giving tithes and offerings" (Malachi 3:7). They will naturally no longer rob of the hearts of people, because they can guide the people to the cross, being united with them, to make them one with Him. Paul says in Romans:

> That I should be the minister of Jesus Christ to the Gentiles, ministering the gospel of God, that the offering up of the Gentiles might be acceptable, being sanctified by the Holy Spirit.
> _____ Romans 15:16

Differently from the priests of the law, Paul robbed nothing from God as a priest of the gospel. He has the Gentiles sanctified by the Holy Spirit and offered them all as tithes and offerings acceptable to God. Today's preachers must think deeply whether they are giving the church members to Him as tithes and offerings. If so, they are the priests belonging to Melchisedec, the priests of the gospel. In this way, the priests and the people will be equally blessed by God.

From the Tithe of the Law to the Tithe of Abraham

The writer of Hebrews compares the mortal Levites to Melchisedec, who has eternal life, in order to identify the difference between the law and the gospel.

> And here men that die receive tithes; but there he receives them, of whom it is witnessed that he lives. ⁹And as I may so say, Levi also, who receives tithes, paid tithes in Abraham. ¹⁰For he was yet in the loins of his father, when Melchisedec met him.
> _____ Hebrews 7:8-10

The writer of Hebrews implies that it is important to pay tithes of the law, but it is much more important to give the tithe of Abraham.
Also he says that Levi, receiving tithes of the law, paid tithes to Melchisedec because Abraham his father gave a tithe to him.
Why did the writer of Hebrews say this? It is, as Abraham gave a tithe to Melchisedec and was blessed, so Levi who is in the loins of

his father should pay tithe (of Abraham) to Melchisedec and be blessed by him.

If we give tithes of the law in the church, we should be satisfied at that level. Without neglecting it, we also should give the tithes of Abraham to Melchisedec (i.e., Jesus Christ) when the time comes and we should be blessed by Him. This blessing is our salvation, becoming one with God by the Holy Spirit. The tithe of Abraham is the *reality*, not the *shadow*, which is greater.

Jesus' View to the Tithe

We can find other Scriptures verses that clarify the relation between the tithe of the law and the tithe of Abraham. Chapter 23 in Matthew is always quoted when people argue about tithing. It is the only time Jesus spoke about tithing, so many people read and study it with interest.

But the problem is that they do not have the spiritual eyes to read and understand what Jesus means. As a result, whether they are against the tithing or for it, they cite the same text in support of their argument. How can it be correct for those who have no eyes to read the Scriptures to say that tithes are abrogated, and will it be correct for them to defend that tithes still hold good?

In fact, Jesus does not say anything about abrogation or validity of the tithe of income here, but explains the relationship of the tithe of the income (the law) and that of Abraham (grace).

Jesus says to the scribes and Pharisees:

> Woe to you, scribes and Pharisees, hypocrites! for you pay tithe of mint and anise and cummin, and have omitted the weightier matters of the law, judgment, mercy, and faith: these ought you to have done, and not to leave the other undone. ^{24}You blind guides, which strain at a gnat, and swallow a camel.
> Matthew 23:23-24

The scribes and Pharisees paid a tithe of their income because God prescribed it through the law. However, as Jesus rebuked them, we, as believers in Jesus, quickly conclude: "Ah, they paid tithes but without pure heart, omitting judgment, mercy, and faith. However, I am not so."

Moreover, we consider judgment, mercy, and faith a sort of appropriate mental attitude when we pay tithes. Of course, we have to be sincerely-minded when offering something or doing something related to God, for sure. However, judgment, mercy, and faith represent the tithe of Abraham, not the mental attitude we should have when we tithe.

Although the scribes and the Pharisees were eager to pay the tithes of the law, they never knew the tithe of Abraham, which is the reality the tithe the law pointed to. They were rebuked because of this.

Then how can judgment, mercy, and faith be the tithe of Abraham? It is as follows:

Judgment (*krisis* in Greek) refers to Jesus coming to us and judging our old self on the cross. Mercy (*eleos* in Greek) refers to the resurrected born-again life in Jesus through God's mercy. Faith (*pistis* in Greek) indicates the faith of Jesus that will abide in our born-again bodies. Accordingly, judgment, mercy, and faith represent the process by which a person meets Jesus and is born again as a new man. This is so we can give ourselves to God as a living sacrifice, which is the tithe of Abraham.

The scribes and the Pharisees were only interested in their financial tithing and they showed no interest in the spiritual meaning of tithing and were ignorant of it. As a result, by paying the tithes of the law, they only increased their self-righteousness by believing they were following what God had commanded them to do. This is the *gnat* they found in the tithes (v. 24), but they missed the judgment, mercy, and faith, which is the tithe of Abraham. And that is weightier matter, the *camel*, which they should have found in tithing. Thus, they were rebuked.

Jesus continues to say, "These ought you to have done, and not to leave the other undone." Here, "these" indicate judgment, mercy, and faith, and "the other" refers to tithe of the income. Therefore, this word is frequently quoted as a reference that Jesus said to tithe even in the New Testament time. However it cannot easily be interpreted in that manner.

Judgment, mercy, and faith refer to the gospel, and tithes of mint, anise, and cummin refer to the law. Jesus did not say, "Do these (i.e., judgment, mercy, and faith) and additionally do the other (tithe of mint, anise, and cummin)," because the two, that is the law and the gospel, cannot coexist in our hearts. Only one of "these (gospel)" or "the other (law)" can exist in us. This means that if we are under the law, we can never be under the gospel.

If we are under the gospel, we do not leave the "other (law)" undone by having "these (gospel, grace)" done, because the "other" has been perfected in "these." To explain further, to have "these" done refers to the situation in which we are born again and offer the tithe of Abraham, and then, the "other (law)" is fulfilled in us. This way, "These ought you to have done, and not to leave the other undone" is fulfilled. Consider Matthew 5:17: "Think not that I am come to destroy the law, or the prophets: I am not come to destroy, but to fulfill."

Therefore, Jesus' saying, "These ought you to have done, and not to leave the other undone" means "You should be born again and be those who give the tithes of Abraham."

Epilogue

There are two types of tithes: the tithe of the law, meaning money, and the tithe of Abraham, indicating the born-again man. The tithe of the law is the duty God commanded and also works so that we may hope for good things to come. Here, the good thing refers to offering ourselves as tithes of Abraham.

We begin our faith with the tithe of the law, and we should be born again as those who pay the tithes of Abraham in due course. This is the revelation of the Hebrews when its author mentions Levi paid tithes to Melchisedec through Abraham.

When we have offered the tithe of Abraham, then we who were of the priests of the Levites will be of the priests of Jesus Christ, and the tithes established by the law will be fulfilled in us.

Therefore, let's pay the tithe of Abraham!

The Tithe That Always Abides, Part II
– Is the Tithe of the Law Taken Away?

Hebrews 10:8-9
Above when he said, Sacrifice and offering and burnt offerings and offering for sin you would not, neither had pleasure therein; which are offered by the law; ⁹Then said he, See, I come to do your will, O God. He takes away the first, that he may establish the second.

I will now explain the question of the maintenance or abolition of tithing in the present time; the tithe of income.

In the above passage, God has no pleasure in the sacrifices and offerings given to Him under the law. People generally use this passage of Scripture to support their argument that since Jesus has come the law has been taken away. Moreover, we may wonder whether it would be appropriate to apply the word He gave to the Israelites several thousand years ago to the present day.

Many people are concerned about the tithe and study it because it relates to the all-important idol of today: money.

However, the problem they have is they approach the Scriptures to find reasons not to tithe because it is burdensome. Therefore, they fall into their own trap and draw a conclusion that "the tithe has been annulled since Jesus came." They publish books as if they have discovered something great, and they make their ideas public. Their opinion, that people do not need to pay tithes, may sound like very good news to those who are reluctant to pay in the first place, but as a matter of fact, it makes them reject their blessings to come.

Tithing has not been invalidated. Of course I am talking about the tithe of income. The tithe abides always, regardless of time.

I shall explain this with the following three sub-sections.

- ✓ Has the Tithe Been Taken Away Because it is Old Law?
- ✓ Is the Law Taken Away Since Jesus has Come?
- ✓ The Tithe of the Law of the Tithe of Abraham

Has the Tithe Been Taken Away Because it is Old Law?

Some people who are against tithing say, "Will it be right to apply the law about the tithe that was given to the Israelites some thousands of years ago to us today? As the European countries have already abolished tithing, it is appropriate to abandon it."

It is said that some European countries have absorbed the tithe into the government system, and contemporary Jews do not tithe. However, the Scriptures are the Word of God to *me*, and as such the tithe is the covenant between God and *myself*. We need to be sincere to the Word of God, and do what we are supposed to do according to the Scriptures regardless of what others do or do not do. If the European countries and the Jews have done away with it, it is their own decision. They cannot be our example and their decision cannot be biblical. We ought to follow what God and the Scriptures say.

I will explain the title question from the biblical point of view. The Old Testament gives the law for the Israelites to keep, such as tithing, worshipping at the tabernacle, performing the sacrifices, having priests as intermediaries, male circumcision, almsgiving, fasting, prayer, committing no murder, eating no swine's flesh, keeping the Sabbath, levirate practice, etc. The Israelites had the shadow of things to come, which is Jesus Christ. The Scriptures, the Word of truth, are not only applicable to the people of Israel; they are applicable to all human beings. The "people of Israel" refer to us who believe in Jesus and seek the truth. Those who are commanded by the law of God and have to keep it are none other than us.

However, some of the things the Israelites did under the law are not performed by us currently, for example, levirate, circumcision, "an eye for an eye and a tooth for a tooth," keeping the Sabbath, and not eating swine's flesh. We have a hazy idea that we do not keep those things because Jesus has come. However, that is because of the reasoning of the present day, environments, and culture. God accepts those changes, and you will know if you ask Him.

Then the question comes, "Can the tithe be regarded as such an item to be discarded?" No. Sorry! It is because the tithe has a very special and clear purpose that it may not be taken away; that is, to pay for the service of the Levites who serve in the tabernacle. Accordingly, the tithe will last as long as the tabernacle and the service workers remain in this world.

Do you wish to believe that the sacrifice system has been abolished along with the Levitical priesthood? That is correct but the sacrifice system has been developed and revealed in another form, so it still exists and it will always. The tabernacle is present as the church, the sacrifice as service and church life, and the priests as pastors or ministers. These will never be abandoned. The tithe of the law is our duty to give according to its original purpose.

📂 The Offering of Sacrifice Always Valid

In the Old Testament time, people were forgiven their sins and had their relationship with God restored through the offering of sacrifices. In fact, all the other requirements of the law refer to only one thing; that is, the forgiveness of sins.

The offering of a sacrifice has been progressively developed and revealed from the tabernacle to the temple, from the temple to Jesus Christ, and from Jesus Christ to the church, and the corresponding form of sacrifice has also been changed. For example, nowadays we worship God not in the tabernacle but in the church, and the sacrifice of the law has been developed and revealed to be the church life of today. Thus the sacrifice did not disappear.

As the people of Israel are temporarily forgiven for their sins through the offering of the animal sacrifice, we are forgiven forever for our sins by offering Jesus on the cross through church life. The sacrifice in the Old Testament time is the figure of our current church life, which is led by Jesus.

Now I will describe how the sacrifice institution in the past matches today's church life.

Tabernacle Matches Church

The church corresponds to the tabernacle in the past. As God was present in the tabernacle, God abides in Jesus Christ, and God lives in the church, the body of Christ. As the Lord has met the people of Israel in the tabernacle, God who is a spirit meets church members in the church. People are forgiven for their sins in the tabernacle in the past and in the church today.

Sacrifice Matches Service and Church Life

The service and activities in the church correspond to the sacrifice in the tabernacle in the past. The people of Israel, led by the priest, were forgiven by offering a sacrifice in the tabernacle. It was the shadow of the sacrifice of forgiveness of sin. We are going the way of forgiveness of sin led by the pastor who has Christ in him, in the church. When we are born again through the death of Jesus and our old self on the cross, we can offer ourselves as a living sacrifice. It is the perfect spiritual sacrifice; in other words, the spiritual tithe. Our sins are forgiven.

Therefore, the sacrifice in the Old Testament corresponds to the sin-forgiveness by Jesus in the church.

Priest Matches Pastor

The pastor of the church is a priest of the tabernacle. In the tabernacle, the priests receive the offerings from the people and did what they ought to do so that all the offerings may be acceptable to God. The priest of the law is a figure of Jesus Christ, the high priest, who forgives our sins. Jesus Christ works the duties of the priest through the pastors of gospel who have Christ in them.

Some people think that the office of the priesthood has been destroyed since the sacrifice of the law has been taken away in the New Testament time. But they are in the wrong. Paul the apostle says, "That I should be the minister of Jesus Christ to the Gentiles, ministering the gospel of God, that the offering up of the Gentiles might be acceptable, being sanctified by the Holy Spirit" (Romans 15:16). Paul, who brought the Gentiles to know God through being born again, refers to himself as a minister (priest) of the gospel. Notice in this process he is offering the Gentiles as a living sacrifice.

He connects himself, a pastor, to the priest and also connects his work of having the Gentiles forgiven and offered as a sacrifice to God. In addition, he matches the church he established with the tabernacle. The sacrifice of the tabernacle may be destroyed or modified depending on the times and conditions, but the sacrifice as reality remains forever in this world and so does the priest.

Some of the pastors are of the priests of the law like those who are rebuked in Malachi, and others are priests of the gospel like Paul in the New Testament.

Tithe Abides Always

As I have described above, the tabernacle, sacrifice, and priest now abide as in the forms of developed revelations. This sacrifice will last as long as this world exists. If not, we will lose the opportunity and way by which we will be forgiven our sins by Jesus. This must not happen. Therefore, as initially intended, the tithe of income will abide with the purpose of paying for the services of the priests working in the tabernacle, and reminding the people of their offering of themselves as tithes. The tithe abides always.

Is the Law Taken Away Since Jesus Has Come?

Consider the following passage from Hebrews.

> Then said he, See, I come to do your will, O God. He takes away the first, that he may establish the second. _____ Hebrews 10:9

The majority of believers believe that the tithe is no longer applicable since, "Jesus, the gospel, has come so the law and its requirements are no longer relevant." And "We are living in the time of being saved not by works but by faith."

They judge those who give tithes as being under the law, and praise those who do not pay them as free men under the gospel. They can say what they please, but it is not as simple as this. Jesus came to earth to begin the New Testament time or the gospel time—the time of Good News. By His coming, the chronological reference was changed from BC (Before Christ) to AD (*Anno Domini*: in the year of the Lord).

However, Jesus who is the truth is to come personally to each of us. And it is erroneous if you think that Jesus has come to you as He came to earth in the past. He came to His disciples and to those who were around Him only in those days. Your gospel time will begin in your life only when you meet Jesus individually.

Therefore, now some people still live under the law because they have not yet met Him personally, and others live under the gospel because they have met Him in their individual lives. You may now be under the law even though Jesus came 2,000 years ago, if you have not met Him in your life.

What is more, we easily conclude that we have met Jesus or He has come into our heart when we attended church for the first time. But that is also not true. We know within ourselves whether we have met Him or not, without asking others. Most people who have lived for decades or even a whole lifetime, although they attend church regularly, have not met Jesus personally. They are those who are under the law. Knowing this, most of the believers are under the law, who are to abide by the law. Under this situation how can we say the tithe of the law is taken away?

Moreover, imagine if you finally meet the living Jesus whom you were longing to meet, so now you are under grace. Then what do you think He will say to you regarding the tithe? Will He say like this? "I know you worked hard to pay tithes regularly although you are not rich. Now that I, the *reality* of the tithe, have come, you may stop tithing."

Not at all! He may demand that you, who have escaped paying tithes, now pay them. Maybe He will tell you to pay all the tithes that are left unpaid. The tithe of income abides always, before and even after the coming of Jesus to you individually.

📂 The True Meaning of Being Taken Away

Jesus has come, but the law or the tithe has not been taken away in the manner we may believe. When you receive Jesus, you will be born again with a new life. In this instance, your old self is destroyed. The *shadow* is gone and destroyed, and the *reality* has come. Thus, tithes, sacrifice, temple, prayer, fasting, and worship have been fulfilled within you.

Now God does not force you to do those things as duties. For example, regarding the church service, your previous viewpoint that you were obliged to attend is no longer relevant and you attend with joy for the purpose of praising God and hearing the Word of God.

You attend service as usual before and after you are born again, but after you are born again your legalistic viewpoint on the service has been removed. Likewise, your previous viewpoint on the tithe, which was only limited to the material possessions, is destroyed, and now you can view it with fresh eyes. But the tithe of income remains as it has always.

The "Tithe of the Law" of the "Tithe of Abraham"

What will the born-again men who became the tithe of Abraham think about the tithe of income? Will they think that it is taken away? No. They are born again as "tithes of Abraham" offered to God. Therefore, for the rest of their lives they are to save neighbors to be born again and be given as tithes of Abraham. In fact, their being born again will be justified and complete when they bring neighbors to be born again. Therefore their being born again is combined as one with being born again of the neighbors. This is the principle of loving your neighbor *as yourself*.

If you are born again now, it is for you to save your neighbors.

There can be no other purpose for your life, and you will do this work as a member of the spiritual church.

Not to digress too much, I want to mention one thing at this point. When I say the born-again man should be able to save his neighbors, some may be reluctant to agree because the act of salvation belongs to Jesus only. Yes that's right. But Jesus is working inside of the born-again men as Christ. So if you are born again, you should have Christ and can do what Jesus did because of the Christ gene in you.

Jesus said in John 12:24, "Truly, truly, I say to you, Except a corn of wheat fall into the ground and die, it stays alone: but if it die, it brings forth much fruit."

The first corn of wheat refers to Jesus and many corns coming from the first one refer to the disciples. The first corn of wheat and many corns should be the same wheat that can produce much fruit. So if Jesus is the life-giving spirit, the Savior, then we also should be the life-giving spirits, the saviors, if we are truly born again as disciples.

Back to the subject, when the born-again pay tithes, we pay them not in order to keep the law, but as a way of sharing eternal life with others, that life that comes from God. This is the *life of love* itself that those, in whom the law is taken away and fulfilled, live. Even though the law is fulfilled in you, the tithe of the law still remains. This is not what you should do, but you will naturally do so. If you correctly understand this principle of life, it does not stand to reason at all to say that the tithe of the law is taken away.

Epilogue

To sum up the issues concerning tithes and tithing: those who are under the law in the church should tithe and those who are under grace also tithe with the heart of loving neighbors. Therefore, the tithe of income abides always in the church.

We know that some eggs are fertilized and others are not. Even if the hen sits on the unfertilized eggs a long time, they do not hatch. They will be given to people and other animals to feed them. On the contrary, the fertilized eggs have a seed that will hatch when the hen has incubated them for a period. When the chicks grow up, they can produce more eggs.

The tithe we sow to God is like that of the chickens. A tenth of the income corresponds to the fertilized egg. We should be wise to incubate it and reap more. Some people do not pay tithes and also prevent others from tithing, thereby distorting the Scriptures. If we are tempted in this way to eat the fertilized egg we will totally lose the opportunity to be fruitful and multiply. Know the heart of God that shows us to sow to reap and have the correct communication concerning the tithe.

The tithe has continued from Old Testament times until today, both under the law and under grace. I pray that all the readers might experience God and reap abundantly through the tithe.

Two Mites of A Certain Poor Widow

Mark 12:41-44

And Jesus sat over against the treasury, and beheld how the people cast money into the treasury: and many that were rich cast in much. ⁴²And there came a certain poor widow, and she threw in two mites, which make a farthing. ⁴³And he called to him his disciples, and said to them, Truly I say to you, That this poor widow has cast more in, than all they which have cast into the treasury: ⁴⁴For all they did cast in of their abundance; but she of her want did cast in all that she had, even all her living.

Offerings in the church cannot be separated from God. In order to accurately understand the two mites of a poor widow in the text, we first must know God who is concealed within the whole concept of tithes and offerings.

People frequently link this passage with the previous verse: "Which devour widows' houses, and for a pretense make long prayers: these shall receive greater damnation" (Mark 12:40). They interpret this passage of Scripture as Jesus calling down damnation on the scribes and Pharisees for causing poor widows to lose their houses through the enforcement of offerings. If they understand it in this way, they take the humanistic view and shall discourage the poor from tithing.

As will be explained, Jesus says, "Give offerings as the widow did." However the humanistic preachers say, "Do not let the widows give such offerings," according to their common sense and the teachings of man. Those who do not know God will preach this, but this amounts to the Word of God being transformed into the doctrine of man. Who on earth is Jesus in this case?

According to the text, Jesus applauded her for giving so much of her meager resources but did not compliment the wealthy people who had also given into the temple treasury. Does this mean that we should give out of our poverty but not out of our abundance? Of course not! He applauded her because He found her faith and obedience hidden in the two mites. Also in the same vein, the rich men were not applauded because they cast into the treasury without faith.

I will now reveal God who is hidden in the offerings of these two types of believers.

Two Mites of the Poor Widow

Here the mite is *lepton* in Greek. One *lepton* corresponds to 1/64 *denarion* (one *denarion* corresponds to a day's wage for a worker). If we estimate that one day's wage was $100, one *lepton* will be calculated as $100/64 (=$1.56). Therefore, two *lepta* (=$3.12) are a very small amount of money.

He says that her two mites were all that she had. When she gave all her living to God, she also gave her life to Him and relied upon Him. Therefore, the two mites represent money having the same value as the life she gave to God in obedience to His leading. Likewise, when the widow living in Zarephath, appearing in Chapter 17 of 1 Kings, gave her last meal to Elijah, it matches the case in which this widow gave two mites to Him. Both of them gave all their living to Him.

This widow could offer all her resources, all her life, to Him because she already communicated with Him and walked with Him. She gave her life to God as He led her. Those people were blessed by Him.

Read Matthew below.

> He that finds his life shall lose it: and he that loses his life for my sake shall find it. _____ Matthew 10:39

Who is he that finds his life? It is he who pretends not to hear God and disobeys Him so as to keep his life when the Lord tells him to give two mites as an offering. Such a man rejects the Word of the Lord who gives life so that he may save his life of the flesh, but consequently loses new life. On the other hand, he who gives two mites when he is led by God, like the widow, will get a new life due to his obedience.

Jesus applauded her offering not because of the offering itself but because her obedience with all her life was reflected in her offerings. Jesus saw from her obedience even to death that she could follow and obey Jesus to the cross to destroy her old self for being born again. Jesus applauded her for this reason.

If a person had given all his living through his own blind daring without being led by Him, he would not be applauded because it did not come from God. We must first communicate with Him and then we will be correctly led regarding offerings. The widow gave all her living to Him. How could she do that, and how did He communicate with her when she gave the offerings?

Below is a precious testimony from a church member.

"Five to Seven" Offerings of a Church Member

Some years ago we had our church remodeled. The pastor thought it would be close to impossible to do this given the limited finances of our church members. However, despite his anxiety, they gave sufficient money for the remodeling project and finally we had a nice clean church.

One of our lady church members, being led by God, wanted to give offerings on this occasion. She was moved to offer five thousand dollars while listening to the pastor's sermon concerning offerings for church remodeling. But it was a very big sum, well beyond her capacity to pay, and she instantly ignored it by saying, "I'm not sure it came from God," within herself.

Meanwhile, the children attending Sunday school also joined in the remodeling offerings. Her son brought home an offerings envelope but left it lying on the floor. She said to him, "Hey, you should be more serious about the remodeling offering. Give all you have with all your heart."

This kid, looking sad, answered her, "If I offer all of my allowance to God how can I buy ice cream or a notebook?"

She thought his worry was useless and said, "Son, don't worry. If you need some, just let me know. I'll give it all to you."

Next morning he put all his pocket money, fifty dollars, into an envelope for the church remodeling offering. Seeing what he was doing, she recalled what she had told him: "If you need some, just let me know. I'll give it all to you." She realized that God had given her a word. She also realized that her son's fifty dollars offering matched the five thousand dollars that she had been prompted during the service to give. She realized then that the prompting had been from God. It was too much for her, but she tried to obey by giving that amount of money in obedience to Him despite the fact that she had no savings.

She thought about canceling an insurance policy but realized that she would lose the money she had already put into the policy. Therefore she tried to find another solution. She considered a bank loan but realized that she had no bank account. She wondered how she could come up with the money.

On the same day, one of her relatives living in the country visited her and he gave her son twenty dollars of pocket money. Watching this, she was just about to tell her son, "Look, God makes you full the instant you give to Him. Well done." However, even before she spoke, her son put the twenty dollars into the offering envelope in which he had already put fifty dollars and said, "Mom, I'll give this to God too."

Finally her son had offered all his living of seventy dollars to God for the remodeling offering.

Upon seeing him, she fell in deep trouble. Because when her son gave fifty dollars, she painfully accepted the prompt of five thousand dollars as God's, but then her son offered seventy dollars; did that mean she had to give seven thousand dollars? When she came to this point, she became angry and began to have serious doubts even about five thousand dollars, not to mention seven thousand.

"From five to seven? How can God be so changeable? Once He said five, shouldn't it be five to the end? Shouldn't He be steadfast like a rock, as the truth?"

However, she mitigated her anger and finally decided as follows: "He could give seventy dollars because he had it, but I will do my best to make an offering of five thousand dollars."

She went to the bank to ask how much she could borrow on her credit card. She thought she would be lucky if she could borrow three thousand dollars at best, and in that case, she would try to borrow from somewhere else to make five thousand dollars.

However, when she heard from the clerk at the teller's window, she was shocked. To her great surprise, the clerk said that she could borrow up to seven thousand dollars, exactly the amount in question. At this reply, far from being delighted, she grumbled in her heart.

"What? How can he say that I'm eligible for seven thousand dollars? I have no transaction history with this bank and I have no job. Is he insane? The bank's financial position deteriorates because they lend money in this way. How stupid!" She felt angry with the clerk since now it appeared that she should give seven thousand dollars as an offering while she could not even bear to give five thousand.

Ignoring all, she came back home with five thousand dollars borrowed and, feeling very uneasy, made up her mind to give five thousand dollars.

Cares weighed heavily upon her and, not knowing what the matter was, she went to see the pastor to ask for his advice. After hearing her story, the pastor spoke to her.

She realized that God had told her to give seven thousand dollars' worth of offering for the church remodeling. And she had ignored God for reasons she had considered valid. Therefore, with a sorrowful Godly heart, she got an additional loan to make seven thousand dollars and gave all the money to the church as a remodeling offering.

Let me tell you how God worked in this story.

First, God's voice is small.

God first moved her with a five thousand dollar offering and He confirmed this through her son's offering of fifty dollars. She prepared five thousand dollars in obedience to His inspiration while her financial circumstances were very difficult. He made up her mind to give that large an amount of money based on her communication with Him, through His gentle touch in her heart. Her faith was great and God was pleased with her.

His voice, or touch, is always very small as if it flits through our mind. Therefore, if we do not wish to obey Him, we can easily neglect it saying, "I'm not sure if He stirred me up or not." However, the person who truly loves Him obeys the small touch at any cost. Who will not obey if He speaks in a loud voice and with threats?

The *smallness* of His voice distinguishes those who truly love Him from those who do not. This is the reason why His stirring up, or voice, is always small. If we think deeply, we will realize that we have ignored His small voice every day.

Second, an even greater God was revealed.

Anyway, God was very pleased with the lady who had shown pure love for Him, and God wanted to reveal Himself in an even greater measure. So He sent her a message to increase the amount of the remodeling offering from five thousand dollars to seven thousand dollars through the increase of her son's offering from fifty dollars to seventy dollars. He also confirmed it through the unexpected card loan of seven thousand dollars. How wonderful He is!

However, not knowing His will, she only borrowed five thousand dollars at first. She unwittingly disobeyed and accordingly felt uncomfortable in her heart. Finally, she correctly understood what He intended to say and could obey Him through consultation with the pastor. This is the spiritual thrust of this story.

God is well pleased with her not because she was tormented by poverty, got a loan and gave it to God, but because she lived a life of communicating with Him and showed obedience to Him as He led her. This kind of offering is called the offering of two mites. Now we will understand that such an offering is not as easy as one might think.

The widow in the text was commended by Jesus for the same reason. This is the God who is hidden in the two mites offering of the widow.

The Offerings of the Rich

In contrast to the widow, there are rich men who lack communication with God. They gave offerings too. They gave a lot more than the widow in terms of the sum of money, but she was commended and they were not.

What is the difference between them?

📂 Who is the Rich?

To see the difference we first must know who the rich are. The rich in the in the Scripture does not simply refer to the people with material wealth. The rich are those who think they lack nothing in their lives even without God and who, accordingly, do not lean on God for mercy. In this sense, they are called rich.

Furthermore, the rich are to do many good works in order to get respects from men of the world, neglecting listening to God who is present. When the rich do such good works on their own, they come to accumulate the memories of these good works in their mind as possessions, which are their self-righteousness. Based on such possessions, the rich will receive the respect of men and will judge and despise others who fall short of their possessions.

Read the following passage from Luke.

> The Pharisee stood and prayed thus with himself, God, I thank you, that I am not as other men are, extortionists, unjust, adulterers, or even as this publican. [12]I fast twice in the week, I give tithes of all that I possess. _____ Luke 18:11-12

The Pharisees are typical rich men. Therefore, the "rich" refers to the men who have a lot of self-righteousness, living without retaining God in their knowledge. Their offerings are not well received by God for sure. This is why the offerings of the rich are not commended compared to the widow's.

As said, the rich have no communication with Him when they give offerings, attend church activities, or live their everyday lives.

They never invite God into their deep thinking and decide on their own how to live. But they are mistaken. They are walking in the way of death because they exclude God who is life from their lives. We will have another chance to discuss the rich man in Part Three, "The Rich Man and Lazarus."

You may think that if they come to church and give offerings it indicates they feel some sense of emptiness in their hearts and try to rely on Him. In a way, yes, but it is superficial. Those who sincerely trust in God have Him in their heart and communicate with Him like the widow.

Of Their Abundance

Jesus said that they did cast in of their abundance and He was not satisfied with what they did. Why is it so wrong that they cast in of their abundance?

What does it mean to "cast in of their abundance?" The rich, having no communication with God, decide the amount of money to give as offerings on their own and give it within their capability, because they have to be responsible for their lives. Therefore, they always have to leave *something* to live by behind after giving offerings. This is what Jesus refers to as *abundance*.

Think about the case of the widow. She cast in offerings even beyond her capability, leaving nothing, as God told her to do so. She knew by faith that her life and living was dependent upon God, not on money, so she cast in all that she had when God moved her heart.

In principle, the rich cannot but cast in offerings out of their abundance and that is the way that all the rich give offerings. Such offerings cannot please Him because these offerings are not led by God but by themselves.

Context...

Earlier I mentioned the flow of the current text with the verse, "Which devour widows' houses, and for a pretense make long prayers: these shall receive greater damnation" (Mark 12:40).

The rich in this passage represent the scribes who were mentioned in the above verse. They devour widows' houses because they do not know God in every work. If they gather offerings, it will be just offerings as money without God, which means that they snatch the widows' houses by taking advantage of God's name.

But those who know God, even if they advise the widows to give offerings, are able to see God working in the offerings and the widows who give will be blessed by God. Consider Elijah who took the last meal of the widow at Zarephath to bless her. Those who know God gather the offerings from the widows and they do not devour their houses.

The current text does not comfort the widow who is robbed of her possession, but enlightens the rich who are giving offerings without communication with God, unlike the widow. The text is linked to the previous chapter and verses this way.

Epilogue

The text speaks about offerings but it describes two groups of people who have two kinds of faith, which is displayed through the offerings that they make.

The *first* group consists of those like the widow who believe in God through their walk with Him, and the *second* group includes those, like the rich, who believe according to their own thinking.

As stated, the offering includes the faith of those who offer, and thus, the offering reveals the faith of the givers. When Cain brought an offering to God in Genesis 4, He did not have respect for Cain and his offering, but in the case of Abel, He had respect for Abel as well as for Abel's offering. We can learn from this that the offerings given to Him equal the faith of the giver. The offerings of the rich match the offering of Cain; and the offerings of the widow match the offering of Abel.

We should give offerings in the manner of the widow's two mites, which testify that we correctly believe in Jesus. However, it does not mean that we have to give all that we have now with firm resolution. If we can give "two mites" as offerings, we ought to be guided by God, and we must obey His touch. Even if we give all our living without His stirring up of our hearts, or failing to understand it, we cannot but give the offerings of the rich.

What offerings are you giving now?

I Pray You, Give Whatever Comes to Your Hand, to David

1 Samuel 25:4-17

And David heard in the wilderness that Nabal did shear his sheep. ⁵And David sent out ten young men, and David said to the young men, Get you up to Carmel, and go to Nabal, and greet him in my name: ⁶And thus shall you say to him that lives in prosperity, Peace be both to you, and peace be to your house, and peace be to all that you have. ⁷And now I have heard that you have shearers: now your shepherds which were with us, we hurt them not, neither was there ought missing to them, all the while they were in Carmel. ⁸Ask your young men, and they will show you. Wherefore let the young men find favor in your eyes: for we come in a good day: give, I pray you, whatever comes to your hand to your servants, and to your son David. ⁹And when David's young men came, they spoke to Nabal according to all those words in the name of David, and ceased. ¹⁰And Nabal answered David's servants, and said, Who is David? and who is the son of Jesse? there be many servants now a days that break away every man from his master. ¹¹Shall I then take my bread, and my water, and my flesh that I have killed for my shearers, and give it to men, whom I know not from where they be? ¹²So David's young men turned their way, and went again, and came and told him all those sayings. ¹³And David said to his men, Gird you on every man his sword. And they girded on every man his sword; and David also girded on his sword: and there went up after David about four hundred men; and two hundred stayed by the stuff. ¹⁴But one of the young men told Abigail, Nabal's wife, saying, Behold, David sent messengers out of the wilderness to salute our master; and he railed on them. ¹⁵But the men were very good to us, and we were not hurt, neither missed we any thing, as long as we were conversant with them, when we were in the fields:

[16]They were a wall to us both by night and day, all the while we were with them keeping the sheep. [17]Now therefore know and consider what you will do; for evil is determined against our master, and against all his household: for he is such a son of Belial, that a man cannot speak to him.

What correlation is there between offerings and salvation? Is there no correlation simply because offerings are physical possessions while salvation is a spiritual matter? The answer is that these two questions correlate even though one is physical and the other is spiritual, and I shall explain why.

There are two kinds of offerings.

The first are the offerings we give on our own. We decide whether we would like to give and how much we will give. In this case it is correct to say that these offerings have no bearing on our spiritual salvation

The second type of offering is made according to God's leading. We give this offering not by ourselves but in obedience to our living God. The widow's offering that we read about in the previous message belongs to this category. Such an offering has the spiritual value of obedience to God or faith other than the value of the material possessions offered. Therefore, offerings do not directly fulfill spiritual salvation but the heart of obedience of those who give.

Since we do not know the way of salvation at all, we must obey and follow God to be saved. Only those who are obedient to God will be saved. If we give offerings as guided by God, it means we are obeying God. To see our obedience in offerings, we are proved to be obedient to God in all matters, which will eventually constitute the salvation. This is the reason why the offerings of material possessions relate to spiritual salvation.

The above text is partially quoted from Chapter 25 of 1 Samuel. It deals with the period when David was in the wilderness of Paran, escaped from King Saul who was trying to kill him. At this time there was a rich man in Maon called Nabal and he had a wife called Abigail. She was a woman of good understanding and of beautiful countenance, but he was churlish and evil in his doings.

When Nabal held a feast to celebrate the shearing of his sheep, David sent out his men with a message asking Nabal for some food because he had protected Nabal. But Nabal rejected David's request and sent the men back in shame. David got angry and prepared to attack. Hearing of this, Abigail made haste and took food supplies and met David and his men without letting Nabal know.

She said to David that he should not shed blood because God would appoint him ruler over Israel. David changed his mind about the attack and returned to his camp, and ten days later God smote Nabal and he died. Afterwards Abigail became one of David's wives. Here we find Nabal and Abigail who reacted differently to David's request. Nabal was ruined and Abigail was glorified.

Now I will explain the difference between the faith of Abigail and that of Nabal through their attitude towards possessions and I shall also describe how offerings are connected to salvation.

Folly Is With Nabal

Three major characters appear here. Nabal, who was rich but churlish and folly was with him; Abigail, who was of good understanding, wise, and of beautiful countenance and who was his wife; and the famous David.

Regarding what they symbolize, David is the type of Jesus Christ we can find a lot in related Scriptures. As David is the type of Jesus Christ, we can easily guess who Nabal and Abigail symbolize. These two persons represent the believers. Some of us are with folly, and some are of good understanding. Which group do you belong to? Of course your name will not be identical to Nabal or Abigail, but you can see whether your mindset and reaction are identical to that of Nabal or Abigail.

I will describe the folly of Nabal in three points.

First, he did not know that David had protected him.

David sent his young men to Nabal and said to him that he had taken care of him and he asked him to "give whatever came to his hand" to them for they came in a good day. As he said, the shepherds and cattle of Nabal were preserved without any harm because David had protected them. But Nabal did not know this and he did not accept it even when they explained it to him. He thought that his possessions were kept safe because he managed and controlled all his possessions well.

There is little difference between Nabal and us. God has blessed us and we succeeded in this life so far. But we tend to think that we made it because we are smart and excellent, not appreciating and understanding His blessing. If we are really so, we have the same mindset as Nabal.

A certain family experienced hard times that they, on many occasions, did not know where their daily meals would come from and they started attending our church. Some years have passed and they have prospered and have been able to buy a house of their own. Naturally it is because God blessed them. But not realizing this, they thought they had succeeded because of their own ability and business sense. And they tried to exercise their pride in various ways, and when it was not accepted in the church, finally they left.

We pray to God and Jesus when we are at risk, but we frequently forget Him when we are well-off as a result of His blessings.

Second, Nabal did not think highly of David.

When David sent his servants to Nabal to ask him to "give whatever came to his hand," Nabal displayed an indifferent attitude. He would not have rejected David's request if he had respect for David. Why did Nabal belittle David, a man of God? It is because Nabal had no communication with God. And he failed to sense David was being trained by God as the new king, having only guessed that David was a worthless servant who ran away from his master (Saul the king). We will know David the man of God when we communicate with God, and if not, we will fail to know who he is, as Nabal failed.

If we meet this David, "a man Jesus," in the church as the pastors or leaders, while in communion with God, we will be eager to hear him and will cherish his message.

But if we neither communicate with God nor know Him, we will be indifferent to the sayings of the pastor and to the activities in the church. For example, if we are advised to give offerings by the pastor, we will be stingy like Nabal, and we will grumble about the church activities because we think we are robbed of our time.

What is more, I do not know whether this kind of real pastor is available in the churches nowadays, but, when the pastor rebukes us for our worldly thinking and behaviors, we will belittle the pastor, dismissing him as a flawed man, just as the Jews belittled Jesus as a son of carpenter. In the text, Nabal considers David as a mere servant who breaks away from his master.

How can such a Nabal and those believers who think in his way give offerings to God and church? How can they follow "a man Jesus" to the cross for salvation? They will not obey the man of God so the salvation and blessings of God are far from them. Those believers are represented by Nabal.

Third, Nabal was destroyed because he could not see the hand of God who tried to save him.

When Nabal declined to offer David any food, David prepared to make war against him but changed his mind after listening to Abigail. But Nabal died. Nabal had been placed under the protection of David. If he was a man of sense he should have welcomed that protection, but he rejected it and he met with catastrophe. Through the intervention of Abigail, Nabal escaped being slaughtered by David, but was doomed to die in the end.

In God's sight, Nabal was already doomed to die. Therefore, He tested Nabal's faith through David for the purpose of saving Nabal. But he could not perceive David, and accordingly refused David's demand. God wanted to deliver Nabal out of death through David's request for help, but He cannot save him since Nabal turned down David, the savior.

How was it possible that helping David would lead to Nabal's salvation? Because by helping David, by thinking highly of him and obeying him, as a result Nabal could have been united with him to go through the cross and would be saved. The man who can forsake *all*, including money, on account of David, and follow him, can be saved through the cross. It is quite natural that Nabal, who did not forsake even mere money on account of David, could not be saved. Nabal was destroyed not because of the punishment of God, but because of his refusal to the Savior.

A church member was stirred by God to give offerings for the church remodeling. Nobody told her to do it but she said that she received God's voice in her mind. At first she intended to obey Him. But she put it off from day to day because she was not well-off, and His message gradually grew dimmer as time passed. In the long run she could not give it and after that time, she was pressed for money more than ever. She had to live in a very small rented house and also had to hide herself from creditors.

She suffered hard times because she rejected His voice. It will be a great mistake if we understand that God will punish those who do not give offerings. He wants to help those who are in need, but He does not bless anyone blindly. He wants to see if the person concerned deserves blessing, that is, does he have faith? Then God can help and bless him as he has faith to receive the blessing.

God touched her about giving offerings in order to bless her like the widow woman in Zarephath. But she, having neglected His will, followed her own way and failed to be blessed by Him. She, like Nabal, declined to help David, and had to face miserable consequences.

"Give, I pray you, whatever comes to your hand to your servants, and to your son David" does not imply taking something from Nabal. It is the voice of Salvation. Nabal ignored this and he was ruined. Because he was completely preoccupied with carnal matters and had no communication with God, it was inevitable that he would respond in this way to David. Nabal believed in God superficially, not substantially. His end was to be destroyed as destined.

If we sinners also refuse His hand of deliverance, we fall as we are doomed initially, even if He does not have us destroyed. If the pastor, the man of God in your church, says to you "Give, I pray you, whatever comes to your hand unto your servants, and to your son David," it is His hand of deliverance. Just follow with all your heart, having communication with God.

Wise Abigail

Unlike Nabal, Abigail communicated with God. And she knew that David had protected what they had and he would be appointed as ruler over Israel later. She showed David wholehearted kindness. When she went to see him, she unsparingly prepared food for him and his company. She really wanted to give whatever came to her hand to David.

When she left to meet David with the food, she did not talk it over with Nabal (1Samuel 25:19). This shows us that providing David with food was very important to her. If she had tried to persuade Nabal about this matter he would not have agreed and she would have been too late to intercept David. Also, if she had not really wanted to get food to David, she would have discussed it with Nabal, knowing that he would have prevented her from assisting David. In this way, they would have been destroyed altogether.

As for us, when moved by Him about giving offerings, some of us, like Abigail, value it and obey it in defiance of all difficulties, but others pray like this: "Lord! Touch my husband, the unbeliever, and let him first instruct me to give offerings, as I do not want to quarrel with him, but have peace. Then, I'll do it."

That was Nabal's prayer. If you truly have a mind of obedience to God, like Abigail, you will just do His bidding.

Abigail went with food and met David and his men on the way. She prevailed on them. David changed his mind and decided not to attack Nabal. Abigail saved the whole family and their possessions from disaster.

I know some in the church who are lavish in giving to the Lord. They have a high regard for the church just as Abigail thought highly of David and they know that they will be blessed in the world and that they will be saved as they treasure the church. They are always generous in time, activity, and offerings in the church. They intercept the calamity coming to themselves and their families through such giving to the Lord and they are blessed.

The story of Nabal and Abigail demonstrates how our faith grows. We all start with the faith of Nabal. Then those who are used up and have found no satisfaction in their current faith of Nabal will seek God and communicate with Him and pray to believe in Jesus correctly. God will send David, "a man Jesus," to them. They will not do to him everything they wish, but will obey. Through him, they will develop the faith of Abigail.

Through her walk with God she was saved, escaped misfortune, and also became well-off. True blessings follow as we turn to God and Jesus. This is what entering the kingdom of God is all about.

I shall explain this.

Abigail and the Kingdom of God

Consider the following passage.

> I pray you, forgive the trespass of your handmaid: for the LORD will certainly make my lord a sure house; because my lord fights the battles of the LORD, and evil has not been found in you all your days. [29]Yet a man is risen to pursue you, and to seek your soul: but the soul of my lord shall be bound in the bundle of life with the LORD your God; and the souls of your enemies, them shall he sling out, as out of the middle of a sling. [30]And it shall come to pass, when the LORD shall have done to my lord according to all the good that he has spoken concerning you, and shall have appointed you ruler over Israel; [31]That this shall be no grief to you, nor offense of heart to my lord, either that you have shed blood causeless, or that my lord has avenged himself: but when the LORD shall have dealt well with my lord, then remember your handmaid. _____ 1 Samuel 25:28-31

This passage highlights that there is something more important than the fact that Abigail gave food to David and averted a calamity. Abigail knew that David would be protected in the bundle of life, and be appointed as the ruler over Israel. Abigail, who walked with God and followed David, became his wife.

This signifies that while Abigail, the believer, followed and obeyed Jesus for healing her spirit on the cross as His disciples did, she believed that the life of Jesus would be protected and grew in her heart and finally Jesus would come into her as the ruler, bringing the kingdom of God. David, king of Israel, comes at this time into her heart as the Holy Spirit. To come as king means that she received Christ into her heart and He leads as her king. This is the coming of the kingdom of God and her salvation.

She asks David to remember her when he becomes king. It sounds as if she asks him to favor her when he sits on the throne just as she gave food to him. Does she mean this? No, she is simply articulating a natural law. She is asking that she may reap what she has sown. It is her confession of faith in which she will finally receive eternal life by helping and obeying David.

Like Abigail, we should sow in the manner that Jesus would remember us when He comes in the kingdom of God.

Contrasted to Abigail, Nabal did not understand what he was doing at that time. He believed in Jesus, expecting that he would reap what he did not sow. Naturally he would reap nothing.

Read the following verses from Matthew.

> Many will say to me in that day, Lord, Lord, have we not prophesied in your name? and in your name have cast out devils? and in your name done many wonderful works? ^{23}And then will I profess to them, I never knew you: depart from me, you that work iniquity. _____ Matthew 7:22-23

The genuineness of truth, salvation, and the kingdom of God must be verified here and now, because in the last day, at the judgment, we will only reap what we have sown now. We must check whether we are currently going the way of Nabal or the way of Abigail.

She was finally remembered by David, and she became his wife (1Samuel 25:42). She offered everything unsparingly for the work of Jesus and she consequently received Him in her as king, which means becoming the bride of Jesus Christ. This confirms her salvation which started by giving simple food to David.

Epilogue

The essential difference between Nabal and Abigail is that she feared the living God and obeyed His word, while he did not.

They who have no knowledge of God in them, like Nabal, will hesitate to give offerings and all other things related to God to the church, because they have no God. In case they do it eagerly, they do it that they may be seen by men.

On the contrary, those who communicate with and fear God will take part in every activity in the church with joy. Such believers are ready to follow "a man Jesus" to the kingdom of God and for the salvation of which the Scriptures speak.

Offerings by themselves do not save us, but those having communication with Him give offerings. If we do not make offerings that are led by God, it means that we do not have communication with Him, the Savior. In this case, we are still far from salvation.

I pray that all of us should follow the example of Abigail and should therefore be remembered when Jesus comes as king into us.

Now Part One of this book is finished. I have explained "Communication with God" and "Tithes and Offerings" through such communication. The key is to communicate with God is seeking His will.

However, although we say that we wish to follow His will, we are substantially led by the ideas given by the evil one in us. God's will is transformed in us by this evil one and our communication fails. There is an evil enemy who brings us who would do good to ruin.

I am going to explain the identity of this enemy in Part Two.

See you there!

PART TWO
EVIL IS PRESENT WITH ME

We have studied in Part One that if we would do good, we should do the good that is caused by God, and in order to do so, we should communicate with Him.

However, such communication is not so simple. We disobey unwittingly and are unable to communicate with Him as we have seen in Part One in the cases of Eli, Ahab, Saul, and those who neglect the voice of the Lord to give offerings in the church. We act that way because evil is present in our hearts and it interrupts or distorts communication with God.

Paul the apostle expresses that status "when I would do good, evil is present with me" in Romans 7. Simply speaking, my heart's desire to seek to communicate with God who is the "good" itself in us is "good," and my heart's desire to stay away from Him is "evil." However, we do not know the reality of this evil that is within us. Accordingly, we are trying to find and label and blame things outside of us that are evil so that we don't have to point a finger at the evil inside us.

We can have perfect communication with Him when we have correctly recognized this evil in us and have conquered it through Jesus.

In Part Two, I will give light to the reality of the devil, Satan, demons, the antichrist and other evil spirits that interfere with our communication with Him:

3. The Origin of Evil; Devil, Satan, and Demons
4. Antichrist and Evil Spirits

3
THE ORIGIN OF EVIL; THE DEVIL, SATAN, AND DEMON

The Origin of Evil

When we read the Scriptures and find the word "evil," we easily can think of the devil, Satan, and demons. We want to fight against these evils and overcome them. Therefore, we have fought with them over a long period of time and we are still fighting against them even now. And we will do so in the future too.

We, however, do not know what they are. How can we fight with something that we do not know? Impossible. It is just our hallucinations that we fight against them so far. As a matter of fact, we have been already been defeated by evil, and have offered ourselves to it— soul and body—as its slaves.

Many scholars have studied the realities of the devil, Satan, and demons, but have failed to disclose what exactly they are. Their realities have been hidden during the progress of human history as well as in Christian history. It will be natural for mankind to have no idea of the true nature of evil if even we, the believers who have the Scriptures that reveal the truth, could not grasp such a thing. Now I will accurately describe their deeply hidden realities.

The devil, Satan, and demons are a contrary concept to God, so they should be considered together with God. For example, if we think that we know "light" we should get to know the concept of "non-light," or "darkness," in juxtaposition. We cannot know what light is without knowing what darkness is. Therefore, if we do not know what the evil being is, it means that we do not know God, the good, at the same time.

Under this circumstance of ignorance, we have been eager to believe in Him. Do you think that we ever believe in Him correctly?

God Who Is the Absolute Good

📂 **The Good and Evil In Our Thoughts**

We define what is good and what is evil in this world, and label those who do the good things we defined as good, and those who do the evil things we defined as evil. For example, we define "donation" good and "stealing" evil. We label him who donates a "good man" and him who steals an "evil man." This is the general concept that we have about the good and evil in this world.

Accordingly, people attempt to confine themselves to the good which they defined, and also force their neighbors to do the same. For example, "love" is defined as good, so we try to love and ask people to love day and night through education or whatever activity. Yet we and they cannot love. The history of mankind has proven that man can never be made to love through coercion.

What is more, will a man be a truly good person if he donates? Will a man be an evil person if he does not do that? No. The Pharisees, for instance, were rebuked by Jesus as evil even though they donated, helped the poor, kept the Sabbath holy, and prayed. However, the disciples who were together with Him did not keep the Sabbath holy but were not condemned (Matthew 12:2).

We can know from the above that good or evil is not decided by doing the good or the evil work established by man, but is decided based on the person who does the work. According to the truth, a good man cannot do evil, and an evil man cannot do good at all. That is, a good man naturally performs good deeds, and an evil man naturally performs evil deeds.

Read the following passage.

> For a good tree brings not forth corrupt fruit; neither does a corrupt tree bring forth good fruit. ⁴⁴For every tree is known by his own fruit. For of thorns men do not gather figs, nor of a bramble bush gather they grapes.   _____ Luke 6:43:44

Therefore, if we wish to do good we should be a good being first, basically; then, following, whatever we do is good. Jesus has come to make us good beings to do good.

📂 The Absolute Good

I will describe what the Scripture of truth says is "good." In truth, the "good" does not mean a certain law for us to abide by, but, rather, it is a person who is God Himself. Moreover, the good is not something that has a certain rigid mold, such as the law, but it is the personality of God, which is formless. People try to fit all mankind into their definition of good, but in vain. However, all mankind can be and should be fitted to God, the good, and they will be good.

Mark 10:17 begins the story of a young man who had great possessions. He approached Jesus and asked Him, saying, "Good Master, what shall I do that I may inherit eternal life?" And Jesus said to him, "Why call you me good? there is none good but one, that is, God."

This man thought Jesus was good. He called Him that way because he had seen Him do many good works, such as healing the sick, raising the dead, and giving food to the people. However, Jesus says there is none good but one, that is, God. God is good itself and the origin of every good. And God is always good, is not evil at any time. God is absolute good.

Jesus is good not because He did good works for the people, but because He has God, the good itself, in Him. Jesus wishes to reveal this truth to us through the dialogue with this young man. We also can be good men like Jesus by becoming one with God through Jesus.

God is the absolute good which is good anytime, in any case. We should share the good through Jesus; then we will do good always.

The Origin of Evil

Having discussed the absolute good of the truth, now I will explain evil, which is a contrary concept to good. The three stages whereby we realize evil in this world are as follows:

- ✓ Evil is the Concept of the State: "State Evil"
- ✓ The Reality of Evil of the World: "Active Evil"
- ✓ The Doer of Active Evil: "Evil Man"

📂 **Evil is the Concept of the State: "State Evil"**

When we attempt to discuss *good* and *evil*, we frequently set up God as good and the devil as evil. However, when we begin to think that good and evil collide and fight with each other, few go on with that attempt because it is very crude to think that God Almighty comes into conflict with the devil.

Nevertheless, the idea that God is the good and the devil is the evil is not wrong, and we can meet the truth if we go a little more deeply. The struggle of the good versus the evil only happens in this world, the world of non-truth. There is no war between the good and the evil in the world of the truth of God.

Let me explain further. There is God and God is the reality. In order for "There is God" to make sense, there should be the antonym concept of "There is no God" at the same time. That is, "There is God" takes its meaning only with the counter concept of "There is no God." Therefore, the fact that "God exists as a reality" is sustained by the relative concept of the state of the non-existence of God.

God is "good" and the absence of God is "evil." The absence of God is the origin of evil. In principle, evil is available because of the existence of God, the good. The good is the "reality," but evil is the state of the absence of good.

God is the reality that exists by itself. Reality has power; that is, a dynamic force. However, evil as a state does not have this force. It is because evil means the concept of the state in which the good, the reality having power, has emptied its position.

Evil does not fight with good nor could fight against it. Where there is good, there is no evil; and where there is no good, evil. Evil is always subject to good and its movement.

This is like the relationship between light and darkness. Light is the reality and darkness is the "state of no light." The former has power but the latter does not. Therefore, they do not collide with each other. When light has come in, darkness goes out, and when the light has left, the darkness comes by default. There can be no discord between the movements of the two. In fact, there is only one movement of the light; therefore, there cannot be any conflict between the two.

As discussed, "evil," or "darkness," does not struggle with "good" and "light." Therefore, the former are not wicked or bad as we generally think, but, rather, help the good be the good and the light be the light.

Accordingly, evil refers to the "state that is without the good," which exists because of the existence of the good that is reality. This evil is called the "evil as the concept of a state" which can be neither good nor bad. I may call it in short, "State Evil."

Godlessness	GOD
(Evil, Darkness)	(Good, Light)
	MANKIND
	in Eden

The heavens and the earth are the creation of God who is the good. They are united as one with the good, stay within it, and receive power from the good to work according to the rule of life of the good.

When we are created as an Adam (a man) in Eden, before depravity, we belong to God, the good, having nothing to do with the evil.

📂 The Reality of Evil of the World : "Active Evil"

Only mankind, among all creatures, has left the good and digressed from the life of good. Separated from God and coming out of Eden, men are born depraved in this world. And the depraved men who exist in the state of the absence of God, the good, in their minds, are under the "evil."

Godlessness (Evil, Darkness)	GOD (Good, Light)
MANKIND in this World	

When a man is depraved, he by default accepts evil and is combined with it as one. Then the man moves instantly as the slave of evil in this world. Evil, which is only the state, now gains power and becomes a reality through man and thus becomes active. That is, man is the channel through which evil appears in this world with power. Therefore, this world in which men, having left God, gather and live together, lies in evil.

Read 1 John 5:19: "And we know that we are of God, and the whole world lies in wickedness."

"Wickedness" here is *poneros* in Greek, which means "evil." And "in wickedness" does not mean that something is wicked according to the morality of this world. It speaks of the status of the hearts of all men (the whole world), which are without God, the good (*agathos* in Greek). Also, we can find that same truth in Luke 4:6 where the devil said to Jesus that the power and glory of the kingdom of the world was "delivered to" him. As such, the whole world lies in the devil, the wickedness.

Men live in the absence of God in their heart, and that life is allowed by God temporarily only while we are on earth. Our natural life is evil, so our lives are in vain and full of emptiness. All mankind in this world is under active evil and their lives are evil from the viewpoint of God.

📂 The Doer of Active Evil : "Evil Men"

People having left God, the good, for this world define the good on their own and lead lives according to their concept of what is good. That may be good objectively, but it is unavoidably evil because only fallen, or depraved, man perceives it.

Godlessness (Evil, Darkness)	GOD (Good, Light)
MANKIND in this World	MEN Born Again

The depraved man can neither understand the good nor apply it, because his base is evil already. If he does good, this good is evil also. He is the doer of active evil.

Not knowing this, depraved men fight against God, alleging that they know and have good.

In the parable of the lord of the vineyard and laborers in Chapter 20 of Matthew, the lord gives a penny to the laborers who came early in the morning and bore the burden and heat of the day and he gives the same to the laborers who came at five p.m. and worked one hour. Those who came first complain. Then, the goodman of the house says, "Is it not lawful for me to do what I will with mine own? Is your eye evil (*poneros* in Greek), because I am good (*agathos* in Greek)?" (Matthew 20:15, parentheses mine). The goodness of God, who is likened to the lord of the vineyard, appears evil to the eyes of men.

Likewise, in the parable of the prodigal son in Chapter 15 of Luke, the good of the father runs counter to that of the older son. According to the good of the father, the father takes the fatted calf and has a feast for the prodigal son who has come back. But the father's good acts as an evil to the older son. The Pharisees clashed against Jesus because men did not know the good of God.

In addition, people, the evil men, are in discord with each other because of their individual good, which is depraved. Assume that some six hundred million people live on earth; each has his own standard of good. It will be apparent for the subjective good that works for its own profit is opposed and contrary to another's subjective good. Therefore, each person will judge others, quarrel with them, and make war against them based on the criteria of good they have and insist on. Men are evil, and we are evil men.

Unknowingly, we fight against God who is the truth. If the good of God, who is all of all and has the sole dynamic force of life, conflicts with the good of men which is non-truth and nothing but a lie, the men will be extinguished promptly. But He perseveres in our absurd hostility while we are on earth so that He may give us opportunities to repent and then save us.

He already knew that men would fall when He created them, but He included our depravity in the process of creation. Therefore, when a man leaves God after creation, God will re-create him through Jesus Christ when he truly repents. By this second creation, the man is made perfect according to the image of God. Jesus speaks of this creation as being born again. Therefore, evil and sinful human beings are under His providence of creation.

Analogy of Stove

To help you understand the origin of evil and the principle of its realization, I will liken God to a hot stove.

Imagine a hot stove. This stove is the reality that furnishes heat to people. It only supplies warmth. In the warmth the stove supplies, its antithetic concept of coldness is inherent. But they have no confrontation with each other. Coldness cannot fight against the stove which produces the warmth, because the stove is a reality having a dynamic force and the coldness is only the state of the absence of the stove/heat. Therefore, when the stove comes on, coldness is gone naturally, without struggle.

And as long as people stay near the stove, they will not have any coldness, which remains only as a concept. Problems occur as people leave the stove. Those having departed from the stove suffer coldness in reality. In this instance, they are apt to blame the stove for not giving them warmth. This is how we complain about God saying, "If the God of good exists, what is this evil we see around us?"

The nature of a stove is not to produce coldness. It only generates warmth.

Then, what reality is it that gives this coldness? There is no other wicked reality that produces the coldness. But people bring the coldness unto themselves by incurring the state of "absence of the stove" by leaving it. Therefore, the very author of "actualizing coldness" is the people themselves, not the stove.

Those having departed from the stove are at once dominated by the coldness. They feel cold, shiver, have pain, and realize no satisfaction at all. They quarrel and fight with their neighbors in order to acquire their own warmth. And the world tries to solve that problem by setting good regulations and laws. But they will only fail. All their problems and troubles are caused by one single reason: that is, the coldness. Therefore, only if they get back to the stove, the coldness and matters arising from the coldness will disappear at once. Returning to the stove is the only and fundamental solution of the problem of the people.

As the "coldness concept of state" is brought into concrete existence to those who have departed from the stove, the "evil as concept of state" is materialized in this world because of the departure of man from God; that is, the depravity of man. As a result, the reality of evil of this world is the fallen man himself.

Fallen man feels cold and emptiness in his life. This represents the lives of those who have left God. The Scriptures call them "born sinners" in this world. You will realize that returning to God is the only solution for all mankind.

Epilogue

God is good. Evil exists as a relative concept since God is good.

This evil makes the good become the good. There is no reality of evil, but the "state of absence of the good" is evil. Evil is incidental and it is not wicked or bad.

When the man has departed from God and has fallen, evil as the concept of a state becomes realized and active. Therefore, evil is introduced to this world as a reality through men. Evil in this instance appears to be good in the eyes of the fallen man. And they live doing evil thinking they are doing good. They are evil men.

With this basic knowledge of evil, in the next chapters I will describe the identities of the devil, Satan, and demons appearing in the Scriptures.

The Devil

The Greek of the devil is *diabolos*. Our general thinking about the devil will be something like the following:

"The devil is a supernatural spirit appearing in the shape of an ugly-looking man, a beast, or monster. He is a fallen angel, he stands against God, and works with the intention of demolishing God's will. The devil owns evil and unclean spirits as his workers. He is a tempter, a false accuser, and a destroyer of Christians."

Our knowledge about the devil may not be distant from the above description, if not the same. But the devil in Scripture is quite different from such a general understanding. Next I will explain the devil according to Scripture.

This message will reveal who the devil is. And this revelation is the plan of God to destroy the works of the devil within you.

Who is the Devil?

The Devil as a Common Noun

First, this word is a common noun meaning a slanderer or a traducer. Let us read the following Scripture verses.

> Even so must their wives be grave, not **slanderers** (*diabolous*), sober, faithful in all things. _____ 1 Timothy 3:11

Without natural affection, truce breakers, **false accusers** (*diaboloi*), incontinent, fierce, despisers of those that are good, _____ 2 Timothy 3:3

The aged women likewise, that they be in behavior as becomes holiness, not **false accusers** (*diabolous*), not given to much wine, teachers of good things; _____ Titus 2:3 (parentheses and bold, mine)

In the above passages, the devil (*diabolos* in Greek) is translated as "false accuser" or the common noun, "slanderer."

🗁 The Devil who Perverts God

When these common nouns of slanderer, or traducer, are used in relation to God, they shall mean the devil.

In fact, the devil is evil of men which I described in the section on the origin of evil. Evil described therein is the devil. Recalling the previous section regarding evil, the process in which the devil is brought into existence in this world from the origin which is a "state" is as follows:

a) The devil as the concept of a state → b) The devil within man → c) Man devil.

These three stages are distinguishable but are one, just as cause, process, and result make up one equation. I will now describe the nature of the devil in three stages.

Stage 1 : The Devil as the Concept of a State: State Devil

God is good and the devil is evil. God is light and the devil is darkness. In the like manner of the evil, the devil is the state of "non-existence/absence of God" which is already inherited in the "existence of God." God does not do away with the devil essentially. No, He cannot exterminate him because his existence, even as a state concept, is a principle. And this devil as the concept of a state does not resist God, and he is neither good nor bad at this stage.

Stage 2 : The Devil in a Man: Active Devil

After depravity, men are united in heart with the devil in this world. When the devil is united with man, then the devil will take active power of the man, and can fight against God, the good. Thus, the devil is bad and realistically evil.

Regarding taking power of men, the devil and men are substantially united into one, and mankind is subject to the devil. Under this circumstance, mankind can feel God through his conscience (Romans 2:23-15), but in most cases His voice is so weak it is neglected. Therefore, the thoughts of the man who has the devil in him would be "godless" all the time.

That man is described as the one who does not retain God in his knowledge. Consider Romans 1:28, "And even as they did not like to retain God in their knowledge, God gave them over to a reprobate mind, to do those things which are not convenient."

Regarding the principle of the oneness of the devil and the man, the devil, which is the state concept, cannot force himself into the man with his own power. But to reject God is to pursue "godlessness," and by this rejection in his heart, the devil comes into him by default. The Scripture describes the devil as if he works actively, but such active power is, in fact, the movement of the heart of the man, which flows in a Godless way.

This is illustrated in the devil tempting Jesus (chapter 4 in Matthew and chapter 4 in Luke), the devil having put into the heart of Judas Iscariot to betray Him (John 13:2), and the devil, as a roaring lion, walking about, seeking whom he may devour (1 Peter 5:8). All these passages describe the flow of the heart of the man concerned, but do not mean that the devil has active power independently. The devil will only have power relying on the power of heart of the man concerned.

Stage 3 : Man Devil

Accordingly, he who does not behave himself according to the knowledge of God in his heart, moves as the devil wishes, he is a "man devil." The depraved human beings, the sinners, are his slaves and are the men devils (1 John 3:10).

The devil put into the heart of Judas Iscariot to betray Jesus (John 13:2). This means Judas decided to act in concert with the godless thought in his mind. This Judas is he who has become one with the devil, and he is none other than the devil. Therefore, Jesus pointed out that Judas is a devil (John 6:70). And on another occasion, He also called Peter "Satan" (Matthew 16:23).

Therefore, when a man receives the idea from the devil, that is, godless thought, and conducts himself to work for the devil as his slave, that man is the "man devil."

Thus, the "devil as the concept of a state" is finally materialized as an active force to fight against God in this world.

In summary:

First, term "devil" is a common noun, and he is a slanderer and traducer.

Second, the devil is he who slanders and falsely accuses God, and he is a being having the personality of a man. The devil according to the second definition refers to the following three stages:

1) The "state of the absence of God" which is a contrary idea to "existence of God." The devil in this instance is neither good nor evil.

2) The "godless thoughts" in the heart of the man which were formed when man is depraved and united with the "devil as the concept of a state." The godless thoughts are the "devil in the man."

3) Man who acts according to those ideas given by the "devil in him." He is the "man devil."

The devil is brought into concrete existence through the above three steps; that is, "a state of the absence of God," → "Godless thoughts in man," → the "man behaving himself in the Godless way." These three are not different. They are one equation stating the cause, the process, and the result during which the devil became active in one man in this sinful world.

Some Principles Relating to the Devil

I will now explain some important principles about the relationship between the devil and the man, which will give you an insight about the identity of the devil.

📂 Will I Be Independent When I Leave God?

When we leave God, why do we belong to the devil instead of being independent by ourselves? It is because we are inherently God's creatures. The creatures can have life and maintain it only when they belong to the Creator. If we depart from Him, we will not be independent but belong to the "state of absence of the Creator." We will be cut off from the supply of life and will be subject to death.

For example, suppose a man has manufactured a car. It will run properly as long as it is maintained and cleaned by the manufacturer. But if it is abandoned and neglected, it will be nothing but a junk because it cannot run by itself. And it will gradually rust and waste away. This is the point. The car which is a "created thing" has to belong either to the man who has created it or to the "absence of the creator." The former is life of the car, and the latter is the death of the car.

As described, the man who is the creature has to belong either to God or to the absence of God. There is no independent status of man on his own as a creature in this sense. Our lives will function properly and appropriately only when we are in the right place in God. This "belonging to God" is the freedom of the creatures which will be given to us through Jesus. If we abandon God and remain that way, we rush to death.

📂 I Am Not Me But Another Man

"I" living in this world as a sinner am taken captive by the devil, which is "me" and "me captured by the devil" coexisting within me. For example, if I am captured by a kidnapper, I have the "original me" and the "captured me" inside me. My actions are controlled and transformed by the kidnapper regardless of the intention of the original me. In this case, I am me, but I am not me at the same time.

This scene shows the real spiritual state of the sinner living in this world who left God. If we think about ourselves, we know that we want do good, but we do evil. We are sin-possessed; we will all agree that we hate our sin-possessed selves.

Paul says in Romans 7:17, "I do not understand what I do. For what I want to do I do not do, but what I hate I do."

Paul, who does what he hates, is "another man," not Paul himself. And yet, he is Paul after all. Therefore, I, at the present time—while I remain as a sinner—am not "I" but "another man" captivated by the devil/sin. And yet "another man" is "me" also.

Some may say that when we do evil, it is the devil's fault and not ours, because we are taken by the devil. But the devil is nothing but the "state of absence of God" in our mind. Since the man himself selects such a state and agrees to it of his own accord, the choice to do evil is his.

We have to destroy "another man" in me, the old self, on the cross through following Jesus.

True Identity of Devil Is Only Revealed by Jesus

This subject will be hard to comprehend if we have not substantially met "a man Jesus" in our lives. However, it is the most important part in the way of following Jesus, and it will be more efficient to understand this concept in connection with the identity of the devil.

We have no correct knowledge about the identity of the devil. We do not know who and what the devil is. In this situation, we cannot fight the devil. However, we were told to fight against him so we insist that we are fighting against him. How can we fight with the devil when we do not know him? In fact, while reading this book even, we are already taken by him. Therefore, even the saying "Fight against the devil!" comes from the devil. Such a saying is merely an empty lie because we do not know the devil.

While not knowing who the devil is, we tend to defend and justify our deeds prompted by the devil. We can find such illustration from the Jews who persecuted the disciples of Christ. The Jews did not know they were working for the devil, but assumed they were working for God.

Consider 2 Corinthians 11:14, "And no marvel; for Satan himself is transformed into an angel of light."

Satan refers to the believers who are seized by Satan, and are under the law. They know and claim that they do the good works of an angel, but the following is what they do, of course unwittingly.

Read John 16:2. "They shall put you out of the synagogues: yes, the time comes, that whoever kills you will think that he does God service."

Likewise, if we have had no idea of the devil's identity, we have done service to him unwittingly so far, thinking we do God service.

Here we can see that the devil deceives us with so-called false good deeds. It is impossible for us to distinguish good from so-called false good. If we no longer want to be deceived by the devil, we need to meet "a man Jesus," who is testified to by the Scripture. He will show you who the devil is and lead you to the cross to destroy your old self, which is yourself captured by the devil. Without meeting Him, we cannot get away from the devil which is a part of us.

🗁 You Win If You Do Not Agree

Once we know the devil, it is very simple to fight with the devil. To win we are first to know what is the will of God; if we know it, we can follow. It is as simple as that. Consider the case in which Jesus was tempted by the devil. The thought of the devil came into His mind, but He refused it and did not unite Himself with it. That is, He did not allow the devil to have control over Him. The Son of God refers to a man who is exposed to the thoughts of the devil but discerns them and does not act in concert with them.

However, this is not a simple matter, which can be solved by determining in our mind not to do so. That is because we are one with it already. When we meet Jesus, He will give us the knowledge about what the devil is, and then we will be disciplined and trained to overcome him on every occasion. We can only discern the devil correctly after the crucifixion of our old self and the resurrection thereafter as a new self through following Jesus. After the death of the old self on our cross, we will have the power to identify the works of devil, and rule over them. This way, God makes our enemies our footstool through Jesus.

For your information, even after the cross, i.e., being born again, we cannot prevent the thoughts of the devil by the roots from coming into our mind while living in the flesh, because it is the natural principle of the mind of the man who is in the flesh. Therefore, every man in the flesh is exposed to the thoughts of the devil, whether we are born again or not.

Nevertheless, we who are healed by Jesus have the Spirit of Christ after the cross; we are one with Christ. Therefore, like Jesus we will no longer be deceived by the thoughts of the devil which comes to our mind through the desire of the flesh and the glory of the sinful world.

Next, I will explain about the thoughts given to Jesus by the devil who tried to tempt Him.

THE DEVIL HAVING TEMPTED JESUS, PART I
- MAN SHALL NOT LIVE BY BREAD ALONE

Luke 4:1-4
And Jesus being full of the Holy Spirit returned from Jordan, and was led by the Spirit into the wilderness, ²Being forty days tempted of the devil. And in those days he did eat nothing: and when they were ended, he afterward hungry. ³And the devil said to him, If you be the Son of God, command this stone that it be made bread. ⁴And Jesus answered him, saying, It is written, That man shall not live by bread alone, but by every word of God.

When I was still young in faith, I read these passages and imagined that an ugly and dreadful-looking devil appeared to Jesus and tempted Him. So I swore within me by saying, "I will never listen to the devil if he comes to me and tempts me this way!" Strangely, however, such a devil has never appeared to me nor tempted me in believing Jesus up to now.

Why not? Is it because I am so holy that the devil cannot even touch me? Sorry, no. It is because the devil is not like what I guessed and it does not come that way.

If a dreadful-looking devil appears to us and says, "I am the devil. Hear and follow me, then I will give you fortune and fame, even this world," nobody will listen to him. This cannot be the way the devil tempts believers.

Furthermore, strangely enough in this passage, Jesus was taken here and there by the devil when the devil should have been shivering with fright when he saw Jesus. Surely we are mistaken somewhere in our understanding about the identity of the devil. Now we will reveal his true nature.

In fact, the nature of the devil who tempted Jesus is not that of a stand-alone spiritual being, but the "godless thoughts" that were posed to Jesus' mind based on the "lust of the flesh, and the lust of the eyes, and the pride of life" (1 John 2:16).

In the text, the devil tempted Jesus in three ways:

- ✓ *First*, to command the stone to be made bread.
- ✓ *Second*, to worship the devil, and all the kingdoms of the world will be yours.
- ✓ *Third*, to cast yourself down from the pinnacle of the temple, and God will give His angels charge over you to bear you up.

I am going to describe who the devil is by explaining the essential matter of the temptations. When the devil is disclosed, Jesus Christ, the counter concept of the devil, will be disclosed naturally. Unfortunately, you will realize that we may not know Jesus correctly, even if we say we believe in Jesus.

The Devil Comes Through Thoughts

The devil having tempted Jesus is the godless thoughts that are open to all fallen people born in this world in the flesh. All men without exception with a fleshly body are exposed to such thoughts. Jesus, who is without sin, is in the flesh like us (Romans 8:3), so He is not an exception.

In the passage, the devil does not appear as a terrible figure but he shows himself as a thought in Jesus' mind. Accordingly, the devil works by injecting his ideas into the minds of mankind. The expression for the devil to "inject ideas into the mind" means that we push the will of God out of our mind and simultaneously draw the thoughts of the devil in. That is, we can call the thoughts of devil into us or thrust them out depending on how we determine our mind. After all, the movement of the devil is not caused by a stand-alone reality, but the result of our mind abandoning God. Therefore, the devil is *me* thinking and acting outside of God.

Having not understood that the devil resides inside us and works this way, we may have beaten down many people under the pretext of destroying the devil. In this way, we have sincerely served the devil. Considering how the devil works, the war is not an actual bloody fight, but a spiritual fight inside us. It is the fight of whether to follow the will of God or the thought suggested by the devil. If we decide to follow God's will and act accordingly, we will win this war.

Likewise, the devil comes to Jesus in this way and wishes to obtain His approval and make Him his own. When the devil came, Jesus did not yell nor work miracles so as to thrust him away and overcome him. He simply did not agree in His mind to the godless idea and rejected it. Jesus won the victory over the devil in this way.

When Jesus, as the Son of God, was tempted by the devil, He was neither well-off nor in peace. He was tempted while almost starved to death after the forty days' fasting. Who will not be thankful and obedient to God while he has enough food and feels cozy? He, who puts trust in God and follows Him under the condition in which he feels cold and hungry as if God has forsaken him, is the one who really believes in God as His Son.

Let us have a closer look at the temptation scenes.

Stone Made Into Bread : Will of God vs. Lust of Flesh

Jesus also has the lust of the flesh to eat and live on earth since He is a man. The lust itself to eat is not against the will of God. We have a natural desire to eat when we are hungry. However, He, as the Son of God, or if He is the real Son of God, will not to eat in spite of the hunger since God does not allow Him to eat.

He starves to death unless he eats now after having fasted forty days. The bread in this instance means the life of the flesh. Jesus had to choose either to eat bread in order to save His fully human life or to continue to fast in obedience to the Word of God even if He might lose His human life. While He is placed in that extreme situation, the devil says to Him to make bread and eat it. This means that the thought to eat, which is against God in this instance, arose in His mind.

📂 The Devil Perverting the Will of God

Everyone will obey if they can afford to do so. Here, Jesus fully knew that God wanted Him to go on fasting, but He was faced with the condition in which He would starve to death unless he ate bread.

Nobody will disobey the will of God when he truly knows God. Therefore, the devil deceives people by changing the original meaning of the will of God in a plausible manner so that they disobey Him.

In Part One of this book, we discussed that during communication with God we should know the heart of God correctly in order not to fail like Eli, the priest, Ahab, the king, and Saul, the king. But as we have known thus far, the devil is so deceitful that we can never defeat him by ourselves. I will explain how deceitful the devil is through the devil who tempts Jesus.

You will recognize that overcoming the devil is not a simple matter which can be achieved through our suspicion and efforts, because we are already one with him. Under this circumstance, our communication with God is always distorted and ignored. Therefore, we need to meet a man Jesus who will reveal the true nature of the devil to us. And Jesus will make you to put the devil under your footstool and you will do the perfect communication with God.

Let us continue to study the devil who tempts Jesus. Here, the devil says, "If you are the Son of God, command this stone that it be made bread." This is the thought coming into the mind of Jesus who already knew God wants Him to fast, yet perhaps He wondered: "Maybe I misunderstood the will of God (which was to continue my fast). I'm afraid of dying in vain, having misunderstood the will of God," or

"If I die of hunger here, who'll save the world? God does not want me to starve to death. He told me to fast before, but now it is time to have bread."

From the monologue above, we can find no word of disobedience to the will of God. Everybody refuses to obey when they justify or make excuses for themselves, and finally conclude that God permitted their disobedience. Such disguised thoughts which are against the commandment of God are the devil itself, and when we take them as ours, we are thus deceived by the devil.

When deceived by devil in such a way, we never think we are insubordinate to Him. On the contrary, we will think that we ate food in compliance with His will. For instance, the Jews who persecuted the believers of Christ never dreamed that they followed the will of devil, but they acted that way based on the firm belief that it was God's will to do so. Consider John 16:2, "They shall put you out of the synagogues: yes, the time comes, that whoever kills you will think that he does God service."

The real meaning of that "devil deceives" is that we disobey the will of God to pursue our own lusts of the flesh. In fact, we will realize that it is *we* who disobey God, not the devil. We have no excuse to reproach the devil, others, or situations, but ought to blame ourselves for letting the devil work in us.

Jesus rejected the desire to eat and various thoughts given by the devil, and finally did not eat to follow God's commandment. He was not deceived by the devil, which means that He did not deceive Himself. He obeyed God in this way, and He really is the Son of God.

🗁 Esau Having Dropped Out of Salvation

If Jesus listened to the devil and ate the bread, Jesus could not be the real Jesus who could do the works of God. Because if he is such a Jesus who listens to the devil in times of hunger, neglecting the will of God, then he will eat as usual against the will of God if he feels hungry while he is living in this world as the savior. Such a savior cannot be the Son of God. God also does not call such man as His son.

One of examples of those who failed in such temptation of the devil is Esau.

Read the following passage.

> And Jacob sod pottage: and Esau came from the field, and he was faint: [30]And Esau said to Jacob, Feed me, I pray you, with that same red pottage; for I am faint: therefore was his name called Edom. [31]And Jacob said, Sell me this day your birthright. [32]And Esau said, Behold, I am at the point to die: and what profit shall this birthright do to me? [33]And Jacob said, Swear to me this day; and he swore to him: and he sold his birthright to Jacob. [34]Then Jacob gave Esau bread and pottage of lentils; and he did eat and drink, and rose up, and went his way: thus Esau despised his birthright. _____ Genesis 25:29-34

During the test by God, Esau walked in a way different from that of Jesus. He sold his birthright for a mess of pottage because he was starved to death. The birthright indicates a calling to be a son of God. If, having treasured the birthright as Jesus did, Esau would have obeyed God at the risk of starvation, he would have become His son. However, Esau decided at the time of temptation that food was more important than the birthright given by God.

He said in verse 32, "Behold, I am at the point to die: and what profit shall this birthright do to me?" The devil prompted such thoughts in Esau's mind; generally speaking, Esau may have thought, "Don't you think that you have to first maintain your life if you want to keep the birthright? God won't want you to die in hunger in this condition, too! You'd better eat now!"

This is the same thought that we guessed occurred in Jesus' mind. That is, "If I die of hunger here, who'll save the world? God does not want me to starve to death."

Esau was quite willing to assent to the thought of the devil who had distorted the will of God. Since Esau was very hungry he strongly wished to believe that God would fully understand the situation he faced. This is the true and hidden meaning of Esau's saying, "Behold, I am at the point to die: and what profit shall this birthright do to me if I die here?"

He was, thus, deceived by the devil which, in fact, is the way his mind, ignorant of the knowledge of God, worked. Therefore, the man who is ignorant of God is always open to the devil, and will behave as his slave.

Esau might want to keep the birthright; he did not know the real identity of the devil. Therefore, being deceived by the devil, he honored the food more than the will of God each time he felt hungry. He spent his whole life this way, and he was forsaken by God. God did not forsake Esau, but it was Esau who forsook God by deceiving himself. Being deceived, he did not even know that he was going the wrong way. His whole life was like that, without repentance to God. This is the meaning of "he was rejected: for he found no place of repentance" (Hebrews 12:17b).

📁 Your Birthright

When you confess Jesus as your Savior in the church, it means you are given a spiritual birthright. How much do you value that birthright? You will be born again as sons of God if you have the proper understanding about the devil and are not deceived by him. And you will not be deceived as long as you retain the knowledge of God. Otherwise, you are destined to be deceived by the devil that comes to you through lust and desire of the things of the world, and will lose your birthright unwittingly, like Esau.

Such temptations, whether you obey or disobey God, are given to you every day. However, most believers do not even think about the devil, because they have never retained the real sense of God in their minds. Therefore, we are totally ignorant of such temptations given to us in everyday life. Or, even when we hear the voice of God, we constantly deceive ourselves by justifying or prioritizing daily eating and living.

For instance, when God stirs us up in our minds to give offerings, we ignore it by thinking, "It is too much to offer. Absurd. It cannot be of God. Even if it is God's, He will understand my poor situation. He is on my side."

Or, if one of our relatives has a wedding ceremony coinciding on the Sunday service, we rush to conclude that, "It happens on Sunday. It is the intention of the Lord to allow me to skip the Sunday service today."

Having these thoughts, we make no great disservice to God. However, if we behave in this way as deceived by the devil, fighting against God, our birthrights will be taken from us, if we do not repent.

Esau represents the man who believes in Jesus not knowing what the devil is and how he works to the end.

The Way to Acquire Both

Thinking deeply, we can find that all things in this world and happenings are under the control of God and they are the results of His plans. The fact that the devil appeared and tempted Jesus was the plan of God. God sent the devil (Luke 4:1) to Jesus.

Under this circumstance of temptation, God forbade eating while, on the other hand, the devil urged eating. Jesus, who fasted forty days, did not eat according to God's will, but did not die of hunger, either. Jesus was accepted by God through obedience, and got the bread as well. He received both God's approval and bread by selecting the best choice first, which was obeying God.

Likewise, if we obey God and do as He wishes, we will not lose anything in this world, and furthermore, we will be accepted by God as His children. By choosing God, the spiritual matter and the worldly matter are solved concurrently. However, if we follow the devil, we may temporarily escape the hunger but we will feel hungry again, and never be satisfied. Moreover, when we abandon becoming the son of God, we give up our spiritual birthright. If we give up our spiritual birthright to obtain the bread of the flesh, we lose everything after all.

We should treasure the birthright that we received when we came to church.

Stone Made Into Bread : The True Messiah vs. The False Messiah

So far, we have seen the obedience of the Son of God during the devil's temptation to sin when He was starving.

Now I will explain another aspect of the devil's temptation which is embedded in the devil's speech. The Scriptures reveal the true Messiah through the dialogue here. The devil says, "If you be the Son of God, command this stone that it be made bread." This means that, "If you, Jesus, are the real Son of God, the Messiah, you should be able to solve the problem of the lack of food for mankind. If you are Him, give food to the poor in this world."

If Jesus did so, He would have been well received by the people, but He did not do so. As described, Jesus, the Son of God, did not value the bread of the flesh more than the will of God, which is the truth.

On the contrary, the devil gives the priority to the bread of the flesh he will eat in this world. With such thoughts, he cannot but lightly esteem the birthright. Moreover, the devil considers the birthright as a means of eating his fill in this world; that is, he tries to live well through the blessings of God by believing in Jesus. For this purpose, he values the birthright, if he is able to value anything. He is an "Esau" who lightly esteemed his birthright and sold it for one morsel of food.

Let us think how the devil tries to persuade Jesus with his righteousness and the goodness of godlessness.

📂 The Devil's View About the Messiah : The False Messiah

We who are spiritually blind can only see the matters of this world: we are concerned only about how to eat and live well now. For instance, we think food is our top priority while living. And we all have a natural warm heart to give bread to hungry people. And to our shock, the devil is also saying that.

The devil's suggestion comes as a thought in the mind of Jesus, perhaps as follows:

"If you are the Son of God, make bread and give it to the hungry people. Then they will appreciate you and follow you. Are you not hungry and facing death? Many people in this world suffer pain due to hunger, much as you suffer now. Nobody could have solved this problem. If you turn away from their sufferings, you are not the Son of God. If you are able to feed them to their fill, you'll be respected as the true Son of God, the Messiah."

When the devil misrepresents and fights God, he does not blaspheme Him openly. He always speaks about God and acts in the name of God. Therefore, the devil comes to us as God or as the angel of God. However, he expresses a distorted God. The God the devil knows is He who can make the hungry people eat their fill. Therefore, the devil says that if Jesus is the true Son of God, He must do these things.

The Scripture describes the Jews as the devil who insists that the Son of God should be so.

Consider the following passage from John.

> They said therefore to him, What sign show you then, that we may see, and believe you? what do you work? [31]Our fathers did eat manna in the desert; as it is written, He gave them bread from heaven to eat. _____ John 6:30-31

What the Jews mean is as follows:

"Jesus! What sign do you do so that we may see and believe that God has sent you? Our ancestors ate manna coming from heaven when they were hungry in the wilderness with Moses. Can this be the confirmation that God deeply cared for the food our forefathers would eat? If you have also come of heaven, will you not show the sign of giving us food as God did through Moses?"

As I said, the Jews anticipated that God would solve the matter of food when the Messiah came. Surely they had the same thought as the devil tempting Jesus in the text. Here you will now realize also that the devil in the Scriptures is not an ugly-looking spirit, but a human being who may be showing a warm heart.

The Jews read the Scripture but understood it according to the thought of the devil, with virtually humane hearts, but without retaining the knowledge of God. Naturally, their interpretation of God from the Scriptures, who they believed in, was the God of the devil who they created. They never dreamed that the God they worship is the perverted God of the devil. Quite naturally, Jesus had to say to those Jews, "God is not your father, but the devil is." But they, failing to perceive the fact, had to confront with Jesus with all their strength (John 8:41-44).

I heard a woman, whose husband was a pastor, say, "If Jesus comes on earth now, He will visit the hungry, the poor, and those who work for peace in this world." We can easily catch what kind of Jesus she has in mind: It is the Jesus who gives physical bread to the hungry and the poor.

With this thought in mind, many people share food with others in order to practice the love of Jesus. They think they must live that way as His disciples.

Yes, true. Nobody says it is wrong to share bread. We ought to do it, however, without neglecting to give them spiritual food which will make them one with God. Messiah gives us spiritual food for our eternal lives, and if He finishes His works by giving only earthly food, He is the fake Messiah whom the devil has in his mind.

Let us see what Jesus, the real Messiah, did in this respect.

📂 Jesus, the Real Messiah

We lead poor and void lives because we have left God and are essentially under the control of the devil. This is the fundamental problem of all mankind living in this world. Therefore, to solve this problem, we have to return to God. As long as we have abandoned God, we will never be satisfied in our lives and will eventually die in sin even if we have plenty of food and money. Of course, it is not Jesus' final aim to give bread of the flesh.

Jesus says in Matthew:

> Therefore take no thought, saying, What shall we eat? or, What shall we drink? or, Wherewithal shall we be clothed? [32](For after all these things do the Gentiles seek:) for your heavenly Father knows that you have need of all these things. _____ Matthew 6:31-32

He says to those who seek something to eat or something to drink that God already knows that men live by bread. As He said through His Word, God supplies food to people through any means. As God feeds the fowl of the air that do not sow or reap, He cares for people more deeply. Sometimes, God allows some people to suffer from hunger so that they may seek Him.

Here, we need to differentiate between the role of God and the role of Jesus. While God is working in that way for the people with the earthly food, Jesus will play His role, that is, to give spiritual bread to feed hungry spirits. Jesus will give spiritual food to us so that we may never thirst or hunger for good, after going through our own crucifixion and resurrection being united with Jesus. Thus, Jesus restores our lost communication with God, to become one with God. This is the one and only way to essentially solve all the problems of this world. Jesus, the Messiah, came to fulfill this work for us.

Do not be confused therefore; Jesus has not come to give earthly, physical food, but spiritual food. Ask for spiritual bread, not earthly bread, from Him and you will get it.

The devil distorts the above truth and tricks us by saying that the Son of God must settle the matter of earthly bread to eat. That is, he turns our concerns to a matter outside of us to gloss over the basic nature of the problem, that is, our separation from God. Therefore, you have gone astray if you follow Jesus with the intention of getting some more bread for the flesh.

Knowing all the devil's wiles, Jesus reveals the true Messiah, which we will discover in the next section.

Bread for the Flesh vs. Word for the Spirit

Jesus refuses the devil's suggestion of making a stone into bread to eat, and says, "Man shall not live by bread alone, but by every word of God," citing Deuteronomy. Simply speaking, we must not live a natural life, one sustained only by bread, but live a born-again life which is sustained by the Word of God, our spiritual bread.

The natural life is the shadow of the born-again life, the reality. Read the following passage:

> And you shall remember all the way which the LORD your God led you these forty years in the wilderness, to humble you, and to prove you, to know what was in your heart, whether you would keep his commandments, or no. ³And he humbled you, and suffered you to hunger, and fed you with manna, which you knew not, neither did your fathers know; that he might make you know that man does not live by bread only, but by every word that proceeds out of the mouth of the LORD does man live. _____ Deuteronomy 8:2-3

The Israelites were tempted while passing through the wilderness in the same manner Jesus was tempted in the wilderness.

First, God wanted to know if the Israelites would obey Him in their heart while being hungry in the wilderness, as written in verse 2. Likewise, God wanted to know whether Jesus would obey Him after having fasted forty days in the wilderness. The former failed and the latter succeeded.

Referring to verse 3, Scripture says God allowed the people to hunger and fed them with manna so that He might teach them they did not live by bread only, but by His Word.

We are puzzled with this statement because it is our common understanding that if God wanted them to learn this principle (man does not live by bread alone), he should not give anything to eat and keep them alive, rather than giving manna (food). Then the people would realize, "Ah! We can live without manna. We truly do not need manna alone to be alive on earth."

But we are mistaken concerning the true meaning of this passage, so we face an oxymoron.

To grasp what this word "manna" means, we need to see what the historical event symbolizes. In the text of Deuteronomy, manna is used as a symbol of the "spiritual" food. When the Israelites were hungry in the wilderness, that situation symbolizes our spiritual hunger in this world. When God sent the Israelites, who were ranging in the wilderness, manna from heaven, it signified that He will work out our spiritual hunger by giving the Word of God (signified by manna) to we who are wandering in this world (signified by wilderness).

Therefore, His feeding them manna symbolizes that He will have them eat the Word of God and, consequently, give them new life. That is, by feeding them with manna, which is the shadow, He wanted to enlighten them about eating the Word of God to have eternal life, which is the reality. However, they could not catch the meaning, but were thankful for the physical aspect of manna as food.

When the Scriptures say, "We shall not live by bread alone," it means that "We shall not live by natural life alone, which is maintained by bread." Therefore, we will have to be born again and become people who live by the Word of God at the expense of all possessions in this world. And this cannot be accomplished without Jesus. Jesus, the Son of God, therefore, has come to fulfill this purpose within us by giving us spiritual food, not earthly food.

📂 Jesus Christ, the Real Humanist

Today's humanists may not esteem God and Jesus highly when they consider God as the One who forbade Jesus to eat for forty days. They may judge Him for having no mercy. Speaking for those who are merciful, indeed, the devil tells Jesus with a tear-provoking and warm word, "You have misunderstood God. Make bread and help yourself to it. Why not?"

We have problems in life, not because we cannot eat and drink as much as we like, but fundamentally because we are in the hands of the devil. Under such a condition, we will finally fight each other, hate each other, envy one another, and turn away from the poor, even if we repeatedly encourage each other by saying, "Share what we have with others," "Gather together to help the poor," and "Love one another." The history of mankind has already proved that these are the useless efforts, lies and hypocrisies.

The people who are slaves of the devil are squeezed and tormented by him to lead a life unworthy of mankind while deprived of mankind's dignity. We are oppressed in the most inhuman manner on earth when our spiritual eyes are opened. As long as we are in such depraved states, we will never be satisfied if we eat heartily, yet we cannot afford to care for hungry neighbors. Therefore, good sayings like "share what we have," cannot solve the problem.

However, we will restore the true dignity of mankind when we receive the Word of Life from Jesus to free ourselves from bondage to the devil. Then, we who were beaten, oppressed, transformed, and bent because of the devil will restore the proper dignity of men in Jesus. Jesus Christ has come to make us truly-freed mankind. Therefore, the true humanist is not he who gives bread but Jesus Christ who gives the Word of Life to set us free.

If you believe in a Son of God who comes only to give bread, you believe in one who masquerades son of God who stays in the thoughts of the devil.

We will continue this discourse in the next section.

The Devil Having Tempted Jesus, Part II
- Do Not Tempt God

The Power and Glory of All the Kingdoms of the World

Read the following passage to discuss the second temptation of Jesus.

> And the devil, taking him up into an high mountain, showed to him all the kingdoms of the world in a moment of time. ⁶And the devil said to him, All this power will I give you, and the glory of them: for that is delivered to me; and to whomsoever I will I give it. ⁷If you therefore will worship me, all shall be yours. ⁸And Jesus answered and said to him, Get you behind me, Satan: for it is written, You shall worship the Lord your God, and him only shall you serve. _____ Luke 4:5-8

Secondly, Jesus was tempted regarding the power and glory of all the kingdoms of the world.

What would the power and the glory of this world belonging to the godless being, the devil, be like? It would be vain and nothing other than chaff and death. In spite of this, people struggle without exception to acquire the power and glory of this world: We long to be a man of great power, we desire to win acceptance from the world, and we want to be admitted into the higher class and lead a better life.

For this purpose, we envy others, speak ill of them, and fight them.

Because we are lost in darkness through our desire to achieve greatness we don't deserve, we are unable to recognize Jesus who has come to deliver us from that world. Far from hoping to be saved from the vain world by following Jesus, we try to obtain the glory of the world with the help of Jesus because it is hard to get on our own. However, this desire for the glory of this world does not come from Jesus, but is an item that is for sale by the devil.

Not knowing what is right and what is wrong, we, the believers, incessantly demand the power and glory of this world from Him, insisting that our activities glorify God. Such power and glory belong to the devil. It is really a matter for regret for us to pursue worldly power and glory in the name of God who wishes to give us the spiritual glory which is eternal life through Jesus.

Jesus can work as the Son of God when He is not tempted by the glory of the world. During His public life, He had many opportunities to enjoy the glory of the world. For example, many people wanted to have Jesus as their king when He came into Jerusalem (John 12:12-13). The power of the world and its glory that we all desire to achieve were substantially laid before Him. But He dumped all such glory and delivered Himself to the cross to obey the will of God. This shows that He is the Son of God who carries out the works of God. We anticipated this obedience on the cross when He turned down the various temptations of the devil.

In the case of mankind, God sometimes allows us spiritual gifts or power so that we may work for Him. Then, other people naturally crowd around us because of that power. In this instance, most of us are tempted by the glory of the world the crowd gives, and then desert the will of God. In that case, we are not the sons of God.

Above all else, before receiving the power of God, we must be tempted in the wilderness, pass through it, and become the perfect sons of God. This process is, in other words, to follow Jesus to the cross. Then we are worth all the power of God: We will have true power by which we can throw away the glory and the power of the world without regret for the sake of the works of God. We will also reject the devil who deceives with the glory of the world, saying like

Jesus:

"You shall worship the Lord your God, and him only shall you serve" (Luke 4:8b).

Cast Yourself Down from the Pinnacle of the Temple

Read the following passage to discuss the final temptation of Jesus by the devil.

> And he brought him to Jerusalem, and set him on a pinnacle of the temple, and said to him, If you be the Son of God, cast yourself down from hence: [10]For it is written, He shall give his angels charge over you, to keep you: [11]And in their hands they shall bear you up, lest at any time you dash your foot against a stone. [12]And Jesus answering said to him, It is said, You shall not tempt the Lord your God. [13]And when the devil had ended all the temptation, he departed from him for a season.
> Luke 4:9-13

In the third temptation, the devil sets Jesus on a pinnacle of the temple and tells Him to cast Himself from it because God shall give the angels charge over Him to keep Him. Jesus refuses the temptation to call upon the angels by repeating, "You shall not tempt the Lord your God" (Luke 4:12).

📂 The Devil Cites the Psalms

First, the devil quoted the Psalms. In this case, will the psalms cited by the devil be the word of God or that of the devil? Or what?

We know the Scripture we ordinarily read as the Word of God. However, the problem is that it is open to anyone, such as the rich or the poor, the wicked or the just, adults or children, etc. And anyone can quote it freely. Even the devil can quote, as we can see here in this case. Therefore, we have to seriously consider the Scripture we read, otherwise we may cite it in the fashion that the devil cites.

Are we different from the devil in terms of citing this verse in this case? Let us see. Jesus countered devil's reference of the Psalms by saying, "You shall not tempt the Lord your God." Judging from what Jesus says, the verses the devil quoted are not used as God meant them to be, but are misinterpreted by the devil. What does the devil misinterpret? Some believers insist that the devil omitted some words i.e., "in all your ways" from the verses of Psalms when he cited the same.

Read the following passage from Psalms.

> For he shall give his angels charge over you, to keep you in all your ways. [12]They shall bear you up in their hands, lest you dash your foot against a stone. _____ Psalms 91:11-12

The devil says, "If you are the Son of God, throw yourself down from here," and he cites the Psalms, as "For it is written, He shall give his angels charge over you, to keep you: And in their hands they shall bear you up, lest at any time you dash your foot against a stone" (Luke 4:10-11). Obviously the devil omitted phrase "in all your ways" which is in Psalms.

Then, will this be the distortion in meaning? I think not. At this moment, the devil is urging Jesus to leap down from the high pinnacle of the temple. In this case, it does not make a great difference if the phrase "in all your ways" is in the quoted text of the devil or not. On the contrary, such omission is disadvantageous for the devil to persuade Jesus to jump down. Therefore, omission of the words from the verse is not the essence of the devil's distortion.

We learned that one jot or one tittle should not be either added or omitted from the Scripture when we cite it, so we tried to judge whether a quotation is accurate or changed by counting the number of words. But to distort the Word of God is not a mere question of several words, because the person who quotes it is the one who changes the Word of God.

If we want to cite the words of the Scripture in the right way, we should first be born again as spiritual men. Then we can cite Scripture as we want in accordance with the understanding of the heart of God, the Author of Scripture, and in that case we do not have to cite word by word. If we read and quote the Word of the Spirit while we are of the flesh, whether we intended to interpret fleshly or not, we will automatically change the spiritual words into the words belonging to the flesh.

Likewise, in this case, the devil does not distort the Word of God by leaving out a few words, phrases, or sentences, but he distorts the Word simply because of who he is. The devil is the distortion itself. Therefore, upon hearing the devil's citation of the Psalms, Jesus does not refute by pointing out that he omitted some words, but instead He says, "You shall not tempt the Lord your God." That is, "it is to tempt God if you, the devil, understand the recited Scripture like the way you read." The devil treats the Psalms verses superficially to imply that when we, the believers, jump down from the high place the angels will come and hold us so that we will not be injured physically. If we read the Scripture in this fashion, we will have miracle-based faith, and such faith will ultimately tempt God. Jesus is pointing this out. Let us continue.

How does the devil tempt God?

What Is It to Tempt God?

What the devil suggests to Jesus in the text is something like this. "Jesus, if you are the Son of God, the Messiah, why don't you cast yourself from the higher place and show yourself not being injured? Then many people will believe in you and will follow you. Isn't this a good method to make people to believe in you?"

Quite frankly, we share the same opinion with the devil. We also wish to have such miracles and power in preaching the gospel, and pray to God to have the "flashy" spiritual gifts such as healing the sick, prophesying, seeing the visions, casting out the demons, and so on.

However, even if people would believe in Jesus from the miracles and wonders done in His name, it is not the true faith that God wishes to give us. Those who have miracle-based faith will trust in God and praise Him when they have acquired what they wanted by God's miracles, but they will grumble and betray Him instantly when they failed to get their desires. To "grumble and betray God" means that they do not see God in every circumstance, as He is always here. A faith like that, and deeds aimed only at achieving our desires, is how we tempt God.

Therefore, the words of Jesus in verse 12 in the text, "It is said, You shall not tempt the Lord your God," can be paraphrased, "What will people do if I throw myself from the pinnacle of the temple but I am not injured? In that case, they surely will follow me and say that they believe in me. But such faith is of their own making, not the kind of faith that would be given through following me to the cross. Naturally, when something bad happens, they will all betray and run away from me, thinking that God is not with them. Miracle-based faith is shallow, and the Son of God is not concerned about generating such faith that tempts God."

To know the meaning of tempting God more clearly, I will explain Deuteronomy 6:16, from which Jesus cited here, "You shall not tempt the LORD your God, as you tempted him in Massah." Let us see the site where the Israelites tempted God.

Read the following passages from Exodus.

> And all the congregation of the children of Israel journeyed from the wilderness of Sin, after their journeys, according to the commandment of the LORD, and pitched in Rephidim: and there was no water for the people to drink. ²Why the people did chide with Moses, and said, Give us water that we may drink. And Moses said to them, Why chide you with me? why do you tempt the LORD? _____ Exodus 17:1-2

> And he called the name of the place Massah, and Meribah, because of the chiding of the children of Israel, and because they tempted the LORD, saying, Is the LORD among us, or not? _____ Exodus 17: 7

The people camped at Rephidim but there was no water to drink. They requested water from Moses and he told them, "Why *chide* you with me (*Meribah* in Hebrew)? Wherefore do you *tempt* the LORD (*Massah* in Hebrew)?"

Evil is Present with Me 175

Verse 7 describes this situation as the Israelites tempting the LORD by saying, "Is the LORD among us or not?"

When God gave the people of Israel the food and beverages they asked for through miracles in the wilderness, they joyfully praised God with timbrels and danced, but they grumbled at Him again when they were in want. This is an example of tempting God to give in to our desires, when we say, "Is the LORD among us or not?"

Referring to the quotation by Jesus, both the case in which Jesus casts Himself down from a higher place to see if God protects Him and the case in which the people did not believe in God, murmur about no water, and quarrel with Moses were examples of tempting God. Because both cases were meant to check whether the LORD is among us or not, and proof of their unbelief. True faith will know that the Lord is always there always regardless of the situation.

Therefore, when the devil tells Jesus to work miracles before the people so that they may believe in Him, it means that he says to make them have the faith of tempting God in their heart. Jesus answered him by saying, "You shall not tempt the Lord your God," meaning that "It will only make people to have God-tempting faith in their minds. This is what God forbids."

However, the devil's word to show the miracle is a great temptation to Jesus because Jesus could have made His life easier by performing miracles so the people would believe in Him and follow Him, rather than have to die on the cross in misery. However, He, as the true Messiah, the Son of God, knows that such shallowness of believing in miracles is not true faith, so He died on the cross to give mankind the true faith of Jesus.

Yes, there are many types of faith, and all of them are of the devil, except the faith that comes into us when we follow Jesus to the cross. When we have that true faith, we will not complain nor betray God even in front of death.

Then why did Jesus perform many miracles during His public life? It was to reveal the hidden truth. For example, He opened the eyes of the blind man. This is to show that a spiritually blind man will open his eyes by His salvation. He drove out the demon from a demon-possessed man, and set him free. This also signifies that Jesus, through His death on the cross, will cast out the devil that seizes us and make us free even now.

As discussed thus far, the devil's false image of the Messiah is what we think, exactly. In fact, he whom we believe in up to now is not Jesus, but the devil disguised with the mask of Jesus. To reiterate, we, the believers under the law, do not recognize the lead of the living Jesus, and will automatically object to my point, thinking, "Then, are you saying that we should stop to give food to the poor, stop seeking miracles and stop praying God to have better positions in this world?"

We respond in such a way because we only know the law that requires us *to do something* or *not to do something* to prove our faith. Please continue to do those good deeds. However, our acts of charity do not change our sinful nature. Then, what should we do to prove and act on our faith in Jesus? We should meet "a man Jesus" who will heal us to cleanse us from our sins. In fact, this Jesus is hidden to those believers trapped under the law.

In spite of this message, the devil will not be revealed to us until we meet "a man Jesus" in person. Pray hard to God to meet this Jesus, the son of man who has Christ in him.

He Departed From Him for a Season

The devil, having tempted Him, departed from Him for a season. When He has driven out such thoughts that once came into His heart, those tempting thoughts depart from Him for a certain period of time, just for a while, literally. While living in the flesh in this world, Jesus cannot help being exposed to the thoughts the devil gives at all times. Those thoughts are incidental to all humans who are born in this world until we die. However unlike other humans, Jesus is the man whom the devil can never ever make Him to give in to temptation. Such a man is the true Son of God.

Epilogue

In summary:
First, the devil represents the godless thoughts that a man invites

into his mind. Scriptures say the devil, as a person, has put such thoughts into the heart. The devil appeared as thoughts in Jesus to tempt Him. But He knew the thoughts of the devil and rejected them.

Second, the devil pursues compassion, or good, in the world of corruption in the name of God in his own way. He says to give bread to the hungry people, and offers the power and glory of the world to the people. But yet a little while, those things will disappear and will be corruptible. Under the devil's influence, the people to miss the everlasting kingdom of God when all their attention is drawn to those corruptible things of the world. He borrows the name of God to deceive them into seeking things of the world rather than heavenly things. The devil deceived them, but it is they who deceive themselves.

Third, we are friends with the devil wittingly and unwittingly. We have thought that the devil is an evil being who has nothing to do with *me* and who is far from *me*. It is a big mistake. We live together with him and our lives are already controlled by him. It is obvious when we think that what the devil requests from Jesus in the Luke passage is exactly what we might request from Him. That is, the Jesus we believe in now is the Jesus who gives bread to the hungry people, who gives all the power and glory of the world, and who reigns over all the people by displaying miracles.

Therefore, do not be deceived that you are on the right trail of the faith because you think you:

- are a believer;
- rely on the law and brag about your relationship to God;
- know His will and approve of what is superior because you are instructed by the law;
- are convinced that you are a guide for the blind, a light for those who are in the dark, an instructor of the foolish, a teacher of infants, because you have in the law the embodiment of knowledge and truth (Romans 2:17-20).

Like the case of the Jews who refused to believe in the Messiah, Jesus, and condemned Him, all the above points may be of the devil if you are not being corrected and healed by Jesus first. Meet and follow Jesus, and He will reveal the nature of the devil in your life, so you can fight against it.

Once again, what is the devil? It is the man who is against God. The sole creatures who are given the power to resist God in the whole universe are not the angels nor the beasts but the men who are created in the image of God. God allowed men to fight against Him as a process through which He might create them in the perfect image of Him. Therefore, virtually, the devil is the human being who is not yet been born again.

The devil is the concept of a state that exists because God exists. Therefore, its existence cannot be annihilated. We must prevent ourselves from being deceived by the thoughts the devil gives us.

Next, we will discuss Satan.

SATAN

Satan appearing in the Scriptures will now be considered.

Who is Satan?

The term "Satan" generally includes two meanings: a common noun, "adversary," and a "person who resists God."

📂 Satan as a Common Noun

Satan as a common noun means "adversary" or "oppose." Below is the word about Balaam in the book of Numbers.

> And God's anger was kindled because he went: and the angel of the LORD stood in the way for an adversary against him. Now he was riding on his ass, and his two servants were with him.
> _____ Numbers 22:22

Here, the "adversary" is *Satan* in Hebrew and is used in the meaning of "to withstand." Therefore, the angel of the LORD in the quoted verse works is "Satan" for Balaam.

Other related examples (prefer the more common term) are as follows:

And the princes of the Philistines were wroth with him; and the princes of the Philistines said to him, Make this fellow return, that he may go again to his place which you have appointed him, and let him not go down with us to battle, lest in the battle he be an adversary to us: for with which should he reconcile himself to his master? should it not be with the heads of these men? _____ 1 Samuel 29:4

And David said, What have I to do with you, you sons of Zeruiah, that you should this day be adversaries to me? shall there any man be put to death this day in Israel? for do not I know that I am this day king over Israel? _____ 2 Samuel 19:22

And he was an adversary to Israel all the days of Solomon, beside the mischief that Hadad did: and he abhorred Israel, and reigned over Syria. _____ 1 Kings 11:25

The term "adversary" found in the above passages is translated from the word meaning "Satan" in Hebrew. Hence, God or His good angel can be expressed as Satan sometimes, depending on the perspective in the context.

The term "Satan" is used as "adversary" in the above cases.

📂 Satan, the Person Against God

Satan is a "unique being who opposes God." The adversary who fights against God is Satan based on the meaning of to "oppose." Therefore, Satan has the same meaning as "the devil who perverts God" that I already explained in the definition of the devil. That is, Satan means: a) the state of the absence of God, b) Satan in a man, i.e., godless thoughts, and c) man Satan. Point a) above is the status of man in Eden, and points b) and c) are the status of man in this sinful world.

In the parable of the sower in Matthew 13, the fowls of the air represent the "wicked one" was substituted with "Satan" in Mark 4 and the devil in Luke 8. Therefore, the "wicked one," "Satan" and the "devil" have same meaning.

Also, Matthew says as follows:

> Again, the *devil* takes him up into an exceeding high mountain, and shows him all the kingdoms of the world, and the glory of them; ⁹And said to him, All these things will I give you, if you will fall down and worship me. ¹⁰Then said Jesus to him, Get you hence, **Satan**: for it is written, You shall worship the Lord your God, and him only shall you serve. _____ Matthew 4:8-10

Here, Jesus calls the devil tempting Him "Satan." Therefore, we can understand that Satan is the same as the devil.

Next I will explain Satan as the adversary of God shown in the Scriptures.

Satan Mentioned in the Scripture

I will discuss some examples of Satan mentioned in Scripture verses. During the discussion, I will focus on the characteristics of Satan rather than explaining the whole related passages.

Satan Having Provoked David

Consider the following passages from 1 Chronicles chapter 21.

And Satan stood up against Israel, and provoked David to number Israel. _____ 1 Chronicles 21:1

Satan here means the "state of absence of God," and he is united with David as David's heart flows to form godless thoughts, which is the meaning of "Satan stood up." The census taken by David was against the will of God and incurred God's wrath because David did not depend on God, but on the number of people and their power. This is manifest from the word of Joab who aggressively opposed the census. Joab said so to David who required numbering the people, as we read in the following passage.

And Joab answered, The LORD make his people an hundred times so many more as they be: but, my lord the king, are they not all my lord's servants? why then does my lord require this thing? why will he be a cause of trespass to Israel? _____ 1 Chronicles 21:3

This can be said in the end: "May the LORD add to His people a hundred times as many as they are, and are they not all my lord's servants? Why does my lord seek to take a census? The LORD will do it all to my lord. It is to rely on the number of men and their power more than God, and if my lord decides to proceed to it, my lord has the people commit sin before God."

But David did not listen to Joab and had the census taken as he wished. Because of this, God was angered and sent a pestilence on Israel.

We think that Satan, not David, must be responsible for this thing because Satan provoked David to take a census. But as I said in the previous chapter about the devil, Satan is not a being that has an independent personality. If expressed with human terms, Satan is the personality of a man who is combined with Satan. In this case, it is David who allowed Satan into his thoughts.

Therefore, God chastens David and the people of Israel about the census without uttering a single word about Satan. God chastened David. David trespassed and therefore, he could not deny the fact that he was trespassing person. If David was wholly God's, he would not have numbered them in agreement with the provocation of Satan. For example, Jesus did not act on the thoughts of the devil but rejected them in the wilderness during temptation. This shows Jesus is the perfect one as the son of God.

David already had pride in his heart at the time he was about to take the census. He thought that he won wars and settled down because he did well in all ways. Therefore, he wanted to confirm his power by numbering the people whom he considered the base of his power. This is the godless thought in his heart; that is, Satan, because all the successes were the works of God, not David and his men. However, David took the census anyway as he agreed with Satan.

The earlier passage in 1 Chronicles says Satan provoked David. However, this passage in 2 Samuel points out that God moved David.

> And again the anger of the LORD was kindled against Israel, and he moved David against them to say, Go, number Israel and Judah. _____ 2 Samuel 24:1

In here, "God moved David" means indirect permission. David was already proud of himself and had the thought in his heart to number the people. God wanted to reveal his pride in order to correct it. David may deny it by saying he was "not proud of myself" if he has the thought only in heart. Therefore, God allowed the evil thought to be acted upon. After all, David took the census. Having sinned, he could no longer make any excuses for his behavior; he had the opportunity to repent and be healed of his pride against God. The writer of 2 Samuel recorded "He moved him" from this perspective. We ought not to misunderstand this.

As the outcome of this event, David built an altar on the threshing floor of Ornan and offered burnt offerings and peace offerings, stopping God's anger. Afterwards, Solomon built the house of the LORD there (2 Chronicles 3:1). This symbolizes that the pride of David was corrected and healed; he had truly become one with God, and he had been reconciled to Him.

God makes the people be tempted and sin through Satan, has them repent, and finally makes them His. In the same manner, He leaves Adam to himself so that he may eat of the tree of the knowledge of good and evil upon the temptation of the serpent. God then hopes Adam will return to Him to be one again through tribulation and repentance in this world. That is, Adam is given an opportunity to repent by God's allowing him to fall.

If we are seduced by Satan, we will undergo the same pain and suffering as David. However, if we realize it and repent to God, our fall will also work for good to us by the growth of our faith.

In conclusion, the word "Satan" here is the Satan in a man, the godless thought in David.

Peter Satan

Read the following passage from Matthew.

> From that time forth began Jesus to show to his disciples, how that he must go to Jerusalem, and suffer many things of the elders and chief priests and scribes, and be killed, and be raised again the third day. ²²Then Peter took him, and began to rebuke him, saying, Be it far from you, Lord: this shall not be to you. ²³But he turned, and said to Peter, Get you behind me, Satan: you are an offense to me: for you mind not the things that be of God, but those that be of men. ²⁴Then said Jesus to his disciples, If any man will come after me, let him deny himself, and take up his cross, and follow me. _____ Matthew 16:21-24

Satan having acted on Peter is the same Satan who provoked the heart of David. That is, it is the godless or anti-God thought in the believers' minds.

Jesus said to the disciples that he must go to Jerusalem, suffer many things, be killed, and be raised again the third day. Then Peter took Him and rebuked Him, saying that should never happen to Him. And to him, Jesus said, "Get behind me, Satan."

On what ground did He call Peter "Satan"? Jesus said so because Peter is the very person who entangled himself with the godless thought, agreed to it, and exercised it. The will of God is for Jesus to be crucified and resurrected. But the thought of the death of Jesus was a terrible thing to Peter because he looked forward to obtaining an important position when He ascended to the throne. If Jesus died, all his efforts to follow Him, forsaking all, will end in smoke. Contrary to the will of God, Peter thought that Jesus had to survive richly in this world. This is Peter's godless thought, Satan, caused by the greed.

However, Peter never knew that Satan gave that thought to him. If he had known it, he would not have conducted himself that way. Knowing this, Jesus provoked Peter to expose his hidden thoughts so that He may rebuke and correct him in this respect. This case corresponds to the case in which David acted on the godless thought and took a census.

The Satan in this passage is the man who took the godless thought as his. Peter took that thought as his and acted, so Jesus explicitly called him Satan.

Satan Himself Is Transformed Into an Angel of Light

Consider the following verses of 2 Corinthians.

> And no marvel; for Satan himself is transformed into an angel of light. [15]Therefore it is no great thing if his ministers also be transformed as the ministers of righteousness; whose end shall be according to their works. _____ 2 Corinthians 11:14-15

In this passage, Satan represents people who serve Satan as his head of the body. That is, those who accept the godless thoughts in their mind and behave accordingly. They are called ministers of Satan.

Then, what does it mean for them to be transformed into angels of light? Let's consider the case of Pharisees and the scribes. They preached the Word of God, but they transformed it into the commandment of men, the morals and ethic codes, by applying superficial meaning of the law. In this case, outwardly, they are the angels who preach the words of God, but inwardly, they are under the control of Satan. They convert the Word of God into the doctrines of depraved men when reading and teaching the Word of God.

Of course, they do not realize that they are preaching men's doctrine, but God's Word. This way, they unwittingly disguise themselves as angels of light. Therefore, if someone says to them that they are "Satan," they will become angry because they believe that they act according to the Scripture and for the sake of God.

We will also do the same thing as the Pharisees did, if we are not healed completely by Jesus on the cross. We will inevitably disguise ourselves as angels of light. This undesirable thing happens because we mistakenly think that we have believed in Jesus and are born again at the time we went to church. The truth is that we have to meet Jesus in person and should follow Him for due seasons to the cross to be born again.

When we have incorrect knowledge like the Pharisees, and act on it, we will be judged for those works. Excuses such as "I didn't know" will not be valid. We have to wake up now.

Satan in Job : Angel of God

Read the following passage.

Now there was a day when the sons of God came to present themselves before the LORD, and Satan came also among them. [7]And the LORD said to Satan, From where come you? Then Satan answered the LORD, and said, From going to and fro in the earth, and from walking up and down in it. [8]And the LORD said to Satan, Have you considered my servant Job, that there is none like him in the earth, a perfect and an upright man, one that fears God, and eschews evil? [9]Then Satan answered the LORD, and said, Does Job fear God for nothing? [10]Have not you made an hedge about him, and about his house, and about all that he has on every side? you have blessed the work of his hands, and his substance is increased in the land. [11]But put forth your hand now, and touch all that he has, and he will curse you to your face. [12]And the LORD said to Satan, Behold, all that he has is in your power; only on himself put not forth your hand. So Satan went forth from the presence of the LORD. ⎯⎯⎯ Job 1:6-12

I wish to discuss the case of Satan appearing in Job specifically, as it is quite different from the existing concept we have. In this passage of Job, Satan is an angel of God. Many people fail to grasp the identity of Satan in Job because they are fettered by the term "Satan." The Satan appearing in Job represents not an angel who fights God, but an angel who obeys the word of God. The name of Satan here is labeled from the viewpoint of men because he gives calamity and suffering to Job.

Egged on by this Satan, God took away the possessions and children of Job and struck him with sore boils to drive him to the brink of suicide. According to the traditional thinking about Satan, we understand this story as that God who has power to control the acts of Satan gives permission to bring hardship to Job.

However, you will soon find that such understanding is heavily mistaken because God is not deceived and egged on by Satan to do Job harm unfairly. In fact, it looks like God regrets this when He says, "You moved me against him, to destroy him without cause" (Job 2:3). However, if this "regret" means God thinks He made a mistake, He cannot be God, because it will mean Satan, who is superior to God, made fun of Him. Will He be God if He is inferior to Satan? However, we make Him such a poor God according to our erroneous understanding.

This Satan is different from our fixed idea about Satan. As we can see here, he attends the meeting of the sons of God and presents his opinions. This means that this Satan is one amongst the sons of God, that is, the man of God. Also, he does not fight against Him but obeys His word to save the life of Job when He puts Job in his hand.

Satan cannot naturally obey God and be present with the sons of God. Therefore, this Satan in Job is not the one that we know, but this is a "man of God" through whom God reveals His heart to us. He is a representative of God, and at the same time is God Himself.

God wishes to reveal to us through this dialogue format with Satan the limit of Job's legalistic faith. God says that Job is the righteous man of the east and eschewed evil, which is, however, only limited to the righteousness in the aspect of the law. The dialogue with Satan shows that the legalistic faith of Job must be substituted for faith in Jesus Christ. This is the key point of the book of Job.

I will explain about this a little bit further.

"Does Job Fear God for Nothing?"

Here in Job, Satan points out the fake spot of the legalistic righteousness of Job and reveals it.

> Then Satan answered the LORD, and said, Does Job fear God for nothing? [10]Have not you made an hedge about him, and about his house, and about all that he has on every side? you have blessed the work of his hands, and his substance is increased in the land. _____ Job 1:9-10

Satan makes a charge against Job and says to God, "Does Job fear God for nothing?"

This is a critical question which will divide true faith from fake faith. If one fears God for nothing, then he has the true faith of Jesus Christ, and if he fears God for something, then his faith is fake, which is legalistic. Unfortunately, Job fears God because He blesses his home and possessions, that is, Job fears God for something. This simple question, "Does Job fear God for nothing?" has power to thoroughly reveal faith of Job as imperfect.

Why is that? No man works for nothing or at no cost in this world. We even believe in Jesus or God in this paradigm. Therefore, we obey His Word in order to get what we want, such as the kingdom of heaven, blessings in this world, or whatever else our corrupt heart desires. Such faith is legalistic. However, this is not the faith that God wants to give us. That is, God does not want us to obey His Word because we are afraid of Him or we hope for blessings in this world or the afterlife.

What He wants is that we obey Him because we have the same heart and life as His. In other words, He wants us to do what He desires because we also desire to do it. This can be only fulfilled when we meet Jesus Christ in our lives and follow Him to the cross, and He will come on us as the Holy Spirit after resurrection. When we thus have the Holy Spirit in us, we then have the faith of Jesus, not a legalistic faith like Job had first. When we have such a faith, we are one with God and have His heart. When we have such a faith, we will not fear, or respect, God for something, but revere God without conditions, that is, for nothing. We will love others unconditionally, and will not love others expecting something in return.

How about yourself? Do you fear God for nothing or for something?

Therefore, Job's legalistic righteousness must be eliminated so he can receive the righteousness given by Jesus Christ. God wishes to proceed with this course. During this course, God allows hardship for Job for healing.

Read the following passages.

> Have pity on me, have pity on me, O you my friends; for the hand of God has touched me. _____ Job 19:21

> Then came there to him all his brothers, and all his sisters, and all they that had been of his acquaintance before, and did eat bread with him in his house: and they bemoaned him, and comforted him over all the evil that the LORD had brought on him: every man also gave him a piece of money, and every one an earring of gold. _____ Job 42:11

The Scriptures above say that not Satan, but God has brought all the evil on him. All of these are to give Job the true faith of Jesus, demolishing the legalistic faith of man.

Job's tribulation and hardship signify the death of old self on his own cross led by and united with Jesus. And after that tribulation Job was born again as a holder of the faith of Jesus.

📂 Other Angels Who Work Like Satan in Job

The angels appearing in the book of Revelation do harm to people in the same manner as Satan in the book of Job. They can be considered to do harm to people from the viewpoint of men. However, in reality, they are also true angels/men of God because disobedience and sins within the people are to be burned on the cross by the Word of Christ.

Read the following passage.

> And the seven angels which had the seven trumpets prepared themselves to sound. ⁷The first angel sounded, and there followed hail and fire mingled with blood, and they were cast on the earth: and the third part of trees was burnt up, and all green grass was burnt up. ⁸And the second angel sounded, and as it were a great mountain burning with fire was cast into the sea: and the third part of the sea became blood; _____ Revelation 8:6-8

In the above text, the angels are of God even if it seems to the eyes of men that they are harmful. As another example, in 1 King 22, a spirit has comes forth from all the host of heaven (v. 19). And he works as a lying spirit in the mouth of all the prophets (v. 22). Therefore, the good angel of God can be called by the name of "Satan" and "lying spirit."

Therefore, the matter of whether a spirit is an angel of God or Satan should be decided according to its original nature; that is, whether he is of God, not according to superficial name applied in the text.

Epilogue

Regarding "Satan Mentioned in the Scripture," Scriptures say "Satan" has the general meaning of an adversary, and he also means: 1) the concept of the state of inexistence of God, 2) Godless thought in a man, and 3) man Satan, like the definition of the devil.

In addition, Satan appearing in the book of Job represents the "angel of God who obeys His will," which differs from Satan above.

If you now read the Scripture with these basic concepts in mind, you will not have trouble reading about Satan.

Next, we will discuss demons.

Demon

What Is the Demon?

A demon (*daimonion* in Greek) is also called an "unclean spirit" (*pneuma akathartos* in Greek). I will now explain what a demon is.

📁 Demon As a Common Noun

First, a demon is an unsubstantial apparition.

A demon is characterized as a ghostly figure having no body. Scripture uses the term "demon" by adopting this characteristic. James says that faith without works is faith of the demon. That is, faith to believe in Jesus in thoughts only, faith to believe in a dead God, and faith based on the law; all these types of faith are referred to as faith of the demon, because such faith is full of words but no substance. Therefore, it is prudent to say that such works-based faith is of the demon.

In short, all kinds of faith that we could possibly have without meeting Jesus Christ as a man in our lives is that of the faith of the demon.

> Even so faith, if it has not works, is dead, being alone. [18]Yes, a man may say, You have faith, and I have works: show me your faith without your works, and I will show you my faith by my works. _____ James 2:17-19

> Now the Spirit speaks expressly, that in the latter times some shall depart from the faith, giving heed to seducing spirits, and doctrines of devils; ²Speaking lies in hypocrisy; having their conscience seared with a hot iron;   _____ 1 Timothy 4:1-2

The demons (translated as "devils" in KJV) in 1 Timothy above do not indicate the person to whom the demon whispers in the ear or heart; that is, him who has familiar spirits. They who speak pun-intended vain doctrines are called a "demon" or "seducing spirits."

Who are they, then? They are those who preach the Scriptures as man's doctrines, i.e., the law of men. For example, we heard, "We should love our neighbors as ourselves!" for several decades ever since we come to church, but we still cannot ever love our neighbors as ourselves. Of course, the message comes from Scripture, and we should love our neighbors, but we cannot love in that manner.

However, our teachers will come to us and press in saying, "Love your neighbors as yourselves to the end," which will have no effect. Such legalistic teachings are called the "doctrines of demons."

But those preachers who understand "Love your neighbor" correctly will introduce to you Jesus Christ, a man to meet in your life, who will heal you and make you a new man who can love your neighbor correctly.

Do you see the difference between the two? You have worked hard in a wrong place and have therefore born no fruit. This thing happened because you devoted yourselves to the doctrines of the deceitful spirits.

📂 Demon as a Man Who Believes in Jesus in Thought Only

Second, we define a demon as a) the state of absence of God, b) the godless thought in one's mind or c) a person who acts according to godless thoughts; man demon. Please refer to the definition of devil and Satan, as they are same.

Compare "Jesus in our thoughts" to "Jesus, a man to meet." The former is of demons and the latter is of God, as testified to in the Scripture. We will be confused because we have not yet met Jesus, a

Son of Man, in Scripture. However, now is the time to meet "a man Jesus." Meet Jesus and follow Him to the cross to end the faith of demons even from now on, as it is not too late to achieve true eternal life before death.

In short, the demon has the same meaning as the devil and Satan; the devil, a liar against God, the truth; Satan is an adversary of God; and the demons are phantoms which are not real concerning God who is the reality; these three in common mean the godless thoughts in one's mind or a person who behaves according to such godless thoughts.

Existing Thoughts About the Identity of the Demon

Demons are commonly defined as spiritual beings who go into the bodies of men to make them blind or deaf, and cause diseases or spasmodic symptoms, or controls them to perform weird acts.

Will such demons really exist as independent spiritual beings in this world? Are there demons? These are the questions we have had in our hearts for a long time, even if we do not cite the Scripture. To begin with the conclusion: there are no such spiritual beings as demons.

📂 Spirits After Man's Death?

Some people say demons are the spirits left after men are dead, and they sometimes enter men who say that they feel cold without a body, causing him trouble. However, the demons who go into men and cause diseases do not exist from creation. The expression of "one who is possessed with a demon becomes blind and dumb" in Scripture is the direct quotation of people who have a disease of their neuropsychiatry system. When the disease is cured, people say the demons have gone out.

However, this may be still hard to understand and accept, because some people have witnessed others thought to be possessed by demons who, when ordered, identified themselves as the brother, grandmother, great-great-grandfather of the witness, or old famous kings. Therefore, the witnesses firmly believed that the demons are the spirits of the dead men. However, as said, it is not so. They are multiple selves that are hidden and are not other beings with individual personalities. When a person dies, his spirit goes directly to the realm of the afterlife without wandering around and eating the food of sacrifices in this physical world.

Nevertheless, some people testify that they have seen a certain spiritual and smoke-like vague thing has come out of a man who was possessed with demons during an exorcism, or they may have seen a demon staying near a grave. You must not be mistaken in that I am not saying there is no phenomenon like what you have seen. These things happen, but the reality causing them is not a demon.

Then, who causes it? It is caused by the thoughts of demons created by those who believe in the reality of demons. I will describe this topic in detail later.

🗁 Fallen Angels?

The opinion that a demon is the spirit of a dead man is not supported by scholars. The orthodox theology defines demons as fallen angels like the devil and Satan. They have unavoidably defined the demons this way because they have no idea of the true identity of demons. However, such a definition cannot answer the question, "Can the angels living in the spiritual world oppose God and fall?" If the angels freely fall away from God, the universe will no longer exist from that time on. There is no angel having fallen in that way.

Anyway, such a theory could have been derived from the Scriptures, and we can find the following phrases, like, "the angels that sinned" (2 Peter 2:4) or "the angels which kept not their first estate, but left their own habitation" (Jude 1:6), which might support their assertions. However, they do not represent angels in the world of the spirit, but fallen mankind. In the universe, both naturally and spiritually, only mankind can oppose God for a certain period of time according the purpose and the providence of God.

In reality, demons are neither the spirits of dead man nor fallen angels in the spiritual realm. Then, what is a demon?

There Is No Demon

There is no demon as reality. Let us consider 1 Corinthians.

> As concerning therefore the eating of those things that are offered in sacrifice to idols, we know that an idol is nothing in the world, and that there is none other God but one. [5]For though there be that are called gods, whether in heaven or in earth, (as there be gods many, and lords many,) [6]But to us there is but one God, the Father, of whom are all things, and we in him; and one Lord Jesus Christ, by whom are all things, and we by him.
> _____ 1 Corinthians 8:4-6

Paul mentions the eating of those things offered in sacrifice to the idols. He says that the people of the world think of gods in their own way and offer a sacrifice to their own gods. Therefore, there are many gods and many lords, according to individuals.

However, Paul says that there is only one God and one Lord, Jesus Christ, for us who believe in Jesus. This means that there are no other spiritual beings between the God/Jesus and us. The gods whom the people living in this world imagine never existed. And true believers have no problem eating the things sacrificed to these idols which are merely the products of the notions of men.

The demon that is the topic of this chapter means the "idol" which Paul describes here. The demon may be the god and the lord to those who do not know truth, but in reality, there existed no such things from the beginning.

📂 The Demon Exists If We Think It Exists

Speaking further about these idols, then, we wonder, will it be okay for any believer to eat food offered to these idols because we know they never existed? No. Here, we have an issue to ponder. That is, we know demons do not exist, but demons do exist for those who believe in such things.

Paul continues to say in 1 Corinthians:

However, there is not in every man that knowledge: for some with conscience of the idol to this hour eat it as a thing offered to an idol; and their conscience being weak is defiled. [8]But meat commends us not to God: for neither, if we eat, are we the better; neither, if we eat not, are we the worse. [9]But take heed lest by any means this liberty of yours become a stumbling block to them that are weak. [10]For if any man see you which have knowledge sit at meat in the idol's temple, shall not the conscience of him which is weak be emboldened to eat those things which are offered to idols; [11]And through your knowledge shall the weak brother perish, for whom Christ died? _____ 1 Corinthians 8:7-11

Paul says, there is no idol in this world, but not all men have this knowledge. If some eat food sacrificed to the idol still believing in that the idol exists, their conscience is defiled when they eat it. That is, irrespective of the fact that there is no idol originally, depending upon the faith of the individuals there can be an idol to that individual. The idol is alive in the mind of one who is weak in faith and who does not have sufficient knowledge of the truth. If such a one eats the food offered to the idol, he is ignoring the commandment of God and disobeying God in his conscience so he is condemned. Therefore Paul says, "Take heed lest by any means this liberty of yours become a stumbling block to them that are weak."

The question of the existence of the demon can be considered in the same manner. As I said, no demon exists. However, not all men have this knowledge. Therefore, if some people believe there is a demon, to them things caused by the demon actually happen. That is, their belief creates demons in their own world of mind.

Therefore, they sometimes see the demon or they have the experience of being vexed by demons. But they see the demon or undergo such harassment not because the demon really is, but because they believe in its existence.

If we have understood the truth about the non-existence of demons, they will be gone from our world. And we do not need to fight or get along with the demons that do not exist any longer.

In summary, there is no demon in this world. But demonic phenomena may occur. Those phenomena are generated not by the spirit of dead men or fallen angels, but by the belief of their own. That is, God allows, by the natural law, them who believe in the existence of demons to experience them.

Epilogue

The demon is:
1) an unsubstantial apparition
2) a godless being; that is,
   a) a state of absence of God;
   b) a godless thought in one's mind;
   c) a man who is possessed by godless thoughts; "man demon."

The demon is not the spirit of a man after death or a fallen angel in spiritual world. There is no demon in reality, but it only exists in the world of wrong thoughts of men.

Nevertheless, there are many cases in the Scriptures whereby demons are mentioned. Even so, that does not mean Scripture supports the existence of demons, but it adopts the belief of mankind to explain the unseen things which are spiritual.

Now I will explain some passages of Scriptures which contain demons to show you how it reveals spiritual truth. You will realize that the Scriptures mentions demons not because they exist, but as a medium to explain the truth.

A Man With An Unclean Spirit, Legion, Part I
– Come out of the Man!

Mark 5:1-8

And they came over to the other side of the sea, into the country of the Gadarenes. ²And when he was come out of the ship, immediately there met him out of the tombs a man with an unclean spirit, ³Who had his dwelling among the tombs; and no man could bind him, no, not with chains: ⁴Because that he had been often bound with fetters and chains, and the chains had been plucked asunder by him, and the fetters broken in pieces: neither could any man tame him. ⁵And always, night and day, he was in the mountains, and in the tombs, crying, and cutting himself with stones. ⁶But when he saw Jesus afar off, he ran and worshipped him, ⁷And cried with a loud voice, and said, What have I to do with you, Jesus, you Son of the most high God? I adjure you by God, that you torment me not. ⁸For he said to him, Come out of the man, you unclean spirit.

Quite natural as it may sound, in believing Jesus, we reach a point where, without exception, we begin to believe with our own effort and power. For example, *we* decide to believe in Him, *we* decide to give offerings, to pray, to fast, or to participate in the missionary trips and so on, every moment. Thus, *we* believe. Perhaps all of us and leaders in the church are concentrating to fortify such a belief of ours and make it stand firm. Yes, we certainly need zeal for Jesus.

However, such faith is not the faith that God wishes to give us because that faith rests on *us*: man, not on God. This means that if we change our mind for any reason whatsoever, our faith will suddenly tumble. Consider the case of Peter. He had faith enough to decide to go with Jesus to prison and even to death (Luke 22:33). Nevertheless, on that day when Peter was in the position to follow Jesus to the death, he denied Jesus three times. This is the true aspect of faith that we ourselves believe. Of course, it is not the faith that God wants to give you through Jesus.

Up to this moment, you may have never learned nor known that there is true faith besides the one that you currently know. The true faith is hidden to your eyes until you spend a long time in the existing faith that *you believe*, and now you may be enlightened by this book. The true faith is not of you, but of God, and it is the Holy Spirit given by Jesus after healing your spirit on the cross. The true faith is the *faith of Jesus*. This message will show you what the true faith is, which has to be yours ultimately.

The story begins as Jesus reaches the country of the Gadarenes and meets a man with an unclean spirit coming out of the tombs. He lived among the tombs, tearing apart the chains even though he was bound with them, crying out, and cutting himself with stones. When he saw Jesus coming from afar, he ran, bowed down before Him, and cried with a loud voice.

I will now explain through the dialogue between the man with an unclean spirit and Jesus the legalistic relationship between us and Jesus, and the legalistic faith that we have which we misunderstand as the true and correct faith.

You will see that even if the Scripture uses the terms of demons or unclean spirits, it does not say the reality of demons in this physical world. But the Scripture uses the terms as the tool to reveal the world of truth.

Features of the Man Possessed by an Unclean Spirit

The man with an unclean spirit in the country of the Gadarenes represents the one who can neither see the spiritual kingdom of God nor hear the voice of God. He is the man who does not belong to God, but to the demon. This is the real state of all mankind, the sinners, who have left God and have been born to this world. From this passage, we can tell three main features of the man possessed by an unclean spirit.

First, the man with an unclean spirit lives among the tombs.

The tomb is symbolic of death. Therefore, the man with an unclean spirit, the representative of all mankind, stays in death in this world. The following Scripture verses will show us who are under such death.

Read Matthew 4:16: "The people which sat in darkness saw great light; and to them which sat in the region and shadow of death light is sprung up"; and read John 5:28: "Marvel not at this: for the hour is coming, in which all that are in the graves shall hear his voice."

In the main text, the man with an unclean spirit has met Jesus and, ultimately, became a man without the unclean spirit. This healing is the fulfillment of the above Scripture verses as he who sat on the ground of death could see great light and he who was in the grave could hear the voice of Jesus.

Likewise, we are born to this world as sinners and live as such. That is, spiritually, we are possessed with the unclean spirits and we are in the graves, waiting to see great light, who is Jesus Christ.

Second, the man with an unclean spirit could not be bound with chains.

He plucked the chains asunder and broke the fetters in pieces. He is the sign of the sinners. What do the chains and the fetters binding him signify? It is the commandment of God, the law, which aims to curb wicked acts of the sinners. However, no sinner can keep the law, and so we violate it. Likewise, we are obliged to keep the law in this world, but cannot help but break it.

Third, the man with an unclean spirit cries out and cuts himself with stones.

All people are connected in the unity of membership in God. And all of the brothers and sisters around us are sent by God to help our salvation regardless of whether they behave well or wickedly to our eyes. However, the sinners have no idea of this unity because they do not know God. Therefore, out of ignorance they harm the brothers for their own benefit, but in reality, they are harming themselves by their actions. One good example is that of the Pharisees who ruin themselves by persecuting Jesus, their Brother in God, who would save them. We also will do the same as they did when Jesus leads us to the cross for our salvation.

We have believed like the Pharisees did for a long time, being possessed by the demons unwittingly. I wish to name such faith as legalistic faith; faith that is of man, not of Jesus in its essence. We will only begin to hope for the faith of Jesus when we have found nothing but despair from such legalistic faith as we know in this world.

Now our unrecognized spiritual states are disclosed through the man with an unclean spirit in the country of the Gadarenes. In fact, we *are* him. You may not wish to believe what I say, questioning, "How can the demon-possessed man believe in Jesus?" But, yes; he does. We are to go through a legalistic faith, that is, the faith of the demon-possessed man, first, in order to have the faith of Jesus by following Him in person to the cross.

The Demon Worships Jesus?

"But when he saw Jesus afar off, he ran and worshipped him" (v. 6).

We read this story and generally think that it is wonderful to believe in Jesus, saying, "Jesus is a real man of power. The demons of the spiritual world recognize Him and tremble!" Needless to say, we must respect and fear Jesus as a man of power. But, no matter how powerful He may be, His physical power cannot save us, but only His powerless death on the cross. So if we read this story thinking Jesus is a powerful man who can make even the demon worship Him, we are missing the weightier meaning. The hidden weightier meaning of this story is something that is related to the salvation of Jesus, not a simple praise regarding the physical power of Jesus.

I will explain how this story reveals our salvation through Jesus.

The man with an unclean spirit, seeing Jesus from afar off, ran, worshipped Him, and confessed that He was the Son of the most high God. This picture refers to us who come to church in which the words of Jesus are preached, from a distance, in face of all difficulties.

We come to church to attend the services, join the church activities with eagerness, pray, and worship and praise Him. We know that He has power to send us into heaven, make us rich, heal us from incurable diseases, and cast out demons from us physically. We do and confess this way all because we know Him, as the Son of the most high God. But we do it all possessed by unclean spirits; that is, as sinners.

Why did all these things happen to us, considering that we believed in Jesus and depended upon Him with a pure heart? It is because we try to believe in Him while we are already taken by the unclean spirits. That's why we accept unclean spirits' thinking as ours. Anyhow, we must pass through this faith stage because it is a course designated to reach true faith. If we are satisfied with this legalistic faith, we will not be saved, as such faith will not save us.

Normally we consider our sins are forgiven when we confess Jesus is our Savior, but it is not so. The sin-forgiveness process does not happen instantly when we confess with our lips, but it is a life-growing process which takes time. Look at the case of the disciples. It took more than three and a half years from the time they met "a man Jesus" to the time of Pentecost when they became Apostles who could do as Jesus did. Therefore, we have the belief of our sin-possessed selves if we have not yet met "a man Jesus." We are represented in the text by this man who is possessed by the unclean spirit.

To anyone who is disappointed and fully despaired about his current faith, this message will give him great meaning and he will finally confess like below, as the demon-possessed man says:

"What have I to do with you, Jesus?"

What does this mean?

Faith That Has No Part with Jesus

This man with an unclean spirit believed in Him for a very long time but found that he had no part with Him, and deeply hoped that he would be healed so he could have part with Jesus. He, thus being desolate and used up, was ready to meet the real Jesus. He confessed as follows:

"What have I to do with you?"

This is the confession of the believer who gets to realize that his existing faith is that which has no part with Jesus. Now he is ready to meet Jesus to have part with Him. God, knowing this, had Jesus go into the Gentile country of the Gadarenes in order to meet this man and to cast the demon out of him. Accordingly, this man will get to have a part with Jesus, becoming one with Him by receiving the Holy Spirit.

We believe in Jesus, but we feel emptiness even though we have followed Jesus for a long time. Why? It is because we, who are possessed by sin, believed in Jesus without meeting and being led by Him. Have you met "a man Jesus" in your life? The Scripture says the Savior, Christ, should come in the flesh; i.e., as "a man." Therefore, our faith will be divided into two progressive stages: first, faith before meeting "a man Jesus"; and second, faith after meeting "a man Jesus."

Our true faith will start from the time when we meet "a man Jesus" in our lives, and if we follow Him to the cross, we will have part with Him. This means, when our old self is destroyed on the cross, the Holy Spirit will come into us. Thus, we have part with Jesus Christ.

As for having part with Jesus at the point of the cross, consider the case of Peter. He followed Jesus for three and a half years to become one with Him through His crucifixion and resurrection. Being one with Jesus is revealed at the feet-washing scene during the last supper that Jesus had with His disciples. At the last supper before His crucifixion, Jesus began to wash the disciples' feet, normally the duty of the household servant. In confusion, Peter rejected Him by saying, "You shall never wash my feet," and Jesus answered him, "If I wash you not, you have no part with me," in John 13:18.

The spiritual meaning of His washing Peter's feet is to receive Peter in Him to become one. This is achieved when Peter receives the Holy Spirit after following Jesus to the cross. The washing of feet signifies receiving or becoming one, not serving or servant-ship which is the familiar interpretation of this passage. From that time on, Peter became one with Jesus, in one body or one house. In one body, or one house, they have part with each other. Thus, Peter's faith that has no part with Jesus ended at that time. This is what Jesus did to Peter. Only "a man Jesus" will allow you to have part with Jesus.

This man who was possessed with the unclean spirit eagerly wished to have part with Jesus, so, based on his desperate mind, Jesus could work to cast the unclean spirit out of him. Therefore, Jesus spoke to the unclean spirit.

📂 Come Out of the Man!

Jesus told the unclean spirit to come of out of the man. The man with the unclean spirit and the unclean spirit are one, having part with each other, which can be broken only by His Word, not by man. In this instance, His commanding the unclean spirit to come out of the man represents the process by which Jesus heals him with the Word of God.

Applying this case to Peter, the period of three and a half years in which he followed Him to the cross corresponds to the time in which He applied the words "Come out of the man" to the unclean spirit. From the time when Peter followed Him, forsaking all, the demon in Peter began to be cast out; finally, completely, at the cross. And Peter was made whole on the day of resurrection. He is born again at this time, but still young as a newly born baby. On Pentecost he became an adult who could take up spiritual war with the devil and his angels. Therefore, the words "come out of the man" is not fulfilled instantly, but it requires due season.

📂 Torment Not!

When He told the demon to come out of the man, the demon begged Jesus not to torment them. When demons are cast out, the person concerned is convulsed (Mark 1:26) and feels pain. Therefore, here, the demon begs Jesus not to torment him.

Likewise, when the Word of Jesus casts the demon out of men, those who are with the demon will suffer great pain and torment, because the Word hurts their old self. They sometimes gnash with their teeth, have a mind to run away, or would not listen to the Word when they seek to escape the torment by dozing off. They sometimes take a hostile attitude toward the pastor who preaches the Word and fight openly against him who points out their faults. All these things happened during the period in which believers follow "a man Jesus" for healing.

Such a response to the Word of Jesus by those possessed with the demons is also found in Acts when the Jews were very much distressed upon hearing Stephen's preaching.

> And said, Behold, I see the heavens opened, and the Son of man standing on the right hand of God. [57]Then they cried out with a loud voice, and stopped their ears, and ran on him with one accord, [58]And cast him out of the city, and stoned him: and the witnesses laid down their clothes at a young man's feet, whose name was Saul. _____ Acts 7:56-58

The Jews who were possessed with demons were tormented when they heard the true Word of Jesus. At the end of their patience, they stopped their ears, ran upon Stephen, and stoned him. They were like those who had the same response to the Word of Jesus and crucified Him. Will they not be the demons themselves and also those who are possessed with demons?

They are not yet prepared to be healed by the Word of Jesus. In other words, they have not yet despaired of their conventional law-based faith in the wilderness, needing more time. On the other hand, the disciples fully despaired of the law-based faith they already had, and were ready to follow Jesus against all hardship brought about during the healing by Jesus. Therefore, except Judas Iscariot, they well endured the process and were finally set free from the demon.

In the country of the Gadarenes, the time for Jesus to heal this man with an unclean spirit had come. And the demon-possessed man endured to the last while receiving the Word of Jesus, so he could have the demon cast out of him and become one with Jesus Christ.

Next in "The demons having entered the swine," I will continue to explain the spiritual aspects of this event.

A Man With An Unclean Spirit, Legion, Part II
– The Unclean Spirits Having Entered the Swine

Mark 5:9-20

And he asked him, What is your name? And he answered, saying, My name is Legion: for we are many. [10]And he sought him much that he would not send them away out of the country. [11]Now there was there near to the mountains a great herd of swine feeding. [12]And all the devils sought him, saying, Send us into the swine, that we may enter into them. [13]And immediately Jesus gave them leave. And the unclean spirits went out, and entered into the swine: and the herd ran violently down a steep place into the sea, (they were about two thousand;) and were choked in the sea. [14]And they that fed the swine fled, and told it in the city, and in the country. And they went out to see what it was that was done. [15]And they come to Jesus, and see him that was possessed with the devil, and had the legion, sitting, and clothed, and in his right mind: and they were afraid. [16]And they that saw it told them how it befell to him that was possessed with the devil, and also concerning the swine. [17]And they began to pray him to depart out of their coasts. [18]And when he was come into the ship, he that had been possessed with the devil prayed him that he might be with him. [19]However, Jesus suffered him not, but said to him, Go home to your friends, and tell them how great things the Lord has done for you, and has had compassion on you. [20]And he departed, and began to publish in Decapolis how great things Jesus had done for him: and all men did marvel.

Jesus heard the demons' entreaty and allowed them to enter the swine, so the herd rushed down a steep place into the sea and were choked in the sea, and the man who was possessed with the demon sat there, clothed and in his mind.

Having read this story, we have many doubts. We naturally have the following queries:

"Can the demons enter the swine?"

"Does Jesus fulfill the demons' wishes because He is so generous and gracious?"

"Why did He waste about two thousand swine?"

First of all, all these questions arise because we adhere to the literal meaning of the Scripture, and the Scripture is written to give us the revelation of the spiritual world. That is, it tells us something that relates to the salvation and being born again of our spirits who are possessed with the evil spirits.

Now we will share the spiritual knowledge as to the place where the demon stays, the destiny of those who are one with demon, and those who are set free from it.

Let's go into detail.

The Unclean Spirits Entered the Swine

Jesus asked the demon his name, and the demon answered that his name was Legion because they were many. This does not mean that a regiment or an entire divisional force of demons too great to count entered him. The number of demons is used to express the heaviness, or weakness, of symptoms. For example, Jesus says a man is worse when he has seven demons than he who has one demon (Luke 11:24-26).

In the main text, let us consider some words to see what they signify.

The country of the Gadarenes is a place with many tombs, and it means the region of death, this sinful world.

The swine signify those who are not yet born again. The swine do not chew the cud, and as such are exempted from the list of "clean" animals allowed to be eaten (Leviticus 11:7). Swine signifies the people who receive the Word but accept its literal and superficial meaning without thinking deeply. Consequently, such swine cannot be healed by the Word. Typically, they are Pharisees, scribes, and those believers who did not yet meet Jesus and they were not healed for being born again.

Let us consider what the scenes reveal. The herd of swine was feeding at the mountains. The mountain represents the holy righteous mountain of the LORD in the positive sense, but it also symbolizes self-righteousness of people that is stored high in the negative sense. In practice, people of the flesh stockpile their deeds of self-righteousness such as, "I have kept the Lord's day holy," "I have helped the poor," "I regularly attended the daybreak services," and "I have given tithes (Luke 18:11-12)."

Accumulation of self-righteousness according to the law is their reason for living in this world. Yes, they live on their self-righteousness and it sustains their lives. Such a spiritual status is revealed by the scene of swine feeding at the mountains. That is, the swine, the legalistic believers, are fed with the requirements of the law on a mountain made by the deeds of self-righteousness.

The unclean spirit sought Jesus as much to beg that He not send them out of the country. The demons are destined to stay in the region of death and work there. Therefore, they did not want to go out of the country; reasonable, for they could not go out of that place of death, as the demons and death were together and inseparable.

Jesus shifted the demons staying in the man into the swine so that the man was set free from them and the demons could no longer control him. However, the demons still had someone they could control as they wished, that is, the swine. Jesus sent them into the herd of swine, which is the revelation, rather than fulfilling demons' wish. This scene tells us that the place for demons to stay is the swine: that is, the persons who are not yet born again. The demons live in the swine, being one with them, and they control swine's thoughts and acts. Spiritually, this man possessed with an unclean spirit was a swine before he met Jesus.

The swine possessed with demons runs violently down a steep place into the sea and are choked in the sea. This is the life of the sinners who are not born again. The sinners have believed, but they have faith that has no part with Him. That is the faith of the man with an unclean spirit and is the faith of the swine. If we are satisfied with such legalistic faith, neglecting to have the faith of Jesus, shortly we will face the time when we will stand before the final judgment seat of God. Our remaining time will fly so quickly it will seem the same as that of the swine rushing down the steep place to the sea, to death.

This scene reveals the spiritual status of the man possessed with demons and at the same time those who have the faith that has no part with Jesus. We must now check what type of faith we have.

Sitting, and Clothed, and in his Right Mind

"...and see him that was possessed with the devil, and had the legion, sitting, and clothed, and in his right mind: and they were afraid" (Mark 5:15).

Mark describes the figure of the man with an unclean spirit after the spirit was driven out of him as sitting, clothed, and in his right mind. This picture expresses the comparison between a man who is with an unclean spirit and a man with Christ in him. The former is under the law and the latter is under grace.

First, he now is sitting.

This signifies that he has finished legalistic faith and he is now born again by the Word to have faith of Jesus. When he was with the unclean spirit he was standing, but now he is sitting after being healed. "Sitting" is the term to describe a man under grace compare to "standing" to describe a man under the law. For this, we can consider the case of Martha and Mary in Luke 10:38-42. Martha was busy to prepare various many things for Jesus while standing, but Mary was meeting and hearing the Word while seated. And Mary was upheld by Jesus. Martha represents the legalistic faith and Maria the true faith.

Also, read the following passage from Hebrews.

> And every priest stands daily ministering and offering oftentimes the same sacrifices, which can never take away sins: [12]But this man, after he had offered one sacrifice for sins for ever, sat

down on the right hand of God;   _____ Hebrews 10:11-12

When we serve God under the law, we stand, doing one thing or another like a busy bee. But once we meet Jesus we sit down and only wait for the Word of Jesus by grace on the right hand of God and take a rest.

Second, the man healed of the demons is now clothed.

When he was with an unclean spirit, he was not clothed. At that time, the man believed in Jesus but had no part with Him. He was under the law and not clothed spiritually.

Read the following passage.

Because you say, I am rich, and increased with goods, and have need of nothing; and know not that you are wretched, and miserable, and poor, and blind, and naked: _____ Revelation 3:17

The clothes signify righteousness. We must not put on our own self-righteousness, but God's righteousness, the Christ (Galatians 3:27). If we put on our own self-righteousness, we will be found naked by God, as the self-righteousness is not approved by God. Self-righteousness is the product of the law, so we should not be deceived by it.

When he was demon-possessed, this man was naked, being under the law. After the demon was cast out of him, he was clothed with Christ, being under grace.

Finally, he was in his "right mind."

He who is freed from the demon is in his right mind. This means that he was *not* in his right mind when he was demon-possessed. At that time, being under the law, he wandered from place to place in darkness, not knowing where he was from, where he was going, why he was living, or even why he believed in Jesus.

This is the spiritual reality of us, the sinners, and we think we know something, but we know nothing. This world is controlled by those sinners who are not in their right minds. No wonder life in this world is going to end in sorrow and woe after all. If we meet and follow Jesus to the cross like this man, we will be in our right minds and will live an awakened born-again life in this world.

📂 They Pray Jesus to Depart

They began to pray him to depart out of their coasts (Mark 5:17). "Their coasts" represent this world of death where there are tombs, demons and demon-possessed men, swine, and those who feed the swine. Men and things that are related to death and darkness can be found there.

The inhabitants in that country hate Jesus who is the light, because He is an obstacle to what they do in the darkness. For instance, Jesus cast the demons out of the man, which was to be surely praised above all things, but to them the herds of swine were more valuable so the Gadarenes begged Him to leave their coasts. They thought He was an enemy.

Likewise, when Jesus came to the Jews, especially to the Pharisees and the scribes who were their leaders, they begged Him to depart out of the country. He was a big stumbling block to them and to their religious business which was on the verge of collapse (John 12:19). At long last, they crucified Him to force Him to depart from the country. Moreover, they tried to drive the apostles who preached the gospel of Jesus from their country by calling them heretics. Also, when Paul the apostle met a certain damsel possessed with a spirit of divination and healed her, they cast him into prison (Acts 16:16-23).

In essence, those who are in darkness are to exclude and fight against them who are in the light.

In fact, we are now living in the country of the Gadarenes too. In that country, demons and people who are possessed with demons go on a rampage; swine and those feeding them, work hard according to the law of ethic and morals. Their food is the law which produces legalistic self-righteousness. They join tight with each other according to the law, being heavily laden with religious rules and regulations. Again, do not misunderstand; what I am saying is not that we should not abide by the law, but, without neglecting it, we should follow Jesus. Without Jesus all will be in vain.

Jesus did not stay there any longer. Why not? It is because His time had not yet come. When a man who used to live together with demons as a swine in darkness gets used up and desires to have a part with Jesus like this man in Mark 5, Jesus will come again anytime to find and save him.

Tell Your Friends

Jesus says to the man, "Go home to your friends, and tell them how great things the Lord has done for you, and has had compassion on you" (Mark 5:19).

From now on, the healed man will witness what Jesus has done for him. However, it is not that he will simply confess that he was demon-possessed before, now freed by Jesus. But he will witness the whole process of his salvation revealed by the expulsion of demons. That is, he believed in Jesus under the law, having no rest and experiencing a heavily laden life by the law. Even after having done everything he could, like preaching to others, praying, fasting, serving, or helping others, he found no satisfaction in his heart and felt emptiness in his life. His life was desperate. He felt that he had no part with Jesus even though he tried his best to believe.

Having found himself so, he cried out to God and his prayer went up, and thus he met Jesus, the light, in the world of darkness. He escaped the world of darkness by going through the cross united with Jesus. We must go through the cross being united with Jesus, not under our own power (Romans 6:5-6).

All these things meant that God had pity on him and He had done to him great things.

The friends of the man represent those who are sinners and are possessed with demons like he was. He became a born-again man who had the life of Jesus, and he could lead others in the way of salvation. Such a man can preach the good news to his friends.

I hope that He will also cast the demons out of us in this way.

4

ANTICHRIST AND EVIL SPIRITS

Antichrist

1 John 2:18-23

Little children, it is the last time: and as you have heard that antichrist shall come, even now are there many antichrists; whereby we know that it is the last time. [19]They went out from us, but they were not of us; for if they had been of us, they would no doubt have continued with us: but they went out, that they might be made manifest that they were not all of us. [20]But you have an unction from the Holy One, and you know all things. [21]I have not written to you because you know not the truth, but because you know it, and that no lie is of the truth. [22]Who is a liar but he that denies that Jesus is the Christ? He is antichrist, that denies the Father and the Son. [23]Whoever denies the Son, the same has not the Father: he that acknowledges the Son has the Father also.

In the term "antichrist" (*antichristos* in Greek), *anti* means to "oppose" or "stand against." Therefore, antichrist has the literal meaning of "opposing Christ." The identity of antichrist known to us up to now can be defined as an all-inclusive being that produces all kinds of wickedness. But this sort of definition is not much use because it cannot give us an actual and concrete idea about what that being is.

Considering this is the latest definition of antichrist amongst Christianity today, it is unfortunate that nobody has ever clarified what the antichrist is throughout the history of Christianity. This is a very serious problem because every Christian must fight with it in order to believe, but the believers do not know his identity. How can we expect to fight the unknown antichrist and win? Impossible.

Moreover, if we do not know who the antichrist is (the antonym of Christ), it means that we do not know who Christ is. To tell the truth, we have never known Jesus Christ correctly, much less the antichrist. Consequently, our faith has worked nothing so far.

Next I am going to explain the identity of the antichrist that has been hidden under a veil until today.

Antichrist Arising at the Last Time

The term "antichrist" appears in the book of 1 John. We can find from the passage that the antichrist will come at the last time. People connect the last times to the universal last days and use this antichrist to interpret the Revelation. However, the last times the Scriptures mention of the antichrist are not during the last days of the universe, but during the last days of our own old self before being destroyed on the cross.

Regarding the last times of our old self, we are born to this world with the life of *flesh*, that is, the life before born again (John 3:6). Even when it comes to belief in Jesus, we do believe, according to our own way. When Jesus has helped us out of our difficulties, we will work hard for the church in reward for His help. Or we work hard in the church in case we might need help from Jesus while living in this world. In fact, we, the believers, are in need of Him so we can have rich, peaceful and healthy lives.

However, such legalistic faith, which comes first to all believers, has no part with Jesus. Accordingly we will finally face the limit of such faith, like the prodigal son in Luke. At this limit, if we seek God with our true hearts, we will meet "a man Jesus," who has Christ in him. Then the antichrist hidden in a veil will be revealed to us by Jesus at this time. The antichrist, the head of sin which has been controlling our life of flesh, will face his last times because he will be destroyed on the cross, being united with Jesus.

When you meet Jesus and get to see the antichrist, you will find that the antichrist is yourself, who has been acting like a king, resisting the Christ who is to be your king in you. I am sure that you have never dreamed of yourself as the antichrist, although you have been the antichrist ever since you were born in this world.

Jesus has come to be your king by staying within you. However, you just let Him stay out of you and did not invite Him into you. This means that you substantially reject Him even if you may strongly say you believe in Him. He who rejects Christ is the very antichrist. Consequently, as long as you, who are sin-possessed, reign as king inside yourself, you cannot help but oppose and fight Him; thus identifying yourself naturally as antichrist.

If you can see the antichrist in you, it proves that you have met Jesus because the antichrist is exposed only by Jesus Christ. If you now obey Jesus to take up your own cross and follow Him, the antichrist, which is your old self, will be destroyed on the cross and you will receive Christ in you by His resurrection. Once Christ is received in you, you will no longer be antichrist, but you will be of Christ, "a man who has Christ in you."

📁 Falling Away First

People frequently consider that the antichrist matches the "man of sin" appearing in 2 Thessalonians. The antichrist and the "man of sin" are same, and they mean *me* before being born again.

> Now we beseech you, brothers, by the coming of our Lord Jesus Christ, and by our gathering together to him, ²That you be not soon shaken in mind, or be troubled, neither by spirit, nor by word, nor by letter as from us, as that the day of Christ is at hand. ³Let no man deceive you by any means: for that day shall not come, except there come a falling away first, and that man

of sin be revealed, the son of perdition; _____ 2 Thessalonians 2:1-3

Verses 1 and 2 depict the coming of the Lord Jesus Christ and the coming of the day of Christ respectively. Both days mean the last time of the old world which my old self sees. A "falling away," verse 3, will come first.

What is the "falling away" and why does it come first?

The falling away, that is, apostasy is *apostasia* in Greek which is also translated as "forsake" in Acts 21:21, as follows (bold mine):

"And they are informed of you, that you teach all the Jews which are among the Gentiles to **forsake** Moses, saying that they ought not to circumcise their children, neither to walk after the customs."

In the above text, "forsake" is the rendering of *apostasia* in Greek. The falling away/forsaking at the last time can be interpreted in a like manner. That is, it means to forsake (fall away from) the "Jesus who was formed in my heart incorrectly based on my thinking of 'flesh' until now."

According to the principle of nature, when just beginning to believe in Him, believers are destined to believe in Him in the legalistic manner. They maintain the legalistic faith for a long time. Most of them will die in that faith, but the chosen will see the last times of that faith during their lifetime. At that time, we, the chosen, will recognize that even though we have believed very sincerely, our faith is not of Him but of ourselves, who are fleshly men. Then we will sigh for grief when we recognize our faith of fleshly men:

"Alas! I have believed in Jesus for a long time, but now it is proved fruitless." "I used to believe in Jesus whom I, myself, have created in my mind."

With this enlightenment as a turning point, the existing faith made by the self-created Jesus is fallen away. That's why Paul says "there comes falling away (apostasy) first." And after that, we will abandon the existing way of faith that *we believe*, but we will be led by Jesus to the cross so that we receive Christ in us. Paul calls this "receiving Christ in us" as the "coming of our Lord Jesus Christ" or the "coming of the day of Christ."

As a matter of fact, the one who let the faith go astray so far was *us*, we who are seized by sin. That is, each of us is the man of sin and the antichrist. We will understand this fact when we have reached the last times ourselves. We generally think that "falling away" is negative; however, if we forsake (fall away from) antichrist, then we will follow the way of truth.

🗁 The Man of Sin

The "man of sin" in the following passage from Romans is each of us who are seized by sin.

> For I know that in me (that is, in my flesh,) dwells no good thing: for to will is present with me; but how to perform that which is good I find not. [19]For the good that I would I do not: but the evil which I would not, that I do. [20]Now if I do that I would not, it is no more I that do it, but sin that dwells in me.
> _____ Romans 7:18-20

Paul says he wants to do the good but he does the evil he does not wish. He does not attribute his practice of evil to sin. He mentions the fundamental reason why he does evil; that is, he does evil because he is controlled by sin in him.

Accordingly, we have both the "self possessed by sin" and the "original self aiming at good" within us. We can do good or evil depending on which of the two selves wins over the other. In reality, sinners are totally taken by the sin and can never get away from it through our own efforts. We serve sin as a whole. In this case, the whole "I" is represented by "me who is possessed by sin," which is the "man of sin" in *me*.

We have no concept of this man of sin, but we will finally see who he is when the Lord comes, that is, at the last times when we meet Jesus in person. Reversely speaking, when we can see the real identity of the man of sin, the last times of the man of sin comes.

Sin is separation from God. Sin, therefore, has no personality and it is just a "separation" which is a state concept; like evil, devil, Satan, and demon before men fall. However, if the separation dwells in a man, sin will have the personality of that man. For example, if "I" have separation from God within me, the separation, which is a state, is personified through me. In this case, sin is equal to me, having my personality. This is my "man of sin," which is the antichrist.

I will explain about sin further in the forthcoming Chapter "Evil Spirits—Sin."

🗁 Showing Himself that He Is God

Here, I will add one more important issue in connection with 2 Thessalonians 2:4. The man of sin opposes God and exalts himself above all that is called God or is worshiped; he sits in the temple of God, showing himself as God.

Who will dare do like that? We who serve sin do. We, being sinners, pray to God, fast, give offerings, pray, serve table, keep the Sundays, do missionary works, and think that our sins are forgiven because we are doing such activities. But we will remain as sinners until we meet Jesus and follow Him to the cross to crucify our old self. Even though we believed and worked for God and Jesus so far, in reality, we only used the names of God and Jesus in order to profit ourselves concerning things of this world, being prompted by our old self. In this case, who is God, who is Jesus, and who is the Lord? They are gods made by our old self; that is, the man of sin in us.

Also the Scriptures say that the man of sin sits in the temple of God. The temple of God indicates our heart. However, we do not have God in this temple but we have allowed the sin that is "separation from God" to have a seat in our hearts. If we keep going on in this state, no matter how hard we may try to believe in Jesus, we will only believe in an idol Jesus due to the "man of sin" within us. This shows that sin-possessed *me* opposes God and reigns over *me* as God, when instead, "I" am supposed to be the member of body of God.

Jesus says of the last times in Matthew 24:

> When you therefore shall see the abomination of desolation, spoken of by Daniel the prophet, stand in the holy place, (who-

ever reads, let him understand:) _____ Matthew 24:15

At the last times, we will see the abomination of desolation stand in the holy place. The holy place represents the temple within us where God is supposed to abide. We thought God dwelled in us, but we find the "sin-possessed *me*," i.e., the "man of sin" seated there instead. This is the abomination of desolation Jesus talks about. It leads us to believe in Jesus superficially, legalistically, incorrectly and in thought only, and makes us do good works such as loving, preaching, or helping the poor, in vain. All of these deeds we did for God aimed at satisfying one thing: our greed of this world, not the destruction of the "sin-possessed *me*" on the cross by following Jesus.

When we meet "a man Jesus" at the last time, we will see the man of sin stand in our heart as God. "Sin-possessed *me*," the "man of sin," "old self," and "antichrist" have the same meanings.

Returning to 1 John, I will describe other features of the antichrist.

Antichrist Who Is Not of Truth

John says that antichrists went out from us, which shows that they are not of us (I John 2:19).

We read "they" and "us" in the first part of the above text. In this passage, "they" are of the antichrist and "we" are of Christ. "They" and "we" stay together in the inner world of each individual. However, when the antichrist within us is exposed, we must be separated from the antichrists, and we must cast them out of us. Then, we will be of Christ completely. As Christ has no concord with Belial and truth cannot go with non-truth, Christ cannot dwell in us together with the antichrist. The antichrist must be divided from the truth.

This phenomenon is applicable to this world and is displayed in the same manner. It means that those with the spirit of antichrist are separated from and go out of the church community, which is the assembly of those having the spirit of Christ.

John wrote to those who were with him because they understood the truth. And they knew that he told no lie, and communicated with them in the true sense. To those who are not anointed and do not know the truth, this word makes no sense because they do not have truth in them and thus cannot distinguish what is true and what is not. Only those who know truth by meeting Jesus can hear what he says.

Antichrist who Denies that Jesus is the Christ

"Who is a liar but he that denies that Jesus is the Christ? He is antichrist, that denies the Father and the Son (I John 2:22)."

Of course, Jesus is the Christ. However, this passage does not mean to say that one is a liar if he denies the fact that Jesus who came on earth two thousand years ago is the Christ. Now John speaks an eternal truth, not a one-time fact.

You can acknowledge a certain fact only after it is achieved. For example, imagine your boss said that he will promote you. Nevertheless, you cannot acknowledge the fact essentially until you are actually promoted. In other words, you can only acknowledge your promotion on or after the time you are promoted. Until then, you cannot acknowledge the fact of it, but must deny it by nature, regardless of your will.

Likewise, in acknowledging that Jesus is the Christ, the Savior, you can only acknowledge the fact at the time when you are actually saved by Him and become one with Him. Therefore, he who acknowledges that Jesus is the Christ represents the man who is already saved and become one with Him.

On the contrary, if a person denies that Jesus is the Christ, he is not yet saved, being separated from God. Therefore, he cannot but deny Jesus as the Christ, and he has no truth in him as a sinner. He is both a liar and an antichrist, because he has not become one with the Christ, the truth. This is the intended meaning of John.

The antichrist denies the Father and the Son. The confession or denial of the Son does not mean the act of confession with lips. To acknowledge the Son is for me to be pregnant by the Word, then to give birth to a Son having the life of Jesus. If we do not yet give birth to a Son, we keep on denying Him. And if we give birth to a Son, God will come into us together with the Son; and if not, both of them will not come into us.

This is the meaning of Jesus, "where there is the Son," Jesus, "the Father is also."

Read the following passage.

> That they all may be one; as you, Father, are in me, and I in you, that they also may be one in us: that the world may believe that you have sent me. _____ John 17:21

In short, he who is born again acknowledges the Father and the Son, and the one who is not born again denies the Father and the Son and he is the antichrist.

In addition, to "acknowledge" is translated from the Greek *homologeo*. It generally means to confess, to acknowledge. *Homologeo* etymologically means to "speak the same thing." When a certain thing is fulfilled to us, both the fulfilled fact and our speaking about the fulfilled fact will be the same, so we confess; i.e., "speak the same thing." Likewise, if the Son has come on *me* when "I" am born again by Jesus and He has become one with *me*, likewise, the Son of whom I speak concurs with the real Son. In this case, I acknowledge Him; i.e., speaking the same thing about Him.

Furthermore, to deny the Son is to speak of the Son while "I" am separated from Him. In this case, *my* word about the Son does not agree with the real Son as He is. This means that I do not speak the same thing and I deny the Son.

Therefore, he who acknowledges the Son is of Christ and the one who denies the Son is the antichrist.

Antichrist who Denies that Jesus Christ is Come in the Flesh

> Hereby know you the Spirit of God: Every spirit that confesses that Jesus Christ is come in the flesh is of God: [3]And every spirit that confesses not that Jesus Christ is come in the flesh is not of God: and this is that spirit of antichrist, whereof you have heard that it should come; and even now already is it in the world. _____ 1 John 4:2-3

"Every spirit that confesses not that Jesus Christ is come in the flesh is not of God." This does not mean that we will be of God if we confess that Jesus is come in the flesh in history, and we will be the antichrist if we deny the same.

As we all know, Jesus was incarnated to come to earth in history. He was crucified, resurrected, and ascended to heaven, and then came again to His disciples as the Holy Spirit on the day of Pentecost. This Holy Spirit did not come to people all over the world, but to the disciples only.

The representative man of the disciples was Peter who was one of the Twelve. Peter met Jesus for the first time while working as a fisherman. Peter followed Him, forsaking all, and He was crucified to death in front of Peter when the time came. After resurrection, He, as the Christ and the Holy Spirit, came into Peter's flesh in the day of Pentecost and made His abode in him forever. At that time only, Peter could confess that Jesus, the Christ had come in his (Peter's) flesh.

Therefore, "every spirit that confesses that Jesus Christ is come in the flesh" means the "man (spirit) who underwent the same process as Peter, and received the Christ, the Holy Spirit, in his Pentecost, into his flesh." As we can see here, the flesh in which Jesus Christ comes indicates not the flesh of Jesus, but that of each believer. The relationship between Jesus and the Christ is written in the first section of Part Three of this book.

The "flesh" in the above text is *sarx* in Greek and it describes a man, a body, characterized by the flesh; i.e., bone and skin. The man to whom Jesus Christ has come means the man who has confessed that Jesus Christ has come in his flesh/body. He is born again and is of God. Needless to say, the one into whose flesh Jesus Christ has not come is the antichrist who denies Jesus. Therefore, he is the spirit of antichrist.

Epilogue

The antichrist is not another separate being, but "sin-possessed me" in *me*, which is the "man of sin." Also, he is *my* old self.

The characteristics of antichrist are:

First, he comes out at the last time of my old self;
Second, he is not of truth;
Third, he denies that Jesus is the Christ; and
Fourth, he denies that Christ is come in the flesh of each believer.

God wants to be always with us, in us. However, we always resist the Christ who brings God into us. We are living united with the devil, being separated from God, because we think we are wise, having the wisdom of Adam. We are each living as an antichrist.

What matters is the last time. Then we will be able to hear this Word of Jesus in this book if the last time has come to us. Those who hear will forsake all kinds of false Jesuses and will follow the real Jesus from now on. They are those who are blessed.

Evil Spirits

We have discussed the major identities of evil that work against God. Now I will explain other evil spirits that the Scriptures mention, starting with sin.

Sin

Consider the following passage from Romans.

> For I know that in me (that is, in my flesh,) dwells no good thing: for to will is present with me; but how to perform that which is good I find not. [19]For the good that I would I do not: but the evil which I would not, that I do. [20]Now if I do that I would not, it is no more I that do it, but sin that dwells in me.
> _____ Romans 7:18-20

Ever since mankind ate of the tree of knowledge of the good and evil, he has kicked out God, the good itself, from his heart, and turned to depend on his own knowledge of the good and evil. Consequently, mankind born in this world is sinful, and we live in this world separated from God. Naturally, our everyday lives are a sequence of sinful works.

Sin means separation from God. I will now explain the meaning of separation from God. Consider Isaiah below.

> Behold, the LORD's hand is not shortened, that it cannot save; neither his ear heavy, that it cannot hear: ²But your iniquities have separated between you and your God, and your sins have hid his face from you, that he will not hear. ³For your hands are defiled with blood, and your fingers with iniquity; your lips have spoken lies, your tongue has muttered perverseness. _____
> Isaiah 59:1-3

We can find in the text that there is a separation between God and men due to our iniquities, or sin.

Where and how does the separation exist? Read the following passage.

> And even as they did not like to retain God in their knowledge, God gave them over to a reprobate mind, to do those things which are not convenient; _____ Romans 1:28

God is omnipresent. He is everywhere and exists in any time, but not in our hearts. How can the omnipresent Almighty God be absent from our hearts? As a matter of fact, He is present in our hearts also, but we do not acknowledge Him in our hearts or think about Him at all. Therefore, we have no knowledge of God in our hearts, even if He is there. This is the actual separation between God and us, and we who are in such a state are under sin, or iniquities. And under this situation whatever we do, we sin.

📂 A Man Wearing an Air Jacket

I will now illustrate the concept of sin with the analogy of "a man wearing an air jacket."

If a man who is wearing an air jacket wishes to reach the bottom of the sea, he must dive into the sea with power that overcomes the buoyancy of the air jacket. Otherwise, he cannot get there. Even if he reaches the bottom a litter closer through hard effort, he cannot stay there long but must rise to the surface because he cannot long resist the buoyancy of the air jacket. So no one can reach the bottom with air jacket on.

Here in this example, the bottom of the sea signifies God, or the kingdom of God, and the water is this world. The air jacket corresponds to the distance, or separation from God; that is, sin.

The air jacket is a simple material that has no personality. However, it controls my acts and my position when I put it on, and I control the movement of the air jacket as I move with it on. Therefore, the air jacket and I are interrelated and affect each other, being combined as one. The air jacket, as long as I wear it, will have my personality.

In the same way, sin, which is the separation, will have my personality. When I have sin in me, the original "I" will be transformed by sin into a "sinner."

As it is difficult to stay at the bottom of the sea long, and that stay can never be natural when I wear the air jacket, so it is difficult to do righteous works when I have sin in me. Such works will not be long and can never be natural due to the sin that I am wearing. Actually it is not possible at all. Read Romans 3:10, "As it is written, There is none righteous, no, not one." This is the status of the current believers who are under the law.

Please see the following illustration to help understanding sin in me. This illustration will be referred to throughout this chapter.

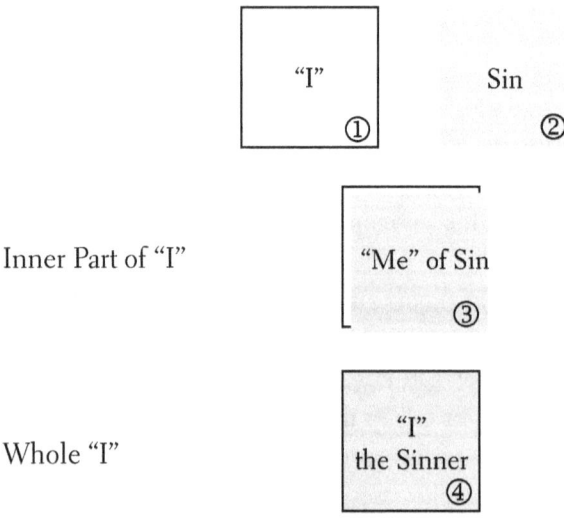

① Original "I" who wants to do good before humans became depraved.
② Sin, air jacket
③ Sin in me ("I"+Sin; Transformed personality of me) = Me of sin = My godless thoughts = Desire in me to do evil = Man of sin = Old self = Antichrist
④ "I" = the sinner

Consider Romans 7:21-24 below. These verses are the realistic remembrances of Paul when he was under the law before being saved by Christ. I will match the numbers shown in the illustrations to the said phrases of Romans.

I find then a law, that, when *I would do good* (①), *evil is present with me* (③). ²²For *I delight in the law of God after the inward man:*(①) ²³But *I see another law in my members, warring against the law of my mind, and bringing me into captivity to the law of sin which is in my members* (③). ²⁴*O wretched man* (④) that I am! who shall deliver me from the body of this death? ___Romans 7:21-24

We generally consider that sin is an act which is sinful, but it is more fundamental than that. Sin is within us, causing all our thoughts and behaviors to be sinful.

Jesus will strip us of our sin (air jacket), replacing it by the Christ, the Holy Spirit, so that we may live freely thereafter without sin. Jesus' forgiveness is such that it is fundamental and once-and-for-all, not temporal or improvised.

Old Self /Old Man

Read the following verse from Romans.

Knowing this, that our old man is crucified with him, that the body of sin might be destroyed, that from now on we should not serve sin. _____ Romans 6:6

In short, the old man/self represents "me of sin"(③). It is the nature of men who are born to this world as sinners. Sin which abides in a man will be eliminated at the cross by Jesus, and at this point the man's old self who has been possessed by sin will be crucified, and then he will have the life of Jesus, which means no longer serving sin.

The Spirit that Works in the Children of Disobedience

Consider the following Ephesians.

Wherein in time past you walked according to the course of this world, according to the prince of the power of the air, the spirit that now works in the children of disobedience: _____ Ephesians 2:2

The prince of the power of the air and the spirit that now works in the children of disobedience are "me of sin" within me (③), who is the personality combined with the sin, or devil. When we were sinners, we had to inevitably follow "me of sin," and at that time, we were the children of disobedience. Therefore, the spirit that works in the children of disobedience is my spirit of sin that worked in me before I was born again.

Spiritual Wickedness in High Places

Consider the following Ephesians.

For we wrestle not against flesh and blood, but against principalities, against powers, against the rulers of the darkness of this world, against spiritual wickedness in high places. _____ Ephesians 6:12

The "high places" mean our hearts, where God is supposed to abide. The spirit of evil, that is, our spirit that is separated from God (③), is in the high places instead of God. It is "me of sin." It is the spirit of the evil in high places.

"A man Jesus" will prompt us to fight the spirit of the evil that controls the high place (i.e., heart) within us, while we follow Him to the cross.

The Angels that Sinned and Left their own Habitation

Consider the following passages.

> For if God spared not the angels that sinned, but cast them down to hell, and delivered them into chains of darkness, to be reserved to judgment; _____ 2 Peter 2:4

> And the angels which kept not their first estate, but left their own habitation, he has reserved in everlasting chains under darkness to the judgment of the great day. _____ Jude 1:6

The angels in the above passages mean not the angels of the spiritual world but us, human beings. The angels who sinned and the angels who left their own habitation indicate the men who are separated from God and remain in sin (③ or ④).

How do we leave God, our own habitation? By not retaining the knowledge of God in our heart, as we live now. This way we have left our own habitation and have sinned. This is the members' separation from the body (God).

We are imprisoned in the everlasting chains of darkness. What are the chains of darkness? We are imprisoned in the darkness of our self-righteousness and self-knowledge of good and evil. Also, we are confined within our self-knowledge and our thoughts about God and Jesus Christ. Such erroneous knowledge, erroneous because all this knowledge is of the sinful world which is under darkness, is the everlasting chain that keeps us in darkness and non-truth.

We cannot escape from this darkness until the judgment of the great day. What is the judgment of the great day? In this instance, the judgment does not mean only the last judgment that will come after death. More importantly, it means the time in our current life when we will understand and realize the wrongness and darkness of our previous knowledge about the truth. This is the last day of judgment brought by Jesus in our lifetime. Then we will repent and follow Jesus to the cross, and will be resurrected, or be born again, as the angels of God without sin, resuming our proper habitation in relation to God.

Epilogue

In addition to the above terms describing evil, many characters opposing God appear in the Scriptures. None of the mentioned serpents, dragons, beasts, or leviathans are additional beings that exist in the spiritual world. All of them are the spirits of human beings (③) that are possessed by sin, or the devil, in us.

This ends Part Two: Evil is Present with Me
The key point to keep in mind is that evil is within us. Evil is separation from God. Such separation will be realized in us whenever we refuse to retain the knowledge of the living God in our heart. By removing this separation fundamentally through following Jesus to the cross, we will be one, forgiven, or sinless, with God and Jesus Christ. Thus, we will be able to communicate perfectly with God and do good. "A man Jesus" will remove the evil in us.

PART THREE
I THANK GOD THROUGH JESUS CHRIST

When we believe in Jesus, it means that we have the hope to be one with God. Jesus will lead us to our own cross to destroy our old self in order to bring the Holy Spirit into us, and thus we become one with God and Jesus Christ. Being one with God is our salvation about which the Scriptures speak.

If we believe the truth without meeting Jesus, we will have no idea about evil and serve it unwittingly, not even making a small attempt to fight it. After reading Part Two, now we can identify evil. However, that will be not enough. We still can do nothing much because the evil in us is more powerful and deceitful than we are alone.

Paul the apostle, remembering his life before being born again, said, "O wretched man that I am! who shall deliver me from the body of this death?" (Romans 7:24). Paul knew by his experience that only Jesus could save him from such a miserable situation. Therefore, he said right next in the chapter, "There is therefore now no condemnation to them which are in Christ Jesus, who walk not after the flesh, but after the Spirit. For the law of the Spirit of life in Christ Jesus has made me free from the law of sin and death" (Romans 8:1-2).

We alone cannot overcome the evil ever, unless we do not meet Jesus in person in our individual lives. Jesus will come to us as "a man who has the Word, or Christ, in him" in our life. Only He can destroy the evil in us. By destroying the evil in us on the cross, we will then be resurrected into the kingdom of God. Now we can do good, as we desired, in Jesus.

"Resurrection" is rising again in the kingdom, "Salvation" means being saved from this sinful world into the kingdom, and "born again" means being reborn into the kingdom, so all these meanings are same.

In Part Three, I will share the insights of the following topics:

5. Jesus as the Word
6. Resurrection

5

JESUS AS THE WORD

JESUS IS THE CHRIST

Jesus is the Christ

Jesus Christ – all along we think that is one name which refers to Jesus. Maybe when we are busy we call Him *Jesus* for short; when we have time, we call Him, more formally, *Jesus Christ*. And yes, they are one, both referring to Jesus of the Bible. However, as we read the Scriptures, we encounter some challenges in this simple understanding like the verses below:

> But these are written, that you might believe that Jesus is the Christ, the Son of God; and that believing you might have life through his name. _____ John 20:31

> Therefore let all the house of Israel know assuredly, that God has made the same Jesus, whom you have crucified, both Lord and Christ. _____ Acts 2:36

John and Peter differentiated "Jesus" from "Christ" as above. Also,

Paul mentioned this concept in Acts 9:22. Surely you will find more Scriptures verses other than these that seem to use different names to describe Jesus.

Are the names "Jesus" and "Christ" same or different? If different, how are they different? Let us consider the names Jesus, and Christ, respectively in order to understand the truth of new life and salvation.

Jesus and Christ are the same, and yet different, like the relationship of our body and spirit, depending on how we see them. As our body, which is finite, so is the vessel of our spirit, which is infinite. Jesus is the vessel of Christ, which is everlasting and eternal.

Consider the following passage from the book of Matthew.

> While the Pharisees were gathered together, Jesus asked them, ^{42}Saying, What think you of Christ? whose son is he? They say to him, The son of David. ^{43}He said to them, How then does David in spirit call him Lord, saying, ^{44}The LORD (*Yahweh* in Hebrew) said to my Lord (*Adonai* in Hebrew), Sit you on my right hand, till I make your enemies your footstool? ^{45}If David then call him Lord, how is he his son? ___ Matthew 22:41-45 (parenthesis and italic mine)

The Jews thought Christ was to be the son of David. But David called Christ (referring to Jesus, the incarnated Christ in this case) as "Lord (*Adonai*)." Jesus was asking them, then how is He David's son? Jesus wishes to reveal the difference between Jesus and Christ. In Jesus, the Christ abides. Jesus is in the flesh, but Christ is the One who existed always; even before the Creation of the heavens and the earth. From the perspective of the flesh, Jesus Christ is the son of David, but from the perspective of the Christ, He cannot be the son of David, because He existed always even before David was born.

Therefore, we can know that the substance of Jesus is Christ. And after Jesus is crucified and resurrected, He comes into the bodies of the disciples as Christ, the Holy Spirit, and thus, they can be saved. In this case, Jesus is proven to them to be the Christ, the Savior. Therefore, Jesus comes first, then comes the Christ in the course of my salvation. When I am saved, the Christ abides in my body.

However, in the Scriptures the terms "Jesus," "Christ," "Jesus Christ," and "Christ Jesus" are used interchangeably to express "Jesus Christ," unless differentiated specifically.

Jesus Is the Word

Jesus is the Word. Read John 1:1, "In the beginning was the Word, and the Word was with God, and the Word was God." The Word is the Christ which we have considered in the previous section. I will touch on aspect of Jesus as the Word through its characteristics of "spoken," "heard" and "written." I will follow the example of the disciples.

🗁 The Word, Spoken

When the disciples met Jesus, they followed Him, forsaking all, denying themselves, and taking up their own cross, to destroy their old selves on the cross. As this expression will appear frequently in this book, I will say this in short as "following Jesus to the cross."

Jesus led the disciples to the cross and resurrection from the dead for their salvation from sin. During that course, the eternal life that is in Jesus was imparted to the disciples. What did Jesus, the owner of eternal life, do to send this life to them? He spoke. He did not inject something to them physically, but only spoke. Likewise, now, if you meet "a man Jesus," He will speak to you to give eternal life.

In this respect, Jesus is the Word which is to be spoken.

🗁 The Word, Heard

From the point of view of the disciples, when Jesus spoke the Word of Life, they heard it. Not all men can hear the spoken Word of Life, but those who are ready to follow Jesus to the cross with true repentance.

> But blessed are your eyes, for they see: and your ears, for they hear. _____ Matthew 13:16

> So then faith comes by hearing, and hearing by the word of God.
> _____ Romans 10:17

As the disciples heard the Word of Life, I hope you can hear the same through this book and be blessed.

📂 The Word, Written

The spoken and heard Word will then be written on the tablets of the hearts of the disciples. This process will be completed on the cross, which began when they met Jesus for the first time.

> For as much as you are manifestly declared to be the letter of Christ ministered by us, written not with ink, but with the Spirit of the living God; not in tables of stone, but in fleshy tables of the heart. _____ 2 Corinthians 3:3

When the Word of Life written on the tablets of their hearts was completed on the cross, they were saved, having the Word, the eternal life, within them. Thus Jesus, the Word, abides in the bodies of the disciples. Now they can *speak* the Word of Life to the neighbors for their salvation as Jesus did. They are the sons of God and His people (Hebrews 8:10).

Likewise, Jesus, the Word, will abide in the body of whoever is saved and born again. You can meet Jesus here and now by meeting such a disciple who has the Word, or Christ, in him. Follow the disciple who is saved and he will show you the way to salvation and you will be saved.

Epilogue

Upon learning this aspect of the personality of Jesus Christ, we have a new understanding of His nature. He is the substance of the Word of God. Even though His flesh, his human personality named Jesus bar Joseph was on earth for a certain period of time in the past, He is on earth even now as the spiritual presence of the Christ, or the

Word of God in the bodies of His disciples, the born-again believers. Therefore, we should meet Jesus as a man and be led by Him to the cross to destroy our old self and gain eternal life. Fall away from the Jesus who only exists in your thoughts and notions.

Who Is My Mother?

Matthew 12:46-50

While he yet talked to the people, behold, his mother and his brothers stood without, desiring to speak with him. ⁴⁷Then one said to him, Behold, your mother and your brothers stand without, desiring to speak with you. ⁴⁸But he answered and said to him that told him, Who is my mother? and who are my brothers? ⁴⁹And he stretched forth his hand toward his disciples, and said, Behold my mother and my brothers! ⁵⁰For whoever shall do the will of my Father which is in heaven, the same is my brother, and sister, and mother.

The whole Scriptures speak about one thing; that is, the salvation offered by Jesus. However, salvation in the Scriptures is expressed in various ways. For example, salvation can also mean going into the kingdom of God, forgiveness of sin, having faith, being born again, the coming of the Lord, being baptized by the Holy Spirit, receiving eternal life, attaining to the resurrection and so on. All these expressions are meant to say "our salvation by Jesus."

Now, as another expression of salvation, we will study "giving birth to a child" through the text.

When we meet "a man Jesus" we will hear the Word from his mouth. As we hear the Word, new life will be conceived in our hearts. While we continue to hear the Word and obey, we will give birth spiritually to a child in due season. The delivery of a child is our salvation. We will discuss salvation in this respect.

In the passage above from Matthew, Jesus calls the disciples His brother, sister, and mother. Occasionally, we see people swear to be brothers with their close friends and other chummy persons and say "You are my brother." Did He also call them His brothers just to show his fond friendship for them? If not, what kind of spiritual background does His context have?

Moreover, while we can understand His calling the disciples "brothers," how can we understand the fact that He calls them His "mother," too? How can they be His mother? We may think that He used this term to mean family members in general who have intimate relationships. However, He is always speaking of such things in a spiritual manner, not as the emotional things of this world. And we will discuss the meaning of the will of God as well.

Family of Jesus

📁 **Earthly Family**

The body of Jesus belongs to this world, but His substance, the Word, belongs to the world that is not seen. That is, He lives both in this world that is seen and the kingdom of God that is not seen. Two worlds overlap in His case. Therefore, He has two families: The first one is of the flesh, which belongs to this world, and the second one is of God, which belongs to the spiritual kingdom of God. In the text, those who came to see Him were the family of the flesh. They are as follows in the passage from Matthew.

> Is not this the carpenter's son? is not his mother called Mary? and his brothers, James, and Joses, and Simon, and Judas? [56]And his sisters, are they not all with us? From where then has this man all these things? _____ Matthew 13:55-56

His family of the flesh includes Joseph, His earthly father; Mary, His mother; and his earthly brothers: James; and Joses; and Simon;

and Judas; and His sisters who are not named.

We wish to be a member of His family because He is the Son of God, the Almighty. However, we cannot belong to His family in the flesh. And it is not so attractive to be a member of His earthly, family, because we know that He did not give any benefits and personal preferences to His family during His public works.

However, unlike His earthly family, Jesus gives preference to the His spiritual family. He gave them the kingdom of God, the Holy Spirit, faith, love, blessing, resurrection, and salvation. Are there any other greater privileges than these in the world? Fortunately, there is a way that we can join His spiritual family. We must do our best to enter His spiritual family.

📁 Spiritual Family

In the present text, Jesus compares the family of God with the family of the flesh. He stretches out His hand toward His disciples and says, "Behold, my mother and my brothers!" He refers to the disciples as His spiritual family.

How can we join His spiritual family? It is possible through the process of being born again. When our old self dies, united with Jesus, on the cross, we will be resurrected and born again as new men. From this time forward, we are born of God as Jesus is, and are counted as members of His spiritual family.

Read the following passage from Romans.

> For whom he did foreknow, he also did predestinate to be conformed to the image of his Son, that he might be the firstborn among many brothers. _____ Romans 8:29

Jesus is the firstborn of God, and those who are born again in the image of Jesus after Him are His brothers, having the same Father; that is, God. At that time, the disciples were in the process of being born again by the Word and will be born again on the cross in due course. Therefore He called His disciples "brothers."

Disciples Are the Mother of Jesus?

Then, how can He call them "mother"? The fact is, at that time Jesus was preaching the Word to His disciples. In the spiritual sense, He was a man having the seed of life, and the disciples were women receiving it. When He proclaimed the Word, they received it in their hearts, becoming pregnant with the (spiritual) life of Jesus, and the Word made that spiritual life grow. When the seed matured at the time of cross, they brought forth a Son, having the life of Jesus. This Son represented their born-again selves; but this Son is also Jesus because that seed, the Word, is of Jesus. Therefore, when the disciples brought forth a Son, Jesus, when the Word of God matured in their hearts, they become the mother of Jesus.

Read the following passage.

> And she shall bring forth a son, and you shall call his name JESUS: for he shall save his people from their sins. _____
> Matthew 1:21

Of course, Matthew wrote this word regarding the virgin birth of Jesus, quoting Isaiah 7:14. Mary gave birth to Jesus at a specific time in history. As written in Matthew, Jesus will save the world. However, this story is also applicable to each of us who hear the Word of Jesus, get pregnant from the seed of the Word that is implanted in our hearts, and give birth to the Son, Jesus, like Mary did. He who brings forth Jesus, spiritually a woman Mary, will be saved by the very Jesus he begot. The child Jesus has saved his mother who gave birth to Him.

Paul the apostle says in this regard in 1 Timothy 2:15, "Notwithstanding she shall be saved in childbearing, if they continue in faith and charity and holiness with sobriety."

Some people mistook this spiritual thing as a thing of the flesh, so they have a high regard of the Mother Mary. They deviated far from the Word. Those who are saved are spiritual Marys who brought forth Jesus, and they are ones who should be regarded highly. The disciples who will hear the Word of Jesus, get pregnant from the seed of this Word, and give birth to Jesus are respectively "Mother Mary." In order to reveal the above truth, Jesus called His disciples "mother."

📂 The Substance of Jesus Is the Word

As I said earlier, the substance of Jesus is the Word. Jesus who came on earth is God incarnate. In the Matthew passage, at that moment, He faced His disciples. As they heard and experienced what He said, they become pregnant with His life and would bring forth a child (John 16:21), who is Jesus, and thus they will have His life that they never had before.

Here we can know that the life of Jesus is transmitted from Jesus to the disciples through the Word, not through any physical contact. Therefore, we can find that the substance of Jesus, which is the Life, is the Word, not His flesh. His flesh is the vessel that contains the Word.

Likewise, the disciples, each of them, will become the vessel of the Word when they give birth to Jesus. And then they can do what Jesus did; i.e., lead others to salvation, as they have the Word in them.

Therefore, Jesus is present around us as the Word in the bodies of the born-again men beyond historic times. Through such born-again men, we can be pregnant with the life of Jesus, and we will deliver Jesus when time comes. At that time we also will be the mother of Jesus and His brothers concurrently.

To Do the Will of the Father

Jesus says, "For whoever shall do the will of my Father which is in heaven, the same is my brother, and sister, and mother (v.50)."

Easily, we can explain this passage like this: "Whoever is eager and diligent to do good works will be considered as my brother, sister and mother. So work hard!"

However, that interpretation is only a superficial and legalistic meaning of the Bible. Without neglecting the legalistic meaning, we should have practiced the weightier meaning of the Scripture. Then, what is the weightier meaning? In order to know that, we must first know the will of God. Without knowing the will of God correctly, we never can do His will. You may automatically think that His will is for us to do good works. Maybe yes, but the Scripture does not say so.

Read the following passage from John.

> And this is the will of him that sent me, that every one which sees the Son, and believes on him, may have everlasting life: and I will raise him up at the last day. _____ John 6:40

According to John, His will is that everyone who sees the Son and believes on Him may have everlasting life; i.e., salvation. Jesus makes those who believe in Him have everlasting life, as the doer of the will of God. In short, to save others is to do the will of God. So if we want to do the will of God correctly, we should be able to save others. On this saying, you may think like this:

"How can we save others? Salvation is can be done by Jesus alone. We only can do good works, not salvation."

No. In that case you cannot do the will of God. Even if you do, you are doing something else, not the will of God.

Think about the disciples who did the salvation works as Jesus did after the Pentecost. The disciples are those who have the Word of Christ in them, and can do what Jesus did; i.e., the will of God.

Read the following.

> Truly, truly, I say to you, He that believes on me, the works that I do shall he do also; and greater works than these shall he do; because I go to my Father. _____ John 14:12

The disciples are those who can do the salvation works, having the Christ gene. That's why Jesus calls them family. They can be us. And we can do the will of God, the salvation of others, if we have undergone the process to have the Word of Christ in us like the disciples.

We should not be confused to think that the will of God is for us to do good works. That is the legalistic reading, which cannot save us. To do the will of God we are to follow "a man Jesus" to the cross first. If you read the Scripture in this way, you have the weightier meaning of the Scripture. If you follow Jesus, you will be saved and will do the will of God thereafter. You are the real family members of Jesus.

Epilogue

Jesus, the Word, came to this world in the flesh. His substance was not the body; the Word that was within Him was the substance. He stays here now in the bodies of the born-again as the Word. When we meet the man who has the Word in him and follow him, we will deliver a son, Jesus. Then, we will be saved and born again by that son to whom we gave birth. We will be His brother, sister, and mother. Moreover, we can do the will of God, which is to save others, as Jesus did.

Shouldn't we be the mother of Jesus who can do the will of God?

An Ax That Was Borrowed

2 Kings 6:1-7

And the sons of the prophets said to Elisha, Behold now, the place where we dwell with you is too strait for us. ²Let us go, we pray you, to Jordan, and take there every man a beam, and let us make us a place there, where we may dwell. And he answered, Go you. ³And one said, Be content, I pray you, and go with your servants. And he answered, I will go. ⁴So he went with them. And when they came to Jordan, they cut down wood. ⁵But as one was felling a beam, the ax head fell into the water: and he cried, and said, Alas, master! for it was borrowed. ⁶And the man of God said, Where fell it? And he showed him the place. And he cut down a stick, and cast it in thither; and the iron did swim. ⁷Therefore said he, Take it up to you. And he put out his hand, and took it.

Sportsmen carry their own individual equipment. For example, the table tennis player carries his own rackets and the golf player his own clubs. If they use another player's equipment, they cannot fully display their competence in the sport because they are not accustomed to another's equipment.

This example is applicable to the Word of God as well. If we wish to use the Word properly, we should first make it familiar as our own. This does not mean that we must go to a theological seminary and study the Scriptures. But it means that we are to follow Jesus to the cross to become one with Him. Then, we can freely use it as ours. If we simply cite the Bible without making it as ours on the cross, we are using the word of others, not the ones we are familiar with, as if they were our own. Naturally, we will be clumsy and poor at using such words.

Regarding the story of the passage, Elisha and the sons of the prophets went to the Jordan River and cut down trees. As one of them was felling a beam, the ax head fell into the water. Elisha cut down a stick and cast it in there to make the iron float and returned the ax head to him.

At first look, it sounds like children's fairy tales, but in depth reveals a very profound spiritual truth about the law and grace and many more. Now I will tell you what they are through each scene.

The Place Is Too Strait For Us

Elisha the prophet and the sons of the prophets try to move to Jordan and build a new house because their current place was too small. He says he will go there with them.

This could be historical fact. Whatever the story may be, it is important for us to know the spiritual meaning of it. What is that? Faith can be divided into two periods: the period of the law and, following, the period of grace. According to the spiritual symbolism, their move from their current place to Jordan signifies that those believers who are under the law move to grace as the time comes.

Regarding the location of their current place, people suggest different opinions. Some says it was Gilgal, others say Jericho. However, the current place of the story, whatever the correct location may be, signifies "being under the law" spiritually.

Their current dwelling place has the feature of being *strait*. The word "strait" is translated from the Hebrew *tsar*, which has the meaning of "anguish," "tribulation," "distress," "opponent," "enemy" as well as "narrow" and "tight." All these meanings are suitable to describe the situation of believes under the law.

They live in a narrow place and are weighed down and worn out by the law, and the things they want to do are intercepted and controlled in many ways. They serve Satan the enemy and live in pain, even if they are with Elijah, which means even if we believe in Jesus we serve Satan the enemy. This situation, which is created by the law, is expressed as "strait."

If we take such a miserable situation for granted, thinking that we will only be freed from it after death, it means that we can endure the "strait" situation further. We are not ready to go to Jordan yet; we have to remain here until we really feel desolate under the law. Only those who feel so will hope to go to Jordan. And they will go into the period of grace, opening their ears to hear the Word of Grace, the gospel. This is the spiritual interpretation of the picture that they wanted to go to Jordan.

In the text, Elisha, the figure of Jesus, goes together with the sons of the prophets when they depart. This signifies that Jesus is in the law and He is in grace also. The law comes before Jesus, but Jesus is hidden even in such law. Jesus says in John 5:46, "For had you believed Moses, you would have believed me; for he wrote of me." As we can see from what He says He was already in the word of Moses. The law and grace are not two separate things, but they are one, like the relationship of the flower and the fruit. Jesus Christ dwells as life both in the law/flower that comes first and in grace/fruit that follows.

Ax

In the passage, the Word of God is likened to the sword (Ephesians 6:17; Hebrews 4:12). And it is likened to the ax here and in Matthew 3:10; it reads, "And now also the ax is laid to the root of the trees: therefore every tree which brings not forth good fruit is hewn down, and cast into the fire."

The trees appearing in the Scripture are the symbols of men. And cutting down the tree with an ax means preaching the Word to people. According to how they react to the Word, two types of people will manifest: those who reject the word and are cast into the fire as in Matthew 3:10, and those who receive the Word and are used as the building material of the church as is shown in this text. The former are under judgment and the latter are saved.

The scene in which the sons of the prophets who came to Jordan to cut down wood signifies the believers are invited to preach the Word to their neighbors. And preaching the Word to their neighbors can be done only by those believers who are correctly born again, that is, those who are in Jordan with true qualifications.

The following accident reveals that some came to Jordan without proper qualifications. They were those who were yet under the law even if they believed they were under grace.

It Was Borrowed

While cutting down a beam, a problem happened: the ax head fell into the water, and he said, being anxious about it, that it was borrowed. Some people explain this story literally, like below:

"An ax head was very expensive in those days. Because he was poor, he had no ax. So he had to borrow one to do the work. But he was a good man so he expressed his grave concern to pay it back to the man who lent it to him."

However, this kind of interpretation, or similar, transforms the Word of God into the nursery story. When reading the Scripture we need to think deeply until we find the spiritual sign which reveals the truth that relates to the salvation of our spirits.

Then, what spiritual sign does this story contain? When he borrowed an ax to fell a beam, it means that he preached to others with the Word that is borrowed. The Word that is borrowed signifies the state of having heard and understood the Word, he did not yet have it as his own through following Jesus to the cross. Such a man can have the Word as the law and knowledge, not as his own.

For example, Jesus says, "Love one another." Therefore, every believer tries to exercise this. It means that he, the believer, has this Word. However, even if he makes an effort to love, he will fail for sure if he does not have the Word as his own by going through the cross. In this instance, he can only pretend or imitate love. It is because he has no power to love. The love is not his, but belongs to others, like Jesus, the apostles and those who are born again. His attempt to love will utterly fail. His ax head falls into the water like the one in the text.

We can see an example of the behaviors caused by the Word that is borrowed in the Parable of the Unjust Steward in Luke 16. This steward under the law heard the word that he ought to forgive the sins of his neighbors and he tried to follow it. However, even if he forgave, he could not do it properly. That is, he reduced their debt of a hundred measures of oil to fifty, and the debt of a hundred measures of wheat to eighty. This was not the forgiveness of sin by the Word, which requires the perfect 100% of forgiveness. He could only imitate the *sin-forgiveness* of the Word as it was borrowed. His ax head fell. Those who borrow the Word are like those who went to Jordan without proper qualifications.

🗁 *Alas!*: The Time of Understanding

The ax head fell into the water. At that instant the son of the prophet said, "Alas, master! for it was borrowed."

He worked hard with the ax, not thinking all the while about the fact it was borrowed. However, when its head fell into the water, only then did he recall that it was borrowed, not his own. He sighed by saying "Alas!" He lamented, not because the ax was valuable, but because he understood that it was an empty trial to fell the beam with the ax that was borrowed. This is to reveal our spiritual situation where we are trying to live according to the Word, but we cannot do so as we wish. For instance, we hear the Word to love, and we try. While sincerely trying to love, the time will come when we realize we do not have the power to love. We have been trying to love with the borrowed Word. We will then sigh, lamenting "Alas!" unconsciously, because we have found that we labored in the wrong way during the past.

However, for those whose times are not up yet under the law, they will not know, or refuse to know, the truth. Whatever they say, the believers are to be fully baptized in the law to true repentance; and only then they can meet "a man Jesus." After our sufficient time under the law, the time of grace will come. And that is the way it should be.

He Cut Down a Stick, and Cast It There

"And he cut down a stick, and cast it in thither (v. 6)."

When he sighed, Elisha came to him and told him what to do. While the son of the prophet was felling a beam he was doing it alone in his own way. When he realized he had problem, he asked Elisha for help, agreeing to do as Elisha said, instead of his own way. Of course, Elisha was with him from the start, but he did not pay attention to Elisha until he had need, then he invited Elisha into his life and agreed to hear and obey.

Likewise, at the beginning, we believe in Jesus in our own way, not hearing what the living Jesus says. Only when we realize we have a serious faith problem will we repent and invite Jesus into our lives and obey Him, forsaking our own way. Jesus was around us all along, but we did not pay attention to Him because we thought we could believe and manage on our own. But now, after our lament, we will believe in Him in His way. From now on Jesus can and will lead us to the way in which the Word becomes ours, which is the cross.

As a solution of the lost ax head, Elisha cut down a stick and cast it into the water and the iron floated. Here the stick is symbolic of the cross (Galatians 3:13). This means that in order to solve the problem of borrowed ax we need to go through the cross.

Jesus leads those of us who truly repented to the cross. Not many believers will know the meaning of going through the cross, led by and united, with Jesus. They might simply think that it making a wholehearted effort to try to love others, but it is only another legalistic effort, as usual. Going through the cross means that we meet "a man Jesus" and follow Him to destroy our old self on the cross. During this time, we have to deny ourselves, taking up our cross (Matthew 16:24), which will appear as hardship and tribulation to the eyes of the old self who is meant to die. However, after the cross and resurrection, united with Jesus, we will have the Word as ours, not a Word that is borrowed.

Consequently, the ax that was borrowed means the Word he has received without passing through the cross. After Elisha cast the stick, the ax floated. The floated ax, the Word, is different from previous one, and is no longer borrowed. The Word he had earlier was mere knowledge in him, but now the Word is written upon the tablet of his heart. This is the true meaning of the word, "He put out his hand, and *took the ax head*" (2 Kings 6:7).

Overall, the fact that the iron floated when the stick was cast is symbolic of his old self that is destroyed on the cross and his resurrection as a new man.

Epilogue

They who are chosen by God will depart from the law for grace. Under the law, people will believe in Jesus, mistaking the ax that is borrowed as theirs. The ax head will fall into the water in due course and they will understand the reason. At that time, they will go to the cross in obedience to Jesus, the Word.

The Crucifixion of Jesus Christ is not just an event that happened a long time ago, but it is the event that is to occur in us now when we meet Jesus. When our old self is destroyed on the cross, the iron having fallen into the water will float as ours. From now on, we will have the life of Jesus, the Word, in us as those who have been born again.

Let us stop borrowing the Word, but have it be ours for good!

O You Dry Bones, Hear the Word!

Ezekiel 37:1-10

The hand of the LORD was on me, and carried me out in the spirit of the LORD, and set me down in the middle of the valley which was full of bones, ²And caused me to pass by them round about: and, behold, there were very many in the open valley; and, see, they were very dry. ³And he said to me, Son of man, can these bones live? And I answered, O Lord GOD, you know. ⁴Again he said to me, Prophesy on these bones, and say to them, O you dry bones, hear the word of the LORD. ⁵Thus said the Lord GOD to these bones; Behold, I will cause breath to enter into you, and you shall live: ⁶And I will lay sinews on you, and will bring up flesh on you, and cover you with skin, and put breath in you, and you shall live; and you shall know that I am the LORD. ⁷So I prophesied as I was commanded: and as I prophesied, there was a noise, and behold a shaking, and the bones came together, bone to his bone. ⁸And when I beheld, see, the sinews and the flesh came up on them, and the skin covered them above: but there was no breath in them. ⁹Then said he to me, Prophesy to the wind, prophesy, son of man, and say to the wind, Thus said the Lord GOD; Come from the four winds, O breath, and breathe on these slain, that they may live. ¹⁰So I prophesied as he commanded me, and the breath came into them, and they lived, and stood up on their feet, an exceeding great army.

We believe in Jesus so that we may be saved and have a new life. The salvation is the change of life from the sinful one, which is to be condemned, to the righteous one, of which God approves. Such change of life is called "being born again" in the Scriptures.

As mentioned, we believers in Jesus are saved. So we come to church, serve at table, give donations, study the Bible, praise, pray, and fast. By doing so, we feel somehow secure because we have done something different compared to what we did when we did not believe in Jesus.

However, this kind of mindset and belief does not hit the essence of faith in Jesus, because believing in Jesus changes our sinful life into a new righteous life. And this change of life is surely not the kind in which we do something different or something additional to our old life. Rather, it is that we destroy our old life in order to have a new life by following Jesus to the cross. We should not confuse working hard for Jesus with following Jesus to the cross to have a new life.

While following Jesus to the cross, if we obey, our new life will gradually increase within us as we hear the Word. The main text above shows us the process of how our spiritual body is being built by the Word.

Let us see what all these things reveal in connection with the establishment of the new spiritual body and how it comes to have life.

The Time has Come for the Dry Bones to Live

Ezekiel the prophet is the symbol of Jesus. God calls Ezekiel the son of man and Jesus also calls Himself the same. Ezekiel prophesies the Word of God in the text, and Jesus also prophesies the Word of God who dwells in Him (John 14:10). The Israelites appearing in this Scripture symbolize we who believe in Jesus nowadays. The dry bones symbolize the Israelites (Ezekiel 37:11) and we who are dead spiritually. This scene is no longer about people in the ancient history of Israel, but about us in this current time.

When you hear this, you might probably say to yourselves, "This saying is for someone else who has incorrect faith, not for me. Because I have believed in Jesus correctly so He has saved me and I am alive and born again. I am praising the Lord." However, this is the way dry bones think. The problem the dry bones have is that they do not know they are the dry bones. Think about the Pharisees: they were typical dry bones, the spiritually blind, but they thought they could see, and didn't realize they were blind (John 9:40).

However, the dry bones appearing in this text are different from the blind men who cannot see themselves. Here, the dry bones realize they are dry bones. This fact is written in Ezekiel 37:11, "Then he said unto me, Son of man, these bones are the whole house of Israel: behold, they say, Our bones are dried, and our hope is lost: we are cut off for our parts."

As we read, the dry bones that will live by the prophecy of Ezekiel say that they are dried, their hope is lost, and they are cut off for their parts. They know they are hopeless dry bones, so they pray hard to God. Only those bones that pray will live through the prophecy and breath given by Ezekiel. Likewise, we also will live through the Word when we realize that we are sinners and truly repent.

How can dry bones that died a long time ago live? Ezekiel answers, "O Lord GOD, you know," which indicates Ezekiel has abandoned his own attempt to reason and trusts that only God can answer. Yes, God will revive the very old dry bones. God will save us, the hopeless forty to fifty year-old sinners through Jesus, once we realize we ourselves are the dry bones.

The Bones Came Together; And Sinews, Flesh and Skin

The passage shows the process of the creation of the new man by the Word.

The bones signify life (Genesis 50:25, John 19:33). And dry bones mean life before being born again. As dry bones, we try to love others as ourselves; however, we realize that it is not possible at all. We have such a good hope and plan to love, but we find our life is simply hollow-cored, like wood pillars eaten up by termites. We are dry bones, and we have dry lives which lead to nothing at the end.

Why are we, our lives, so empty and miserable? It's because we failed to get new life out of our study of the Word. We read and understand the Scripture superficially and legalistically to find out what to do to bring ourselves to life. However, the Scripture speaks about "a man Jesus" for us to meet. And when we meet Jesus, He will reveal to us a fresh meaning of the Scripture and the correct way to new life by prophesying the Word as stated in the text. As we hear the Word that is prophesied by Jesus we will have fresh bodies of new life. We will have bones, sinews, flesh, skin and breath, and then we can love.

The Bones

The bones in the text represent mainframes for maintaining the body. The existing dry bones of the Scripture are products of our thinking, that if we work hard we will receive salvation and blessing in return. However, sinners cannot change their natures by working hard. Consequently, we will remain as sinners, having our lives dry and empty, in spite of hearing the Scripture of eternal life. We read the Scripture with the eyes of the law, and we are under the law.

However, when we meet Jesus and hear from Him, we will realize that there is one new man that we want to be and should be, who is our born-again self. We will become born again when we are led to the cross and receive Him, as the Holy Spirit, into ourselves. To have the knowledge and hope to be a new man is for you to have the bones formed by the Word on the frame of the new man. Therefore, understanding what being born again and knowing how you can be born again is to form the bones of your new man. Being born again and other terms like the kingdom of God, resurrection, salvation, being the son of God, sin-forgiveness, faith, etc., all refer to your new creation in Jesus.

If you continue to hear the Word, you will understand that such bones are inter-connected showing the same "being born again by Jesus" nature. Such understanding is what the bones coming together in the text signifies. At this time, when you find the bones joined together and moving in gear, you will utter a sign of joyful admiration. This is what the noise and shaking expressed in the above Scripture text means.

The above creation process of life occurs in you when you hear the Word and follow Jesus to the cross. This is quite different from a nice sermon that temporarily leaves a good impression on our minds. Only they who have the Word of God, like Ezekiel, can create life by prophesying. They are people like Peter, Paul, John, and so on. Are you now hearing this prophecy of life from one of them? I hope so.

When the bones heard the Word and connected, the sinews and the flesh come up on them, and the skin covered them.

🗁 The Sinews

Sinews connect bones and muscles and allow the bones to work with a single purpose through contraction and relaxation. This means that you are able to link the bones together and express life as you wish. For example, you will be able to explain about the salvation of Jesus in conjunction with resurrection or being born again or faith or the ability to love freely. In this instance, it is like sinews being formed amongst the bones in your spiritual body.

The flesh signifies the experiences that God allows us to pass through every day as we hear the Word and understand it. During this process, your non-truth thoughts, false knowledge and ignorance about the truth will be revealed and be washed away by the Word. The Word we understand must have experiences, and then the Word will be yours. This experience is likened to the flesh.

For example, the Lord may point you out by saying, "You judge others, which you should not do." You hear this and, after thinking, you would confess by saying, "Oh Lord, I judged so. But I will not do it again." However, as soon as we walk out of the place, something happens and you judge others as before naturally. This situation is prepared by the hand of God for you to see that you still judge. At this juncture, you have to truly repent and by repetition, your bones and sinews will get flesh.

🗁 The Skin

The skin that covers the bones and sinews means to smoothly arrange what those who have heard the Word have understood and experienced, and express the same with the truth. But those who have known the truth but have not yet received skin will be poor at organizing the truth and expressing it to others.

For instance, first you know Jesus as the giver of good things in this world, like fortune, good health, and a reputable position in society and so on. So you praise Him. However, when the time comes, Jesus will send you a trial in order to heal you by leading you to the cross. In this case, you may think that "it is judgment for my particular iniquities," or "Jesus forsook me, taking all my good things. He is not right. I may forsake Him too."

But it happened to you because you have matured enough to bear such trials. Jesus will explain it to you and if you understand it properly, you will also speak of your trials to others as natural growth. Thus, you have skin for the newly grown parts of your spiritual body.

Here is example of the skin covering the new man. You may recall in Luke 24 two disciples, one of them known as Cleopas, who were going to the Emmaus. In fact, they were mature enough in their faith to meet the resurrected Jesus, but they did not know what to do or what to say at first. As Jesus spoke to them, they got everything in order and knew what to do and say as born again men. This is the formation of the skin. Finally they will get *breath* at the time of Pentecost.

The skin puts a final touch to the newly created body, except for breath.

Two Steps to Create a Man

Even after the spiritual body was completely formed, it still required the breath of life. Ezekiel prophesied the breath to come into them and they lived (v. 9-10).

The Breath

"Breath" is translated from *ruach* in Hebrew, meaning "wind," "breath," and "spirit." It is the Holy Spirit that will come to you who are newly created by the Word of Jesus.

By the prophesy of Ezekiel, the dry bone went through the process: bones–sinews–flesh–skin to form a new body and, by receiving breath, the body takes life in full. This creation of a new man can be expressed in two steps: The formation of a body, which is the first step, and receiving the breath to live, which is the second step.

You can find this step also when God created Adam. God formed him of the dust of the ground and breathed into his nostrils the breath of life (Genesis 2:7) to make him a living being. Likewise, Jesus created the new spiritual bodies of the disciples by the Word over three and a half years, and finally breathed into them the Holy Spirit to make them live (John 20:22). This process also has two steps: the first is to heal them up to the stage of the cross; the second is His coming as the Holy Spirit in them at the Resurrection/Pentecost.

You also are to go through the same two steps in order to be born again as a new man through Jesus.

The Army of God

The hopeless dry bones are born again as a great army (v. 10).

What does this army signify? It indicates the spiritual soldiers who can perform the will of God. If you are ardent volunteers who want to be used by Him, you should first become His soldiers. And in order to be soldiers, as you have seen so far, you are to hear the Word which will create a new body and bring breath in you. Only such people can be used by God who will do the will of God.

Who are the actual soldiers working for God? They are Jesus, Peter, John, Paul and other apostles. They all have in common the Word in them. They all have the gene of Christ. Therefore, they can prophesy to the dry bones and raise them up as a great army. This is the will of God they do so. You will also do this, if you hear the Word that forms a new spiritual body and sends the Holy Spirit into you.

Epilogue

What are you so busy with today? Doing the works for Jesus and church? Good. Without neglecting them, you should have repented to be able to hear the Word and follow it. If you repent, you will hear and follow the word of Ezekiel, the figure of Jesus. While hearing His prophesies, new spiritual bones, sinews, flesh and skin will be created in you. And finally Ezekiel will prophesy the breath, the Holy Spirit, to come into you, and you will live. You will stand up on your feet, as part of a great army.

    This man should be you!

The Dead Son of the Widow Revived

1 Kings 17:17-24

And it came to pass after these things, that the son of the woman, the mistress of the house, fell sick; and his sickness was so sore, that there was no breath left in him. ¹⁸And she said to Elijah, What have I to do with you, O you man of God? are you come to me to call my sin to remembrance, and to slay my son? ¹⁹And he said to her, Give me your son. And he took him out of her bosom, and carried him up into a loft, where he stayed, and laid him on his own bed. ²⁰And he cried to the LORD, and said, O LORD my God, have you also brought evil on the widow with whom I sojourn, by slaying her son? ²¹And he stretched himself on the child three times, and cried to the LORD, and said, O LORD my God, I pray you, let this child's soul come into him again. ²²And the LORD heard the voice of Elijah; and the soul of the child came into him again, and he revived. ²³And Elijah took the child, and brought him down out of the chamber into the house, and delivered him to his mother: and Elijah said, See, your son lives. ²⁴And the woman said to Elijah, Now by this I know that you are a man of God, and that the word of the LORD in your mouth is truth.

We value the life of man the most in this world, because it is impossible for the dead to come to life again. Therefore, people attempt to extend their lives by any means, and are very much concerned, in mercy, about ceasing to find a cure for humans showing little brain function according to scientific standards. However, even if we consider our precious lives, we must understand that eventually, we all will die. That is, the life that we are giving the highest regard is not an everlasting value to pursue in this world.

Then, what else should we seek to value, other than earthly life, or there is nothing like that? Yes, there is. It is the *eternal life*. During our lifetime, we all should to receive eternal life and, in fact, we are born into this world in order to get that life. If we forsake other valuable things to save our life of flesh, then, how much more—even all—we should forsake to have eternal life?

We all know from whom and how we can get eternal life. We get it only from Jesus. Let us meet and follow Him, forsaking all else, and He will give us life. Thus, our purpose of coming into this world is fulfilled. In believing Him, we should not be deceived by others who say that only after death we will get eternal life. No. We should get it during our earthly lifetime; otherwise it will be too late.

The text is the story of that happened while Elijah stayed in the house of the widow of Zarepath. Her son died and Elijah stretched himself on the child and prayed to God to revive him. She saw what happened to her son, and confessed that he was a man of God and the word of the LORD was in his mouth.

The Scripture does not only mean to say that it was the power of Elijah who revived the life of the flesh, as the child will die again when time comes. It reveals to us that the power of Jesus gives spiritual, eternal, life to those who die believing in Him.

I will now explain the truth relating to salvation that is revealed through this story.

Elijah Calls Sin to Remembrance

The widow murmured and said to Elijah, "What do I have to do with you? Have you come to me to bring my sin to remembrance, and to put my son to death?"

We cannot understand what she is saying.

Is she saying that her son died of the disease that Elijah spread?

Or, does she mean that he came to her to bring her sin of bilking others out of money to light, and this caused the death of her son?

It does not seem to make sense either way. Yes, it is difficult to understand, if we read the story literally as we are fond of doing. As we can guess by now, the Scripture does not simply tell the story of the natural death of a son. The story reveals how we can receive eternal life.

Here in the text, the widow signifies me, the believer; her house my body, and Elijah is Jesus. The Elijah who is staying in the house of the widow signifies the Jesus who is staying with me. Therefore, this is my story.

This reveals the truth of how I can meet Jesus and be saved to get eternal life. The revelation is that, naturally, at the initial stage, I will not have fair knowledge about Jesus so I have incorrect faith that is legalistic. After spending a long time under that faith, when the proper time comes, I will realize that I have had a legalistic faith and be ready to know the truth. By meeting "a man Jesus," I will be truly saved and have the life of Jesus, which is eternal life.

Let us confirm this truth through the story.

📂 The Widow and Her Son

Regarding the death of her son, her son represents her born-again self. Earlier in this book, under the title of "Who is my mother?" we studied that the believer is to give birth to a son, which is the life of Jesus. The son that I bore is myself.

Likewise, the widow's son is the widow herself. This widow had a son but his life was mortal and he died; his life was not eternal. This means that the widow believed in Jesus under the law without true repentance. Therefore, even though the Word that she received made her pregnant and give birth to a son, the son was not of the eternal life of Jesus. And the son died. This is the meaning of the death of her son.

The Word that we hear without repentance is called the law. The law will make us bear a mortal son like the case of the widow here. We need to meet Jesus through true repentance in order to give birth to a son, who will be my everlasting life.

📂 True Repentance

Her son died because Elijah came to her to call her sin to remembrance. This is the revelation of true repentance to meet Jesus.

"True repentance" is total submission to Jesus to follow Him, after experiencing the limit of a godless life like the prodigal son in Luke who was facing death in a far country. The believer who has experienced the life of the prodigal son can follow Jesus without disobedience to the cross. That's why we need true repentance in order to follow Jesus. Reversely speaking, if Jesus comes to us, we will realize that we are the sinners. That is, Jesus will make us the sinners.

Nevertheless, we first are to believe without true repentance according to the providence of God. In such case, our faith should be legalistic in nature even though we think we believe in Jesus, the grace. We believe in Moses, the law, thinking that we are following Jesus. When we meet "a man Jesus," through Him we will realize that we are the real sinners.

Figuratively speaking, such belief in Moses, whether we wanted or not, constitutes the "foundation" of the tower (of faith), and if we realized that fact, now we need to complete the "tower" of faith by following the real Jesus. Jesus is saying in this regard in Luke 14:28-30, "Suppose one of you wants to build a tower. Will he not first sit down and estimate the cost to see if he has enough money to complete it? For if he lays the foundation and is not able to finish it, everyone who sees it will ridicule him, saying, 'This fellow began to build and was not able to finish.'"

The above truth was already revealed through the story of the widow here. The widow is the representation of those who believe in Jesus without true repentance nowadays. The death of her son signifies she realized that, by the word of Elijah, a shadow of Jesus, her faith was not the kind that leads to eternal life. Up until then, she thought she was born again, having a man child by the Word. This can be expressed as "by the coming of Elijah the widow realized that she was the sinner, the dead." Elijah made her a sinner and slew her son.

Consider the case of Peter. When Peter met Jesus, he fell down at

His knees and said, "Depart from me; for I am a sinful man, O Lord" (Luke 5:8). When Peter met Him, he realized that he was the sinner, and this case can be expressed as "Jesus made Peter a sinner and slew him," if I can borrow the expression of this passage in I Kings.

Therefore, "Have you come to me to call my sin to remembrance and to slay my son?" means "So far I did not realize I was a sinner. But now you make me know I am the sinner, the dead. I will follow you, Elijah."

As a believer, we think we are saved and born again at the initial stage of faith, when we hear the Word. However, as time goes by, we will feel empty even if we follow Jesus, and the questions will ceaselessly arise in our mind. "Is the faith that I have the correct one? Am I born again and saved, really?"

At the end of the day, we will painfully realize by the Word of Jesus that our faith we have had in the past is nothing but the legalistic faith we created, not true faith given by Jesus. This is the time that our son is dead, whom we thought alive all along. In reality, this son was born dead, because we gave birth to him by the doctrine of men before we met Jesus. However, we insisted we were alive, out of ignorance; but now we must accept that he is dead.

Elijah had been staying with the widow even before her son died. But, at that time, she could not see him as he was. This means that only at the death of her son she met the real living Elijah. In our case, we are meeting one Jesus, though He appears as two in our eyes; Jesus who is revealed to us before true repentance, and the Jesus who is revealed after true repentance. Of course, the latter is the real Jesus who will give us new life.

Do not wait until you would truly repent to meet Jesus. The day will never come. Jesus is already in front of you now, and it is your decision whether to follow Him, forsaking all else, or not. If you do, you are the believer who truly repented, and you will receive true life.

📂 What Have I to Do With You

"What have I to do with you, O you man of God?" she said. In fact, she said three things here:

"What have I to do with you, O you man of God?"
"Are you come to me to call my sin to remembrance?"
"Slay my son."

These are three aspects of her meeting the real Elijah. She does not demand an explanation from Elijah. But she laments that she believed in Jesus in her own way; in reality, having no part in Him. Her saying exactly matches the confession of the demon-possessed man in the country of the Gadarenes: "What have I to do with you, Jesus, you Son of God most high?" (Luke 8:28).

The believer who is yet under the law will have nothing to do with Jesus, although he comes to church and does various activities in His name. The widow's saying can be summed up this way: "I have believed in you on my own, having nothing to do with you. So I'm still in my sin and you made me find myself dead. Help me out, Lord!" This confession will come out of our mouths when we truly repent, which is the gateway to meet Jesus.

Three Progressive Stages of Life to Revive the Dead

"And he stretched himself on the child three times" (v. 21).

The widow tried to take measures on her own when her son felt sick, but there was nothing much she could do because her son was already died. So she inevitably committed him to Elijah's care. And Elijah revived the son.

So are we. When we have not yet understood who we are, we work very hard to revive our sick faith. We worship, serve tables, help the poor, do Bible study, and go to the prayer house and fast in our own way. However, we will give up when we realize that such endeavors do not work anymore. At this point, we will see Jesus in a different way: not as Jesus in our thoughts only, but as "a man Jesus." Then, we will follow Jesus and leave everything to His control as the disciples did. To what end? To the cross and resurrection.

🗁 Stretch of Three Times

The son is given to Elijah, and now the ball is in Elijah's court.

Elijah did not revive him by exercising a miracle, but rather by the strange motion of stretching three times upon the child. I do not think that this motion itself has reviving power, but it is a sign to reveal the truth. What does this strange motion that brings life back signify, then? It signifies that Jesus raises the dead by the Word in three progressive stages.

Read the following passage.

> Truly, truly, I say to you, The hour is coming, and now is, when the dead shall hear the voice of the Son of God: and they that hear shall live. _____ John 5:25

In the text, Jesus makes the dead live by proclaiming the Word, the voice of the Son of God. Elijah, being the figure of Jesus, makes the dead son alive by this motion. We can understand that the motion refers to the life-giving process of the Word.

How? The stretching three times signifies the three progressive stages of the Father, Son, and the Holy Spirit for us to undergo in order to receive new life of Jesus. At the stage of the Holy Spirit we are receiving eternal life. We also have discussed this three-stage process in Part One of this book; that is, communication stages of God-Jesus-Holy Spirit, if you recall.

The first stage is the Father, a preparatory process under the law, in which we are to be used up enough to follow Jesus, forsaking all. This is how God draws us to Jesus. Read John 6:44: "No man can come to me, except the Father who has sent me draw him: and I will raise him up at the last day."

The second stage is the Son, our healing process by Jesus, during which we follow Jesus to the cross to crucify our old self. This is what is said in Romans 6:5a, "We have been planted together in the likeness of his death." Our sinful old self dies at this moment.

The last stage is the Holy Spirit, a state in which our old self is destroyed and we are resurrected with Christ in us. This is what is said in Romans 6:5b, "We are also in the likeness of his resurrection." At this stage, we are resurrected with new life. The dead man is raised up.

When we have passed through these stages, led by and united with Jesus the Word, we will give birth to a son who is our eternal life. Having this son, therefore, is the evidence that we, the dead, have revived.

The three progressive stages to give life are also found in this passage of Matthew.

> Go you therefore, and teach all nations, baptizing them in the name of the Father, and of the Son, and of the Holy Spirit:
> _____ Matthew 28:19

This passage is frequently called the Great Commission of Jesus. When the disciples are about to receive this commandment from Him, they are already healed by Him during the three and a half years of Jesus' ministry on earth, and have received new life after Jesus' death and resurrection.

At this point, what kind of Great Commission do you think He will give to the disciples? Jesus will tell them to revive all the people with the Word, just as He did to them. Therefore, the Great Commission means, "Make disciples of all nations, letting them perfectly undergo the three progressive stages of life that will raise the dead, as I did to you."

That is, Jesus baptized His disciples in the name of the Father, and of the Son, and of the Holy Spirit. As a result, they are raised up to new life. And now Jesus asks His disciples to do the same for others, because they are also among the living. Elijah baptized this dead child in the name of the Father, the Son, and the Holy Spirit, and revived him.

Elijah prayed God that "This child's soul comes into him again." And God heard the voice of Elijah; and the soul of the child came into him again, and he revived. God will hear you also when you take necessary steps to revive your child, and pray. Then your child will surely revive. Only when your child revives, can you make the child of your neighbor revive in the same way.

What is more, if you think a little bit further, these three stages are actually one; that is, the Stage of the Son. Because the stages are life-growing processes, when you are at the Stage of the Father, you will not know that you are going onto the Son's stage next. Only when you face the Son, "a man Jesus," in your life, that through Him, you will realize you were in the Father's stage until then, and now, you are in the Stage of the Son.

And at the Stage of the Son, when you are healed by the Son, finally, on the cross, and by the resurrection of the Son in you, you are in the Stage of the Holy Spirit, completing the Stage of the Son. Therefore, the beginning of the Stage of the Son is that of the Father and the end is that of the Holy Spirit. In this way, the three stages are virtually one, which is the Stage of the Son.

This is something like *past, present* and *future* meeting together as one in *present*.

The Word of GOD Is Truth

Elijah delivered the son who lived to the woman, and she said, "Now I know that you are a man of God, and that the word of the LORD in your mouth is truth (v. 24)."

The Word of truth revives dead men. Elijah revived the dead child with the Word. This proves that Elijah had the true Word of God and he preached it to the widow. If he had faith under the law, he should have failed to revive the widow's son.

Nevertheless, even if Elijah preaches the true Word of God, when it is heard by those who did not repent truly, the Word of God will be transformed in their hearts as the moral codes of men, the law. In this case, the hearer cannot revive even though Elijah preaches the Word of truth to him.

We can see this case in Hosea 1. God said Hosea the prophet, "Go, take to yourself an adulterous wife and children of unfaithfulness," so he did and had children of unfaithfulness. Hosea, as a man of God, had good seed, the truth, but when it was received by his adulterous wife, his good seed was transformed into the corruptible seed in her. Accordingly, she produced children of unfaithfulness.

In the case of the widow, her time to hear the Word of life had come because she found her son dead. And she could repent and obey the Word of God given through Elijah, and her son revived.

Therefore, in order for the Word that gives life to work, two things must be satisfied: First, the preacher must have the Word of God that is truth, and second, the time for the hearer must be ready and ripe by true repentance. Only then will life transfer between the preacher and the hearer. In this instance, the hearer will live and confess saying, "Now I know that you are a man of God, and that the word of the LORD in your mouth is truth," as the widow said.

Elijah is the man who has the life-giving Word of God. He is a shadow/figure of Jesus and those who have the Christ gene, and they are the men of power who can revive the dead through the three stages of life.

🗁 Distinguishing the Words

The Word of truth revives the dead. And it will be known by its fruits. Many people say they have the truth, the Word, but it will be known only when the dead man, having heard the Word, has revived. Accordingly, the dead man himself who heard the Word and lived can only identify whether the Word is truth. This widow confesses through her experience that the word of Elijah is truth.

However, here are three main characteristics of the Word of truth compared to the law, which we all will agree to when we are revived and saved.

First, the Word of truth makes sense. The Word that is truth has sound logic and testifies by itself to its rightness. On the contrary, the law, which is the doctrine of men, the misinterpretation of the Word of God, has many blind points because it has forcibly combined the contents of the Scriptures together. For example, the Word of truth allows the hearers to enter the kingdom of God actually during their lifetime, which is quite reasonable and sensible, but the law delays the kingdom until after death. Same goes with the understanding about the resurrection and second coming. And the law teaches us that our sins are forgiven by Jesus once-and-for-all, but one the other hand, the law teaches us to repent of our sins repetitively until death, which implies the imperfect forgiveness of sins

When we are taught by the law, we will always have questions such as, "Will this sort of belief about Jesus be all?" "I'll have emptiness as usual even if I follow Jesus." "Nobody has given me sufficient and reasonable answers to my questions about faith."

Carry on! Think deep and long, and you we will have the chance to see the true Word.

Second, the Word of truth requires us to communicate with God. Jesus, the Word of truth, has two aspects; one, a man, and the other, Holy Spirit. Therefore, in order to know Him fairly we should communicate spiritually with Him in our mind. For this reason, if you meet Jesus, He will require you to have communication with God, as this book started with the importance of such.

In fact, the salvation given by the Word is to be one with God, the Spirit. How can we get to the truth without communicating with God at all? Check whether the Word that you currently hear teaches you to have spiritual communication with God.

Third, the word of truth heals us inside. The truth will heal us until Christ is formed in us; compared to the law, which curbs our deeds shown outside. A man healing himself is far from correcting his deeds because his deeds are the output of what is inside of his heart. Therefore, to correct our deeds, we must correct our insides, the spirit, to form Christ, and then our deeds will be automatically corrected to be of Christ (Matthew 23:25-26).

Now you can think about whether the Word you heard is used to control your deeds or to disclose your inside and heal you. The word that heals you is the truth, which will come to you from one who has the Word in him.

Epilogue

When we die we have to leave everything behind that we have possessed in this world, such as family, fortune, fame, and even life. However, there is one thing that we can take along, and that is eternal life. The eternal life Jesus gives us will be all that we should pursue during our lifetime on earth.

Now is the time for us to meet Jesus, the Word. And we ought to entirely leave the dead son to His hand so that we may receive the eternal life at the final stretching of Jesus.

Have your *beloved* son revived!

6

THE RESURRECTION

WHAT IS RESURRECTION?

I have explained about the "communication between God and us" in Part One and the "identity of the devil" which blocks the communication in Part Two. Here, in Part Three, so far we learned about "Jesus, the Word" who gives us life.

Now we have reached the topic of resurrection, which is the final subject of this book. We who are devil-possessed and have no communion with God will be freed from the devil through the healing of Jesus. When we are freed, Christ will come into us and we will then have perfect communication with God, becoming one with Him. This is the resurrection of the dead.

You may be disappointed to hear that the spectacular resurrection of the last day in your thoughts is different from what I explained. However, this resurrection is the truth which will make you a righteous man with eternal life; and it must be something that is beyond the universal spectacular show you may have been taught. Above all, this resurrection is what the Scripture says, and is not my personal view. You will agree with me as we go on.

Resurrection

Resurrection is *anastasis* in Greek, and it means that the dead man comes to have a new life and revives. The resurrection mentioned in the Scripture can be classified in three types as follows: resurrection in the past, resurrection in the future, and resurrection in the present.

Let us consider the resurrections mentioned one by one.

First, the resurrection in the past; the resurrection of Jesus in history.

After the crucifixion of Jesus, the chief priests remembered that Jesus said He would rise again after three days, and they set a guard for the sepulcher. However, He resurrected and nobody could find His dead body. The resurrection of Jesus actually did happen.

However, it is not easy for men to understand and accept His resurrection according to reason. In order to explain His resurrection, some people suggest many easily understandable hypotheses, such as He fainted on the cross temporarily. Nevertheless, He came to earth some two thousand years ago, was crucified, buried, and resurrected. This is the resurrection of Jesus that actually happened in the past.

This resurrection gives us a great meaning that there *is* resurrection. By His resurrection, the uncharted path of resurrection is known and opened to us. We can also be resurrected together with Him because He went before us to open the way. This resurrection serves as the prototype of the "resurrection in the present" to come to me.

Second, the resurrection in the future; that is, in our thoughts which might occur afterlife.

Regarding the resurrection after death, what we traditionally think is this: when we are dead, we do not directly go to the kingdom of heaven or to hell but wait for the last judgment, staying in paradise or *Hades*. When the time of the final judgment of the great white throne comes, the dead will be resurrected and receive new bodies respectively. At that time, many bodies sleeping in the graves will be raised, the sea will give up the dead who are in it, death and *Hades* will deliver up the dead who are in them, and they will be judged according to their works (Revelation 20:13), or something similar depending upon the church denominations.

Some believers have distaste for cremation because they worry that they will be in trouble at the time of resurrection if their bodies are already burned away. They will be relieved to know that they do not have to worry because God Almighty will give them new bodies.

It is your choice to believe that way, but Jesus has not come to teach and give us the resurrection in that manner. This will be manifested clearly by the dialogue between Jesus and Martha in John 11, in which Martha talks about the resurrection of last day, but He mentions the resurrection of the here and now.

To touch briefly on the final judgment, those who failed to undergo the judgment of the great white throne, which is the cross, *with Jesus* in their lifetime, they are to face the same judgment alone *without Jesus* at the time they die. That judgment without Jesus means that they will face eternal death. Therefore, it will be wise for us to go through the final judgment on the cross with Jesus and resurrection with Him in our lifetime.

Third, the resurrection in the present; that is, here and now.

We are very familiar with the previous two kinds of resurrection, but we have practically no understanding of the present resurrection given here. The resurrection of the present is the true resurrection of which the Scripture testifies. That is, when we meet Jesus the Word, our old self is crucified in unity with Him for the judgment of our sin and we will be resurrected in unity with Him into the kingdom of God with a new life.

It is neither the resurrection that happened long time ago, nor it is the resurrection to come after we are dead. But it is the resurrection of the here and now in this world that we are to desire. Jesus has come to us to give this resurrection to us in the present.

I Am the Resurrection and the Life

John 11:21-27

Then said Martha to Jesus, Lord, if you had been here, my brother had not died. ²²But I know, that even now, whatever you will ask of God, God will give it you. ²³Jesus said to her, Your brother shall rise again. ²⁴Martha said to him, I know that he shall rise again in the resurrection at the last day. ²⁵Jesus said to her, I am the resurrection, and the life: he that believes in me, though he were dead, yet shall he live: ²⁶And whoever lives and believes in me shall never die. Believe you this? ²⁷She said to him, Yes, Lord: I believe that you are the Christ, the Son of God, which should come into the world.

They who were dead will have new life when they meet Jesus Christ and they are the ones who are resurrected. The resurrection is, in other words, being born again and receiving salvation. Therefore, in Jesus, we have to have the resurrection in the present.

However, our adversary, the devil in me, is very resourceful as a serpent and he delays all the good things Jesus will give us until we meet our earthly death. For example, he whispers to us that the kingdom of God can be ours only after our physical death; he makes us believe we must constantly be forgiven for our sins, and we can be perfect and holy only after death; he makes us think that a resurrection is coming only after our physical death. By this great deception, all the glory and blessings that Jesus wants to give us now are delayed until death.

Under this circumstance, what glory, what blessing, can we have during this lifetime? No glory. No blessing, ever. Therefore, our life is empty and sinful even if we follow Jesus. It really is a horrible deception which rescinds the whole salvation of Jesus. If we are deceived and agree to these doctrines, we will die in sin. And in such a case, even after death, we will have no glory, no salvation, and no eternal life. All these problems happen because we are deceived by the devil in us, our adversary.

Read the following passage from the book of Matthew.

> Agree with your adversary quickly, whiles you are in the way with him; lest at any time the adversary deliver you to the judge, and the judge deliver you to the officer, and you be cast into prison. _____ Matthew 5:25

Jesus clearly states that we have to solve the problem of sin/adversary in our lifetime. Otherwise, when we face the Judge upon death, we will be delivered to the officer and we will be cast into prison. From what Jesus says, there will be no time for us to make excuses or justify ourselves in front of the Judge upon death. And it is quite clear that we must receive all that God promised us in Jesus, which is actually one, the salvation in our lifetime. Otherwise, we will not be found among the saved and resurrected even after death.

Regarding the background of the main text, while staying at a place beyond Jordan with the disciples, Jesus was told that Lazarus was sick, but He stayed there two more days on purpose rather than directly going to see him immediately. Then, after two days, He went into Judaea and found Lazarus was already dead and had been in the grave four days.

The cited passage shows the dialogue between Jesus and Martha, the sister of Lazarus. It may not look clear outwardly, but in terms of "rising again," the resurrection, Jesus is of a very much different understanding than that of Martha. Now I will explain what the resurrection Jesus discusses truly means.

Your Brother Shall Rise Again

"Lord, if you had been here, my brother had not died. But I know, that even now, whatever you will ask of God, God will give it you" (v. 21-22). Judging from her saying, it seems that Martha trusted the power of Jesus and believed that He could restore those who are dead, including Lazarus. But this fancy confession is in thought only; in reality, she never believed that the dead will rise in the name of Jesus. This will be clear when we scrutinize the dialogue.

Jesus tells her that her brother will rise again now; however, she cannot even think about it, but believes that He will resurrect her brother in the far future, after the physical death. Even if she confesses that Jesus is Almighty and knows the resurrection, in reality she does not know what it is.

Martha thinks of the resurrection at the last day, but Jesus says that the resurrection is the present, which will be shown by the immediate resurrection of Lazarus. And through this sign, Jesus wants to reveal to us that He raises up those who are dead spiritually here and now.

Martha represents each of us, the believers. We also have the same faith as Martha to confess that Jesus is Almighty. And when it comes to the resurrection, we do not even think that it will happen now and here, but we think vaguely that it will be at a certain time in the last days. We may say, "Even if I have no knowledge of the resurrection of the present, I know what the salvation and being born again are, basically." Unfortunately, however, the resurrection is salvation and being born again. Therefore, in case we do not know the resurrection of the present, we cannot either be saved or be born again.

Having found that Martha failed to understand His Word, Jesus says it again.

I Am the Resurrection and the Life

Jesus says that He is the resurrection and the life.

Jesus said to her, I am the resurrection, and the life: he that believes in me, though he were dead, yet shall he live: ²⁶And whoever lives and believes in me shall never die. Believe you this? _____John 11:25-26

With this saying, He does not mean to show off His power and greatness. He says that since He is the resurrection and the life itself, therefore, whomever He is with will have the resurrection and the life.

At this very moment, He stands before her. By this scene He explains that "her being with Jesus" is her resurrection and life. Of course, this "being with Jesus" means that period when Jesus comes into her as the Holy Spirit, after healing her on the cross.

In the same way, before us, the readers, stands the Word, Jesus, who is the resurrection and the life. This scene with Lazarus reveals that we will be one with the Word, having the resurrection and the life, when we hear and follow the Word to the cross.

The *resurrection* and the *life* are connected as one. We will have it after destroying our old self on the cross and we are resurrected. When we are resurrected, we will have eternal life. More explanation follows.

Jesus continues to discuss this concept with Martha.

📂 He that Believes In Me, Though He Was Dead

After saying that Jesus is the "resurrection and the life," He explains to Martha about the resurrection part, which gives new life to the dead.

"He who believes in me, though he was dead, yet shall he live," Jesus says.

We have heard this verse many times and we all might have learned it by heart. However, it is not easy to catch the true intended meaning. A common interpretation is, "If you believe in Me, you shall live (in heaven) when you die," which will mostly fit our current doctrines.

However, Jesus came to make the dead spiritually alive within their lifetime. He says that "the dead are raised" through His works during His public life (Luke 7:22). This means that the dead are raised and given eternal life within their lifetime if they believe in Jesus. For example, He made His disciples, the dead, alive, by giving His eternal life at the time of Pentecost. Therefore, what Jesus means here is if you believe in Him, even though you were dead already, you will receive eternal life during your life on earth.

Then, what is the meaning of "believe in Him"?

To believe in Jesus does not only mean that you trust and rely on Him. But the weightier, true meaning is "to be one with Jesus." You will be one with Jesus when your old self dies on the cross and you are resurrected, united with Him (Romans 6:8). In this instance, Jesus will come into you as the Holy Spirit and, thus you will be one with Him. Now you believe in Him in the real sense, having the faith of Jesus. You who were dead before, now live.

📁 Whosoever Lives Shall Never Die

"Whosoever lives and believes in me shall never die," Jesus continues to say about the "life" part. Please be careful that this also does not mean we will go to the everlasting world after we die if we diligently believe in Him during our lifetime.

In this instance, "lives" means the eternal life we will get after going to the cross with Jesus. Also, he who has this life is proven to be the man who believes in Him.

Therefore, "He that believes in me, though he was dead, yet shall he live: And whosoever lives and believes in me shall never die" (v. 24b-25a) can be paraphrased as follows:

"He who believes in Jesus will have (eternal) life in his lifetime even though he was dead spiritually (this is the 'resurrection' aspect of Jesus), and he who has (eternal) life through believing in Him, his life shall be eternal (this is the 'life' aspect of Jesus)."

Do not be confused! The terms "dead" and "die" appearing in the said verses refer to those spiritually dead, not naturally dead.

When Jesus raises the dead, the process of the resurrection and the life shall be manifested in order. First is the resurrection which makes the dead live; second is the life which is eternal. These two, the resurrection and the life eternal, are actually one. When we are resurrected, united with Jesus, we will have eternal life simultaneously with the resurrection.

The following illustration might help us understand what I am trying to say about the "resurrection and the life."

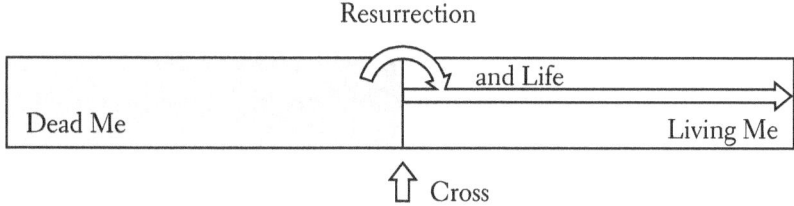

This relationship will be mentioned again when we discuss the "Rapture" later in this book.

Most importantly of all, try to meet the Word, Jesus, who will give you the resurrection and the life by becoming one with you, if you follow Him to the cross.

"Believe you this?" Jesus says to Martha. By this question, Jesus asks whether she understands that faith comes through the process of the resurrection and the life, and whether she has it fulfilled in her.

Yes, Lord

Martha answers as in verse 27 below.

She said to him, Yes, Lord: I believe that you are the Christ, the Son of God, which should come into the world. _____ John 11:27

She responds to Him by saying, "Yes, Lord. I believe that you are the Christ, the Son of God, which should come into the world." When we read her answer, it seems that she believes His word that He will now make her brother rise again, but, in fact, she does not. This will be evident from verse 39, that when He told them to take away the stone, she said to him that he stank—his body was rotting—

for he had been dead four days. She never expected, even in her dreams, that her brother could still live.

She is lifting Jesus high by saying that He is the Savior, the Son of God, and the resurrection-giver, but yet fails to understand the resurrection of the here and now that He really wants to give her. We can find, therefore, that she believes in the Jesus who is different from the real Jesus. She believes haphazardly and only in her own thoughts.

If Jesus asks us, "Do you believe this?" we will obviously say, "Yes Lord." In addition, we have prepared the Apostle's Creed and recite it every Sunday at church, saying, "I believe in Jesus Christ who is the Son of God…" And we will have no hesitation in confessing Jesus as the Christ, the Son of God.

However, what are we substantially expecting from Him when we confess our belief in Him? Maybe our expectation will include entering the kingdom of heaven after death, and the resurrection after death, and full forgiveness after death, and holiness after death, etc. Or we will hope to make much money to build churches, or the power to heal the sick, or people to gather more members of the church, or donations for the sake of Jesus' name, and many other good works we may think of in this world. However, we are missing one thing, which is weightier than all of those: our resurrection here and now, which He wishes to give us.

Actually, Jesus wishes to give us Himself, which is the resurrection and the life, by taking our old self to the cross. However, being deceived by our old self, we pervert His word in the Scriptures and make excuses not to follow Him. What do you think you will get when you choose not to follow Him? Nothing but the death.

What we wish does not match what He wishes to give us. We talk about one thing while He speaks to us about another, and we have difficulty grasping His intention. We can easily guess that He will not feel easy about us. Therefore, if we meet "a man Jesus," we have to expect from Him rebuke for our "imaginary faith" rather than consolation.

Have you met "Jesus Christ, a man," by the way? Heed the spiritual meaning that is revealed by this book. It will tell you the correct way you should go as a believer.

I will now explain additionally two other issues, "Tears of Jesus" and the "Meaning of the Resurrection of Lazarus," because their streams are connected to the text.

Tears of Jesus

Jesus repeatedly told Martha of the resurrection of the present time, but she could not understand it.
Read the following passage.

> When Jesus therefore saw her weeping, and the Jews also weeping which came with her, he groaned in the spirit, and was troubled. [34]And said, Where have you laid him? They said to him, Lord, come and see. [35]Jesus wept. [36]Then said the Jews, Behold how he loved him! [37]And some of them said, Could not this man, which opened the eyes of the blind, have caused that even this man should not have died? [38]Jesus therefore again groaning in himself comes to the grave. It was a cave, and a stone lay on it.
> _____ John 11:33-38

Mary, the sister of Martha, came to Him and wept, saying "If you had been here, my brother would not have died." The Jews, having come with her, also wept. Jesus wept (v. 35).

We can superficially conclude that Jesus wept for the death of Lazarus together with them. However, in consideration of the fact that He waited for his death by delaying two days on purpose when He was notified of his sickness (John 11:6-16), it will be inappropriate to say that He wept because of the death of Lazarus.

Why did Jesus weep, then? It was because the believers trusted His power and followed Him to experience the miracles, but took no interest in their resurrection at the present time that He longed to give them. Due to their attitude, He groaned in the Spirit and was troubled (v. 33), so He wept.

This will become clearer if we read the verse in which some Jews said, "Could not this man, which opened the eyes of the blind, have caused that even this man should not have died" (v. 37)? As they said

I Thank God through Jesus Christ 289

so, "Jesus again groaned in Himself" (v. 38). They also knew Him only as the hero who raised dead bodies, and they judged Him when He fell short of their expectations.

This is the faith of the devil. You will recall that, in the earlier chapter of Part Two, we discussed Jesus who was tempted by the devil. At that time the devil suggested to Jesus to make people accept a miracle-based faith, but Jesus said that doing so was to tempt God. In this case, the people expected a miracle-based faith in Jesus. Seeing this, He groans and He weeps.

Here are questions for you regarding Him.

"Do you know Him as He is, who will take you to the cross for the resurrection, so you obey Him?" And

"Are you mistaken in Him as simply a miracle-doer, and make Him groan?"

The Resurrection of Lazarus Who Had Been Dead Four Days

Jesus raised dead Lazarus from the grave. He did not mean to show His power to raise the dead, or to show His emotional love of Lazarus by this sign, but He wanted to reveal that spiritual resurrection occurs in the present.

In accordance with the signs, the dead Lazarus represents we who have died in sin. The number of days Lazarus was dead, four, signify the period of time during which God allows us to do as we wish until we become totally used up in the Stage of God. From that time on, God will lead us to the next stage of life.

Therefore, Lazarus who has been dead four days, represents us sinners who are dead and have believed in Jesus on our own way, and have become desolate and lost all hope in our self-guided life. Only at this stage will we be able put down our pride in front of God and will obey Him. Now, God can work in us through "a man Jesus."

The story of Lazarus who has been dead four days and rises again is symbolic of we, the hopeless sinners, who will be resurrected by the Word in our lifetime now.

Epilogue

Martha and Jesus were on different pages during the dialogue from beginning to end. Martha was taking Jesus' saying with fleshly mind while Jesus was speaking spiritually.

Martha is us. As Martha could never dream that her brother would be resurrected in this world, we also cannot understand that we will be resurrected here and now. Even though we firmly believe in the past resurrection of Jesus and also believe in resurrection after death without fail, all our belief is empty and void if we fail to achieve our own resurrection now.

We should not waste our lives any longer by listening to the deception of the devil. Now, we ought to meet the Word, "a man Jesus" and be united with His death on the cross and rise again. We will then never die.

Have this life by any means!

Rapture
– Those Who Are Asleep and Those Who Are Alive

1 Thessalonians 4:13-18

But I would not have you to be ignorant, brothers, concerning them which are asleep, that you sorrow not, even as others which have no hope. ¹⁴For if we believe that Jesus died and rose again, even so them also which sleep in Jesus will God bring with him. ¹⁵For this we say to you by the word of the Lord, that we which are alive and remain unto the coming of the Lord shall not prevent them which are asleep. ¹⁶For the Lord himself shall descend from heaven with a shout, with the voice of the archangel, and with the trump of God: and the dead in Christ shall rise first: ¹⁷Then we which are alive and remain shall be caught up together with them in the clouds, to meet the Lord in the air: and so shall we ever be with the Lord. ¹⁸Therefore comfort one another with these words.

This text is frequently used as the source for paintings about the rapture. We can see from their pictures that Jesus in a brilliant aura descends from the clouds in the air with a multitude of the heavenly host, and people on earth are caught up. Painters must have followed sincerely this passage of 1 Thessalonians.

Some preachers say that this world will be in utter confusion since, at the rapture, drivers will be caught up into heaven while driving, and there shall two be in the field; the one shall be taken, and the other left.

Not too long ago in Korea, certain group of people predicted the date of the rapture and gathered in a place and prayed fervently on the day. Some of them sold their entire property, as it would be useless in heaven. However, at midnight on the day, nothing had happened. The believers came out of that place very disappointed, feeling small.

They all were mistaken about the biblical rapture. The rapture the Scripture speaks of is a spiritual event, not a natural one. Famous books of the commentaries and exegeses about this passage say something like this. It may be the final fruits of current Christian theology that has been developed by the brilliant scholars and theologians for more than 2,000 years. However, their understanding is not much different in substance from that of the people above. That is, they also consider a natural rapture. However, they wisely do not specify the date, but say the time will come in the near future. Some say that Paul the apostle also waited for that sort of rapture, but no such rapture happened during past 2,000 years. What is more, Paul never expected that type of natural rapture.

They all are in the wrong from the beginning as they think the venue of this spectacular event will be somewhere in the universe. But it is a spiritual event which will occur inside of us, the spirit.

I prophesy in the word of God that there will be no such natural rapture. I bet, not because I have prophetic eyes, but because it is not the way Jesus comes, according to the truth. Jesus is already with *me* now to raise *me* up through the cross to His kingdom in heaven. Then why should I need to look up the sky for Jesus to come?

Now I will share the insights that I have from the Lord about this difficult passage. The truth is this: The rapture does not indicate physical levitation but it means that we who are terrestrial are changed into celestial and ascend into heaven spiritually. The rapture is another expression of the resurrection, because we who were *dead* are lifted up into the kingdom of God of the *living*. This is the rapture this passage speaks about.

Paul says that the dead have the hope to rise again through Jesus. When the dead rise, the old *me* is raised first, and thus the renewed *me* will have eternal life and will be with the Lord forever. Jesus will give the believers life in this way, so encourage each other to be made partakers of Christ, by holding the beginning of our confidence steadfast to the end (Hebrews 3:14).

In the text, verses 13 and 14 talk about the hope of resurrection of them who are asleep; verses 15 through 17 explain it in further detail; and verse 18 tells us to comfort one another.

Let us go in further.

Those Who Are Asleep Will Rise Again

> But I would not have you to be ignorant, brothers, concerning them which are asleep, that you sorrow not, even as others which have no hope. ¹⁴For if we believe that Jesus died and rose again, even so them also which sleep in Jesus will God bring with him. _____ 1 Thessalonians 4:13-14

We generally think of "them which are asleep" as believers who are dead physiologically, and we thus conclude that a church member in Thessalonica died. So we receive this passage as a soothing message that we should not grieve at the believers' death because Jesus will surely bring them at His second coming. We have experienced the comfort this word gives when we have lost a person whom we loved. This is what we get through the literal understanding of the passage. It never can be bad.

However, if we stop at this surface meaning, we are missing the weightier meaning. The Scripture tells us there is spiritual salvation and resurrection. If we miss them in the Scripture, we will miss our salvation and resurrection as well.

📂 Those Who Are Asleep and Their Hope

"They which are asleep" indicates they who are dead spiritually. In the Scripture, the "dead man" is described as either "he sleeps" or "he is dead," but especially as "he sleeps" when he is believed to revive.

In Matthew, when the daughter of the ruler of the synagogue is dead, Jesus says, "The maid is not dead, but sleeps."

Read the following passage.

> And when Jesus came into the ruler's house, and saw the minstrels and the people making a noise, ²⁴He said to them, Give place: for the maid is not dead, but sleeps. And they laughed him to scorn. _____ Matthew 9:23-24

And in John, when Lazarus died, Jesus speaks that he is not dead, but sleeps.

Read the following passage.

> These things said he: and after that he said unto them, Our friend Lazarus sleeps; but I go, that I may awake him out of sleep. ¹²Then said his disciples, Lord, if he sleep, he shall do well. _____ John 11:11-12

Both the young maid and Lazarus were dead, and all the mourners sorrowed without hope. Jesus could have said that she or he was dead, but He intentionally said "she sleeps" and "he sleeps" because He knew the person would live again now. Jesus wished to reveal to those who mourned that, by raising the physically dead, those who are dead spiritually will be raised up now through Jesus. In other words, the *picture* of rising up of the dead by Jesus signifies that sinners will be resurrected as new men through Jesus.

Paul describes the afore-mentioned picture in detail in the text. All his saying here is spiritual. The scene is such that those who are asleep are resurrected through Jesus here and now, which is known as the rapture.

They who are asleep are sinners and are doomed to death. Therefore, those who realize that they are sinners cannot help sighing out as follows:

"Even if I follow Jesus I feel emptiness and futility in my life, and am not satisfied." Or "No matter how hard I try to do good things, I just can't make it. Will I ever be able to be properly saved?"

Paul comforts those who believe in Jesus by telling them not to despair, because we surely have the hope to solve the problem, unlike non-believers who have no hope. That is, Paul, being those who are alive and remain, comforts the believers who sorrow during the process of following Jesus to the cross.

📂 *You, They* and *We*

To understand the text, we should first know who "you who sorrow," "they which are asleep" and "we which are alive and remain" designate. They all mean one identical life that is growing in Jesus, but with different names, stage by stage. One may still be "dead" (e.g., the child as in 1 John 2), another may be "dead in Christ" (the young man), which I will explain later, and the other may be "resurrected" already (the father) as Paul who is alive and remains.

In this passage, when Paul speaks about the dead/asleep, he calls them "you" or "they," differentiating them from himself. However, at the same time, Paul considers them as himself, even though they are dead and he is alive. It is because they also have the same life as Paul, which is growing in Jesus. Paul once was dead like them, and they will also become like Paul eventually someday as they, including Paul, are all in the course of the same life of Jesus. Therefore, he calls them "we" in verse 14.

Therefore, "you," "they," and "we" in this passage will represent each growth stage of life; the same life of Jesus. It can be "me" or anyone who is in the course of growing in the life of Jesus. "I" will grow in the life of Jesus as follows progressively; "me" who is dead → "me" who is dead on the cross → "me" who is alive.

This will be revealed more clearly as we go further along. We should not be confined in its literality.

📂 The Meaning of "Though Jesus Will God Bring"

"For if we believe that Jesus died and rose again, even so them also which sleep, in (through) Jesus will God bring with him," reads verse 14. This statement is not about the upcoming event in the sky, but the spiritual resurrection/salvation now. Do not look at the sky to find this scene.

Paul says, as we believe that Jesus died and rose again, in the likely manner, we "who sleep (the *dead*)" "in Jesus God will bring with Him (*rise again*)."

The death and rising again of Jesus become ours when we meet and follow Jesus to the cross. When He dies on the cross, our old self who is united with Him will also die. This is "death of death" in our case. Then Jesus will rise again as the Holy Spirit in us and, thus, we also rise again. The death and rising again of Jesus will be ours too, if we follow Him correctly. Jesus comes to the dead to give them eternal life in this way.

In the text, take note that it should *not* read "which sleep in Jesus, will God bring..." but "which sleep, in (through; *dia* in Greek) Jesus will God bring..."

"Through Jesus will God bring with Him" means that God will have our old self destroyed on the cross through Jesus, (which is "the dead in Christ" as in verse 16,) and will let us receive the Holy Spirit, by which we become one with God and Jesus so wherever God goes He will bring us along automatically.

Verses 13 and 14 can be summarized as follows:

"We who are spiritually dead do not need to sorrow (verse 13), because as we believe, through Jesus, God will raise us up and make us abide in God and Jesus always (verse.14).

In order to understand the remaining verses properly, it is essential to know the structure of this passage. In fact, verse 14, especially verse 14a, "Jesus died and rose again," serves as the foundation on which all ideas of the remaining verses sit.

The verses can be divided according to dead and life as follows:

13	But I would not have you to be ignorant, brothers, concerning them which are asleep, that you sorrow not, even as others which have no hope.	
	Dead	*Life*
14	For if we believe that Jesus **died**	and **rose again**,
	even so them also which **sleep**	in (through) Jesus will **God bring with him**.
15	For this we say to you by the word of the Lord,	
		that we which are **alive and remain unto the coming of the Lord** shall not prevent
	them which are **asleep**.	
16	For the Lord himself shall descend from heaven with a shout, with the voice of the archangel, and with the trump of God:	
	and **the dead in Christ**	shall rise first:
17		Then we which are **alive and remain** shall be caught up together with them in the clouds, to meet the Lord in the air: and so shall we ever **be with the Lord**.
18	Therefore comfort one another with these words.	

The words in the "dead" column will have the same meaning to describe the dead, that is, "died = sleep = asleep." Likewise, the words in the "life" column describe the born again man; that is, "rose again = God will bring with Him = alive and remain unto the coming of the Lord = alive and remain = be with the Lord."

Now I will explain verses 15 through 17 which enlarge what is mentioned in verse 14.

We Who are Alive and Remain unto the Coming of the Lord

Read verse 15 below.

> For this we say to you by the word of the Lord, that we which are alive and remain unto the coming of the Lord shall not prevent them which are asleep. _____ 1 Thessalonians 4:15

This verse 15 gives the reason why we should not be disappointed for being the dead. We all know that the current doctrine says "At the coming of Jesus the dead will rise first, then, the living will be caught up." Therefore, we may think in this sense Paul says that the living cannot precede the dead. However, if we understand it that way Paul would be very sad, because it is a great misunderstanding which was caused by taking the spiritual words as literal.

What will be the spiritual meaning, then? "We which are alive and remain" and "them which are asleep" means the same "me." They are "me born again" and "me before born again," respectively. What Paul says is that we should not be grieved for being the dead, because it should come first in our individual life according to the natural principle, and we will be alive if we follow Jesus to the cross. We who are living cannot precede those who are dead/asleep. This issue will be touched on a little bit later.

Who Are Alive and Remain Unto the Coming of the Lord

Now, I will explain why "we who are alive and remain unto the coming of the Lord" is supposed to mean "we who are born again." Here, to "be alive" (*zao* in Greek) means to "have a new life," and to "remain" (*perileipomai* in Greek) is to describe the attribute of the new life which lasts and remains forever. This new life is the "eternal life" that we get at our resurrection, united with Jesus, and it is the "life that never dies," as Jesus says in John 11:26, "And whoever lives and believes in me shall never die." Therefore, "we who are alive and remain" indicates "those who are resurrected unto eternal life."

And "we who are alive and remain unto the coming of the Lord" does *not* mean that "we who are alive in the natural world until the coming of the Lord in the sky." "His coming" (*parousia* in Greek) means the coming of the Holy Spirit into each of us, when our old self dies on the cross and we are resurrected. By this Holy Spirit, we will have eternal life, which is expressed here as "we are alive and remain." If the coming of the Lord, the Holy Spirit, does not occur in us, we cannot be "them who are alive and remain" because the Holy Spirit is the life itself which is alive and remains.

What is more, the word "unto" (*eis* in Greek) is translated into various terms in Scripture. In this case, it would have been better if it was translated as "at" or "by" which implies "time when" or "cause." Because we will come alive and remain "at" (rather than "unto") the coming of the Lord into us.

We can find such usage of *eis* in the Scripture. Matthew 12:41 reads, "The men of Nineveh shall rise in judgment with this generation, and shall condemn it: because they repented **"at"** (*eis*) the preaching of Jonas; and, behold, a greater than Jonas is here." They repented "by" the preaching of Jonas.

Therefore, "we who are alive and remain unto the coming of the Lord" can be re-written as "we who become alive and remain *at* (or *by*) the coming of the Lord."

The disciples show its true example. The Lord came into them as the Holy Spirit at Pentecost. At that time, they became those who were alive and remain *at* (rather than *unto*) the coming of the Lord, the Holy Spirit.

🗁 We Shall Not Prevent

Regarding "we shall not prevent them which are asleep," Paul says we who are alive and remain will not precede them who are asleep. Once again, "they who are asleep" and "we who are alive and remain" are not two different groups of people, but "me." "Me before born again" is the former, and "me after born again" is the latter. The latter cannot precede the former.

All mankind, without exception, is born to this world as the dead, the sinners. This is the providence of God to create the men following the image of Christ by being born again. Therefore, in our individual lives, we first have to go through the period of the dead, and afterwards, through Jesus, we will be reborn as new men according to the image of Christ. This re-birth is being born again (from flesh to spirit), sin-forgiveness (from the sinner to the righteous), salvation (from sinful world to the kingdom of God), resurrection (from the dead to the living) and rapture (from earth to heaven).

Paul the apostle mentions this order in 1 Corinthians:

> So also is the resurrection of the dead. It is sown in corruption; it is raised in incorruption: [43]It is sown in dishonor; it is raised in glory: it is sown in weakness; it is raised in power: [44]It is sown a natural body; it is raised a spiritual body. There is a natural body, and there is a spiritual body. [45]And so it is written, The first man Adam was made a living soul; the last Adam was made a quickening spirit. [46]However, that was not first which is spiritual, but that which is natural; and afterward that which is spiritual.　　　　1 Corinthians 15:42-46

The resurrection of the dead is a part of the process of life, therefore, the thing that is the last cannot come in advance of the first. For example, adulthood can never come before childhood. Therefore, Paul says, "We which are alive and remain unto the coming of the Lord shall not prevent them which are asleep."

In short, verse 15 explains in detail them who are mentioned in verse 14 as "them also through Jesus will God bring with him." They are "us who are alive and remain at the coming of the Lord." And they/we were asleep previously. Thus, Paul says "Sorrow not because we are dead as a process of life and sorrow not, because we will be resurrected through Jesus."

The Dead in Christ Shall Rise First

Read verses 16-17.

For the Lord himself shall descend from heaven with a shout,

> with the voice of the archangel, and with the trump of God: and the dead in Christ shall rise first: ¹⁷Then we which are alive and remain shall be caught up together with them in the clouds, to meet the Lord in the air: and so shall we ever be with the Lord.
> _____ 1 Thessalonians 4:16-17

Paul depicts in further detail the scene of the resurrection of the dead, so-called "the rapture." The text divides the moment of resurrection into two progressive stages. First, "the dead will rise" and second, "live forever." This order and two stages also are mentioned by Jesus in John 11:25, "I am the *resurrection* (first) and the *life* (next)" (emphases and parentheses mine.) To best remember the verse, you may wish to refer to the subject "I am the Resurrection and the Life."

"The Lord himself shall descend from heaven with a shout, with the voice of the archangel, and with the trump of God," reads verse 16. Refer to the following illustration as you read the explanation.

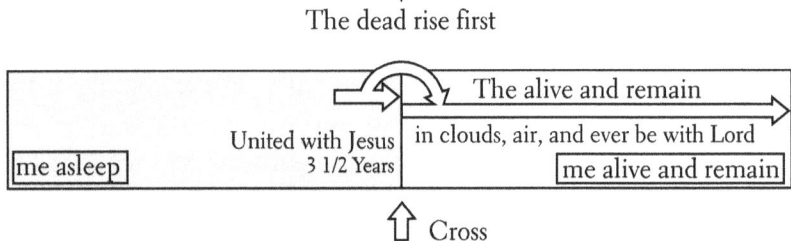

"Lord descends from heaven" means "we receive the Lord in us." This is because, at the moment we receive the Lord in us, our hearts become heaven where God abides. Therefore, "Lord descends from heaven" shall be achieved at the coming of the Lord into us. Yes, this is the scene when the Lord, the Holy Spirit, comes into our hearts at the time of our resurrection, as a result of our following Jesus.

He will descend with a shout, with the voice of the archangel, and with the trump of God. The Word, which is being imparted to us through the deep feeling in the heart, is likened to the shout, voice of archangel, Jesus, and trumpet of God.

As we hear the Word and follow, we will gradually be changed to fit the kingdom of God. That is, the Lord descends from heaven into us. This is the life-increasing process by the Word. While continually growing in this way, we will be resurrected with new life in a final instant. The Word of God in this instance is the last trumpet. At the last trump, the Lord will come into the heart of "them who sleep" completely; therefore, they will be changed (1Corinthians 15:51) to become "them which are alive and remain."

To speak about the case of Peter who is the model of those who are resurrected in their lifetime, he started this process from the time he first met Jesus and finished it at the cross/Pentecost, which took about three and a half years. However, the above description would particularly refer to the crucifixion and resurrection of Jesus. That is, while Peter denied Jesus three times before the cock crowed, he had to watch his beloved Lord Jesus crucified. And the Lord was descending into him as is signified by Jesus' breathing the Holy Spirit to Peter after the resurrection (John 20:22). At the reception of the Holy Spirit, Peter became a man who is alive and remains so.

📂 The Dead in Christ

Regarding "the dead in Christ shall rise first," who are the "dead in Christ?" This will be the key word to interpret this passage. They do not indicate those believers who died naturally before the universal coming of Jesus. To reiterate, the Scripture says resurrection and salvation will happen in our lifetime. Any interpretation of the Scripture that promises things only in the afterlife is simply a deception.

"The dead in Christ" refers to those who met Jesus and followed Him to the cross where their old self died. For this instance, Paul says, "I am crucified with Christ (Galatians 2:20)."

"The dead in Christ" are different from "those who sleep" as in verse 14. "Those who sleep" are dead, yet they need to follow Jesus further to the cross to become "the dead in Christ." And when they are grown to "the dead in Christ" on the cross, united with Jesus, they will resurrect immediately after such death.

Paul wants to say that we, the dead, should grow in Jesus to become "the dead in Christ" in order to be resurrected and to become those who are alive and remain. When we arrange those in the order of resurrection, which is the growing process of life, it will be as follows:

Those who sleep → The dead in Christ → Those who are alive and remain.

Actually, "the dead in Christ" is the case of the "dead" who "died" on the cross united with Jesus. This is the famous "second death," being the death of the death. Read the following passage from Revelation.

"And death and hell (*Hades* in Greek) were cast into the lake of fire. This is the second death" (Revelation 20:14).

The death and *Hades*, which is the place dead men inhabit, are finished by the death of our old self on the cross, and we will be resurrected in the world of eternal life where there is no more death and hell (*Hades*). Read the following passage.

"And God shall wipe away all tears from their eyes; and there shall be no more death, neither sorrow, nor crying, neither shall there be any more pain: for the former things are passed away" (Revelation 21:4).

This is to happen in our lifetime, if we believe correctly.

📂 Shall Be Caught Up Together

Regarding "we which are alive and remain shall be caught up together with them..." in verse 17, in here, "we" are not different people from "them." Both indicate one same person, each of us, in the life of Jesus. Therefore, "then we which are alive and remain shall be caught up together with them in the clouds..." shall mean "born again us" will be caught up (caught up because we have now been born again) together with "us which is not born again." Do not think it is a forced interpretation, and you will know why.

This expression is about the "being born again" point, where the earthly me is changed into heavenly me. At the time when the heavenly me is caught up, the earthly me will be included in it. From that time on, I will not be the earthly me, but the heavenly me ever, because the former is swallowed by the latter and remains inclusive.

For a better understanding, refer to the following epistle of Paul:

> For we that are in this tabernacle do groan, being burdened: not for that we would be unclothed, but clothed on, that mortality might be swallowed up of life. _____ 2 Corinthians 5:4

This verse speaks about the same scene. When we are resurrected to new life, we have the "days of life" at the present time as well as the "days of death" in the past. These days of life will swallow up the days of death in the past and remain inclusive.

This is also the relationship between the law and grace. Jesus said in this respect in Matthew 5:17, "Think not that I am come to destroy the law, or the prophets: I am not come to destroy, but to fulfill." When we are dead, we are under the law, but when we come alive by grace, the law is fulfilled in us who are alive.

Let me give you an illustration. When you graduate university, you enter society. At that particular point of graduation, the school student you will be swallowed up by the society man you. Thereafter, you will live as a society man, having the school student included in you. Being the society man upon graduation is the fulfillment of your school days.

In addition to the current text, we may wish to consider the following passages whereby Paul speaks about the resurrection.

Read the following passage.

> Behold, I show you a mystery; We shall not all sleep, but we shall all be changed, [52]In a moment, in the twinkling of an eye, at the last trump: for the trumpet shall sound, and the dead shall be raised incorruptible, and we shall be changed. [53]For this corruptible must put on incorruption, and this mortal must put on immortality. [54]So when this corruptible shall have put on incorruption, and this mortal shall have put on immortality, then

shall be brought to pass the saying that is written, Death is swallowed up in victory. _____ 1 Corinthians 15:51-54

You will find that the resurrection of which Paul speaks above is the same rapture that we are discussing now.

📂 Clouds and Air

Regarding "... shall be caught up in the clouds in the clouds, to meet the Lord in the air: and so shall we ever be with the Lord":

The clouds are symbolic of the born-again men. Clouds are formed by pure moisture that is evaporated from the water on earth and is lifted up to the sky from the ground. Taking this aspect of the cloud as the sign, the clouds signify those who are tainted by greed on earth, are purified by the Word and are lifted up to have eternal life in heaven. Therefore, when we are caught up in the clouds, it means that we are resurrected and have new life, as symbolized by the clouds. This is the real rapture from this world to the kingdom of God.

As to "meet the Lord in the air: and so shall we ever be with the Lord," the "air" also signifies our hearts. Satan has his seat in the heart of the fallen men so he is called the prince of the power of the air (Ephesians 2:2). When we receive Jesus as the Holy Spirit in this air, Satan, the former prince, gets driven out. From this time on, God never leaves us. That is, *Emmanuel* is fulfilled in us through Jesus.

Comfort One Another

Read verse 18.

Therefore comfort one another with these words. _____ 1 Thessalonians 4:18

Paul says to them who are spiritually dead not to sorrow and lose heart. Only those who do not believe in Jesus will heave a sigh of despair. We do not need to be grieved because Jesus will make us live by resurrecting us. Definitely, through Jesus, we will be changed into them who are alive and remain.

Epilogue

Basically, what Paul wants to say to us with these difficult words is very simple. He wants us, the believers to be comforted, because we have Jesus who definitely will save us by the resurrection.

I will paraphrase the following passage from 1 Thessalonians 4:13-18 according to the description I have provided to you. The resurrection is being born again and being saved.

13 "Brother, do not be ignorant about the dead, and sorrow not like the rest of men who have no hope.
14 (Sorrow not,) because, as we believe Jesus died and rose again, that through Jesus God will bring them alive with him, and
15 (Sorrow not,) because, I say to you as a man who has experienced the Word of the Lord, that we who are alive and remain at the coming of the Lord into us, were dead before. This means that we who are alive and remain (=born-again us) cannot precede we who sleep (=us who are not born again). So we should not be grieved because of being dead at the moment.
16 (Sorrow not,) because when we can hear the word of the Lord as a shout, voice, and the trumpet of God, we will be finally changed and the Lord will descend into us to be one with us. At that moment, our old self will first be crucified, that is, dying in Christ, and will rise first:
17 Then, we will be changed to "us who are alive and remain" (=born again us) from "we who are asleep" (=we who are not born again), meeting the Lord in our hearts as the Holy Spirit, and shall always be with the Lord.
18 Therefore, we have the hope of the resurrection through Jesus, comfort one another.

The whole Scripture tells us about our salvation and being born again. The current text about the resurrection and living surely shows the process in which we are born again from the flesh to spirit. Paul wishes us to be comforted by illustrating the details of the resurrection/being born again process, as above.

Sorrow not, but follow Jesus to the cross to attain the state, "you who are alive and remain!"

The Rich Man and Lazarus, Part I
– Resurrection of the Just and Unjust

Luke 16:19-26

There was a certain rich man, which was clothed in purple and fine linen, and fared sumptuously every day: [20]And there was a certain beggar named Lazarus, which was laid at his gate, full of sores, [21]And desiring to be fed with the crumbs which fell from the rich man's table: moreover the dogs came and licked his sores. [22]And it came to pass, that the beggar died, and was carried by the angels into Abraham's bosom: the rich man also died, and was buried; [23]And in hell he lift up his eyes, being in torments, and sees Abraham afar off, and Lazarus in his bosom. [24]And he cried and said, Father Abraham, have mercy on me, and send Lazarus, that he may dip the tip of his finger in water, and cool my tongue; for I am tormented in this flame. [25]But Abraham said, Son, remember that you in your lifetime received your good things, and likewise Lazarus evil things: but now he is comforted, and you are tormented. [26]And beside all this, between us and you there is a great gulf fixed: so that they which would pass from hence to you cannot; neither can they pass to us, that would come from there.

The basic argument about this passage is whether the story is a real situation or a parable. Some believers understand this story as a real physical description of the scene. They say that Jesus mentions the specific name of Lazarus; this is evidence that it is a real story. They interpret it as proof that the middle state *Hades* exists after death.

Others propose that He only cited the Egyptian myth, and thus it is a parable which does not exactly represent the situation that happens after death. They say that if people at Abraham's bosom can see the torment of people in hell (*Hades* in Greek), seeing their suffering is itself torment. How can such a cruel place be the kingdom of heaven?"

The truth is that the current story is a parable that reveals the spiritual world, as other words in Scripture do.

What does this story truly signify then? This story appears in the final part of Luke 16. Luke 16 begins with the story of an unjust steward under the law who learns of the gospel, but considers the gospel as only another law to obey; subsequently, the steward tries to outsmart the gospel through his actions. In each transaction, he attempts to show his own righteousness, but he neglects to follow the living God, who leads him in everyday life. The unjust steward is not praiseworthy, of course.

Luke 16 further describes the characteristics of those who have faith under the law. They, the Pharisees, are destined to be proud of what they do in front of men and God. However, God does not approve of what they do, because He knows they act to impress men, but neglect to hear the living God. So Jesus says to them, "You do those works because you want to be highly esteemed among men, and that attitude is an abomination in the sight of God."

In this context, the parable of the rich man and the beggar, Lazarus, also demonstrates those who believe under the law instead of believing in grace. The rich man, therefore, represents those who place their faith in the law as the Pharisees do; the beggar, Lazarus, represents those who place their faith in grace.

Let me explain the parable verse by verse.

Who Is the Rich Man? And Who is Lazarus?

We will consider verses 19-21 below.

There was a certain rich man, which was clothed in purple and fine linen, and fared sumptuously every day: [20]And there was a certain beggar named Lazarus, which was laid at his gate, full of sores, [21]And desiring to be fed with the crumbs which fell from the rich man's table: moreover the dogs came and licked his sores. _____ Luke 16:19-21

📁 A Rich Man

Here, the rich man does *not* necessarily indicate a man who earns a lot of money. Instead, the rich man is he who eagerly keeps the law by loving, helping others, praying and fasting, and so forth. These good works are stockpiled in his memory as valuable treasures.

Why are they treasures? It is because when he has them, he will feel satisfied on his own and people will praise and honor him. He can teach others or scold with confidence by saying, "Do as I did," or "Why don't you love others?" And he naturally despises and judges others who fall short of what he does.

For him, what he has done are precious possessions and treasures which lead others to respect him and allow him to justifiably rebuke others and choke them. That is, he can exercise lordship over others based on such possessions/treasures. Understanding this, he will gladly accumulate the treasure of good deeds by keeping the law diligently. He will even voluntarily go into poverty and forsake material possessions, because he knows he will earn the respect of others in return. Indeed, he will receive more than he gives. Why not do this? He who possesses the treasure of self-righteousness is the rich man, according to the Scripture.

Here is another rich man in Matthew 19.

A young man came to Jesus and said What good thing shall I do, that I may have eternal life? and Jesus said If you will enter into life, keep the commandments such as, You shall do no murder, You shall not commit adultery, You shall not steal, You shall not bear false witness, Honor your father and your mother, and You shall love your neighbor as yourself. The young man said to Jesus, All these things have I kept from my youth up: what lack I yet? Jesus said to him, If you will be perfect, go and sell that you have, and give to the poor, and you shall have treasure in heaven: and come and follow me. When the young man heard that saying, he went away sorrowful: for he had great possessions (Matthew 19:16-22, paraphrase mine).

The young man had great physical possessions. However, the word "possessions" has duplicate meaning; that is, one is natural and the other spiritual. Jesus was using, as always, possessions as spiritual meaning, which is the self-righteousness of the young man. As we can know from the dialogue he had great possessions of self-righteousness that came from keeping the laws of God. He had great possessions/treasures like "non-doings" of murder, adultery, stealing, and bearing false witness, and also "doings" of honoring father and mother and loving neighbor as himself. Jesus asked to sell those possessions for him to become the poor (in spirit). He can only sell such possessions by following Jesus to the cross. And if resurrected, he will be in heaven as his treasure and really can follow Jesus by living his life as a true disciple/apostle.

I just briefly explained above text. You can find in detail explanation in *Fresh Eyes to Read the Bible II*. As we can see in the Scripture, the rich and his possessions are not simply meant to say natural richness or physical possessions, but all spiritual. So the rich in the Scriptures signifies to those who have a lot of self-righteousness as their possessions.

A lot of believers think it is hard to understand why the outward acts of loving others, helping the poor, fasting and praying are not approved by God. God does not approve them because all their good deeds are hypocrisies that conceal inward violence and deceit in their hearts.

Just think, if we are sin-possessed, what "good" can we produce, except the "good" of sin? So, most of all, we have to follow Jesus to the cross to cleanse our inside first, which is sin-forgiveness process, then we will do good of God. Read the following verses from Matthew.

> Woe to you, scribes and Pharisees, hypocrites! for you make clean the outside of the cup and of the platter, but within they

are full of extortion and excess. ²⁶You blind Pharisee, cleanse first that which is within the cup and platter, that the outside of them may be clean also.　　　_____ Matthew 23:25-26

    All our good works are not complete if we do them without the sin-forgiveness of Jesus on the cross. And in that case, all our good works will serve as our precious possessions to exalt ourselves before men and God and to judge others who do not do such works. We are the rich in this case.

    We all, the believers, will think that we are freed from sin; that is, our sins are forgiven already. If we have this kind of false sin-forgiveness, we will justify our works for Jesus saying "We work for Jesus in church not to receive sin-forgiveness, but to show our gratitude for being forgiven already. Good. However, that is not the way the born-again express themselves. Because the saying of "to show our gratitude for being forgiven" shows explicitly that our old selves are "trading" with Jesus/God on give and take basis; that is, we take sin-forgiveness from Jesus and in return we work for Him. This is typical legalistic thoughts.

    Furthermore, sin-forgiveness is done only through Jesus, and Jesus is "a man." If we have not met this Jesus and are taken to the cross yet, we still remain in sin. And in this case, we must be gathering great possessions to be rich.

📁 A Beggar

    Another character appears in contrast to the rich man: he is Lazarus, a beggar. He is poor in spirit, imploring God for mercy and grace. The name "Lazarus" means "God helps." Lazarus represents those who are used up by the life of the rich man above, and have truly repented to follow Jesus, by forsaking all and denying himself, to the cross where the disciples met Jesus the first time. This concept will be described hereafter as "following Jesus to the cross."

    In contrast to the rich man who is busy stockpiling his self-righteousness, Lazarus concentrates all his heart on the Jesus he has met; the living Jesus who asks him to focus on following Him. And he will follow only Jesus at this stage. Lazarus represents the man who met "a man Jesus" in his life.

We should ponder on the differences between the rich man and Lazarus. Both of them are believers; the rich man believes for his own aim, that is, to live well in this world and go to heaven afterwards, but this kind of faith is not approved by God. Lazarus believes and obeys what Jesus says to him at the present time even if obeying Him would bring hunger, poverty, humiliation and even death. We should know that the rich man is not a believer in Jesus in a real sense, but Lazarus is.

When Lazarus follows Jesus, Lazarus' thinking and actions will be very different from those of the rich man. He does not lean on the multitude anymore, but leans on only Jesus, seeking His grace. Men such as Lazarus will not be welcomed by traditional believers in his society and will become outcasts sooner or later. Lazarus is such a man.

How about you? Have members of the traditional churches accused you of being different because you follow Jesus? If yes, your path may lead to Abraham's bosom.

What Situation Signifies

Lazarus ate the crumbs which fell from the rich man's table. He was full of sores and even the dogs came and licked his sores.

📁 Crumbs

What do the crumbs symbolize? Both the bread and the crumbs signify the Word, but here bread, or food, that the rich man takes is the law, and the crumbs that Lazarus takes represents the gospel.

The rich men eat their fill with good food: They read the Word through good Bible study materials and efficient training programs, studying abroad at famous theological schools, seminars and workshops with renowned scholars invited. And they have a lot of excellent opportunities to receive the Word, the food, appearing to fare sumptuously. Although they feast well, they have no eye to see the life hidden in the Word, so they only read the Scripture on the legalistic level; that is, they take it only as literal.

The Scripture will reveal, if we read it correctly with spiritual meaning, that we are sinners, and thus we will seek the grace of God to be saved from the sin. However, rich men do not have eyes to read the Scripture spiritually, so they fail, or refuse, to see the sinful status of their spirits.

Even though they fail to catch the hidden weightier meanings, they study and research very hard to understand the words of the Scriptures, which are the vessel to hold the spiritual meaning. The spiritual man benefits much from such studies of the rich men. For example, we are thankful for the brilliant works of the Bible dictionaries, various translations and exegeses of Scripture, archaeological studies about the Bible period, and all kinds of research and studies related to the Scripture. We cannot perform such tremendous works by ourselves, but benefit from those works.

This is what the scene of Lazarus taking the crumbs falling from the rich man's table signifies.

In practice, the today's Scripture could be passed down to us since the Pharisees and the scribes of the Jews desperately transcribed the text with all their elaborate efforts, religiously, from generation to generation. Thanks to their efforts, today we can have and read the words of God in our Christian faith.

However, we, the Christians, think that they are under the law and we are in grace, thinking that they only took the literal meaning of the Scripture, but we can know and read deeper. That is, we think we live by faith, but they live by deeds. In this sense, the Jews are the rich men; we are Lazarus, taking the crumbs falling from the Jews' table.

Nevertheless, you will understand by now that your reading, in principle, is not so much different from that of the Jews. Therefore, if you do not catch the weightier meaning of the Bible from now on, you will remain as the rich man you have been.

Anyway, this is the meaning of Lazarus who manages to live on the crumbs falling from the rich man's table. It seems that he is a miserable man, but he is the most blessed man in God.

📁 Sores and Dogs

Lazarus has sores. This means that he who follows the real Jesus will be attacked by those who are under the law and will suffer pains: They may be condemned and persecuted as an unlawful sect.

Let us look at the cases of the disciples, who, while following Jesus, were frequently under attack and accused by the Pharisees and the scribes because the disciples were different from them, doing unlawful activities which were prohibited according to their interpretation of the Scriptures.

For example, when Jesus went through the grain fields on the Sabbath, His disciples were hungry and picked some heads of grain and ate them. When the Pharisees saw this, they said, "Look! Your disciples are doing what is unlawful on the Sabbath" (Matthew 12:1-2).

And when some Pharisees and teachers of the law came to Jesus from Jerusalem and asked, "Why do your disciples break the tradition of the elders? They don't wash their hands before they eat" (Matthew 15:1-2).

And when John's disciples and the Pharisees were fasting, some people came and asked Jesus, "How is it that John's disciples and the disciples of the Pharisees are fasting, but yours are not" (Mark 2:18)? and so on.

All these accusations and condemnations are the thorns which prick Lazarus and cause sores, through which he is tormented in his heart.

"Dogs come and lick Lazarus' sores." The dogs are not the type of pet dogs on the leash. The dogs in this scene indicate those who do not know the gospel as Jesus said in Matthew 7:6, "Give not that which is holy to the dogs, neither cast you your pearls before swine, lest they trample them under their feet, and turn again and rend you."

The rich man is of this kind of dog.

"Licking" is the metaphor for the acts of comfort to relieve the pains. This scene means some of them, the dogs, may take temporary pity emotionally on Lazarus who is persecuted, and give some words of consolation. However, as they have no understanding of the gospel or of Lazarus at all, they cannot share his suffering or console his pain. Only Jesus will be his comfort and consolation.

Two Kinds of Resurrection

There are two kinds of resurrection in the Scripture.
Read verses 22-23.

And it came to pass, that the beggar died, and was carried by the angels into Abraham's bosom: the rich man also died, and was buried; [23]And in hell he lift up his eyes, being in torments, and sees Abraham afar off, and Lazarus in his bosom. _____
Luke 16:22-23

Both the rich man and Lazarus died and were resurrected, of which the spiritual meaning will now be described.

We all come to this world as the dead, the sinners. We are asleep in the grave. And we cannot even hear God or know if He exists. Under this circumstance, we may go to church and believe in Jesus in our own way. It has got to be our own way, because we have no communication with God. Therefore, we pursue our own benefit and self-righteousness by believing in Jesus. The rich man appearing in this parable represents those who believe in Jesus in such a way.

When we believe in Jesus as a rich man, when we are fully used up in such faith, we will have chance to truly repent and meet "a man Jesus" to follow Him to the cross. At this time we start to have true faith of Jesus. The faith that we had as a rich man is the shadow of the true faith to come which is revealed by Lazarus. We always tend to misunderstand the shadow faith as the true one. So I am explaining repetitively the differences between the two for you to aim and receive the true faith of Lazarus.

Let us discuss the resurrection of Lazarus, which is the true faith.

Lazarus' Resurrection

In Lazarus' case, he also was staying in the grave as a sinner. But he was fully desolate in his faith, unlike the rich man, and had truly repented. He met Jesus and had communication with God through Jesus. He followed Jesus and, as a result, his old self died on the cross, which is expressed in the text as: Lazarus died.

When his old self had died with Jesus, he was resurrected in Abraham's bosom in unity with Him. Where Abraham is, there is the kingdom of heaven (Matthew 8:11-12).

Like Lazarus, some believers around us whose old selves have died by the Word on the cross, are resurrected, and live in the kingdom of heaven with new life here. They truly are the born again men around us who have the Word in them. Try to find them, as they will do what Jesus will do to you.

Rich Man's Resurrection

The rich man also died and was raised. This is not natural death and resurrection. Like Lazarus, his death is a metaphor of death of the old self and resurrection to the new self. But all these are false assumptions.

Then, on what occasion did his old self die and was resurrected? He died when, he thought, he was saved and born again, because such expressions respectively mean "died and rose again"; the resurrection. Most probably that time would be the initial stage when he came to church and confessed with his mouth that Jesus was his Savior. As he thinks that he is already saved and resurrected, what he will probably do is work hard for better rewards after death. There is nothing much else he can do. Therefore, he gets to stockpile self-righteousness so he can be a rich man.

Here, however, he realizes that his resurrection has a problem, because he is resurrected into hell (Hades), feeling tormented. This means that he is not born again and saved correctly. What went wrong? The problem of the rich man is this: He went through the process of resurrection, which includes the experience of the cross, not in reality, but in his imagination only. That is, he did not follow Jesus to the cross in reality. And He received a false resurrection.

The rich man realized that he was in a Hades of torment. What this means is that he learned of the gospel and he knew that he was in the wrong when he believed in Jesus. However, he had not yet reached the point of true repentance at which he could follow Jesus to the cross, forsaking all. This parable reveals the mindset of the rich man. As he does not become desperate enough to follow Jesus to the cross in life, he tries to do other good things of his own to complement his disobedience. He has not yet come to his senses. Such characteristics will be made manifest as we go on.

🗀 Resurrection of the Just and Unjust

It is our general thinking that only the righteous Christians will be resurrected in the kingdom of heaven. But in fact, the unjust will also be resurrected like the rich man here. However, they will be still in Hades even after the resurrection. Then, you may say that the rich man is not resurrected. That is right. But since he insists that he is resurrected; i.e., saved and born again, the Scripture says that he is resurrected, but into Hades. This is the resurrection of the unjust.

Read the following passages.

> And shall come forth; they that have done good, to the resurrection of life; and they that have done evil, to the resurrection of damnation. _____ John 5:29

> And have hope toward God, which they themselves also allow, that there shall be a resurrection of the dead, both of the just and unjust. _____ Acts 24:15

Do not regard "doing good," stated in John above, as keeping the Lord's day holy, helping the poor, not committing adultery, or not stealing, as they have hidden weightier meanings. "Doing good" means following Jesus to the cross to crucify our old self. We who have fulfilled this course of action will come forth to the resurrection of life. This is "good doing" because we are following Jesus, the origin of good.

On the contrary, "doing evil" means, being led by our old self we believe in Jesus, not that we are lead by Jesus. In this case, we might do many various good works people might respect, but they are evil to the eyes of God. Even though we think we are doing good, we are doing evil. The rich man did this "evil work," and consequently came forth to the resurrection of damnation.

Which resurrection do you long for? The resurrection of the just and unjust will happen to us during our lifetimes. However, at the time of our natural death, our state at that instance will be final, be it eligible to the resurrection of the just or of the unjust. So long as we breathe we are given a chance to repent and follow Jesus to the cross to have the resurrection of the just. God is waiting for us to repent, and this is the longsuffering period of God, according to His mercy.

Romans 9:22 reads, "What if God, willing to show his wrath, and to make his power known, endured with much long-suffering the vessels of wrath fitted to destruction?"

Heaven Here, *Hades* Here

Consider the following verse 24.

And he cried and said, Father Abraham, have mercy on me, and send Lazarus, that he may dip the tip of his finger in water, and cool my tongue; for I am tormented in this flame. _____
Luke 16:24

We have found from the parable that death and resurrection do not mean the events that will happen after we are dead, but signify the spiritual things that happen while we are alive. Therefore, we can find in this world both Abraham's bosom where Lazarus has entered and Hades where the rich man is. That is, all these scenes describe the unseen spiritual world of ours; we who are living in this material world in the bodies. So they can see and meet each other if they want to.

Abraham's bosom, the kingdom of God, has come into the heart of Lazarus. The kingdom of God will be in us. Jesus says in Luke 17:20b-21, "The kingdom of God cometh not with observation: Neither shall they say, Lo here! or, lo there! for, behold, the kingdom of God is within you."

And Hades has come into the heart of the rich man. Accordingly, both types of the believers live together in this world and can see each other as the rich man and Lazarus do in the parable.

📂 State of Mind?

Not to digress too much, when I say that the kingdom of God and Hades is here, some people might wonder if I am referring to "state of mind stuff" that is taught and sought by Buddhist monks or other seekers. We must not forget that they try to achieve a peaceful state of mind through their own efforts, like mind control, meditation, fasting, yoga, self-pressing on, healing music, and so on. I guarantee that they will not achieve heaven through these efforts. It is only a kind of legalistic struggle to get out of sin, which will end in vain.

However, entering the kingdom of God is the result of Jesus casting out the devil from us, and having the Holy Spirit in us instead. This is the kingdom. And we may call the kingdom "the state of the spirit" to differentiate from "the state of mind," which is the concern of the mind controllers.

In this lifetime, if you are in the kingdom of God, you will be there eternally even if you die physically; and if you are in Hades now and die physically, you will be there eternally. Therefore, if you are keen to go to heaven in the afterlife, enter the kingdom of God in your lifetime, and you will be in heaven eternally even after your death. This is the only way you can guarantee that you go to heaven in the afterlife.

📂 Joy and Torment

They who are in the kingdom of God in this world live in love, joy, and peace because of unity with God. Paul describes this kingdom as follows:

> I know both how to be abased, and I know how to abound: every

> where and in all things I am instructed both to be full and to be hungry, both to abound and to suffer need. [13]I can do all things through Christ which strengthens me. _____ Philippians 4:12-13

Those who are in Hades are tormented in flame. The flame signifies the desires of this world. The heart that burns to satisfy the desire, or that burns because of failing to satisfy, is expressed as flame.

> Behold, they shall be as stubble; the fire shall burn them; they shall not deliver themselves from the power of the flame: there shall not be a coal to warm at, nor fire to sit before it. _____ Isaiah 47:14

The flame of Hades comes to those who have the faith of the rich man, who is not born again. The flame does not mean the hot bright burning gas we can see. They who are in Hades do not realize that they are in it. They guess that is a certain other place to which people will go to when they are dead, and swear that they would never go there. Those who are in Hades can never go there, because they are already there.

📂 Dip the Tip of Finger in Water

What the rich man in Hades can do is only admire the peace of Lazarus who dwells in the kingdom of God. When the rich man told Abraham to have mercy on him and send Lazarus to cool his tongue, it signifies that he entreats Abraham for a crumb of the peace of Lazarus. But it is not possible.

Good Things of Rich Man, Evil Things of Lazarus

Consider verse 25.

> But Abraham said, Son, remember that you in your lifetime received your good things, and likewise Lazarus evil things: but

now he is comforted, and you are tormented. _____ Luke 16:25

Upon first reading, it seems that the rich man is in torment in Hades because he only pursued his own wealth and did not help others. And Lazarus is comforted because he suffered from diseases and led a miserable life as a beggar. However, the Scripture is written to tell us of salvation of our spirits, not fairy tales or stories. If we read the Scripture in that way, Jesus also will say to us, "You do err, not knowing the Scriptures" (Matthew 22:29), as He said to the Sadducees who read literally.

Then, spiritually, what wrong did the rich man do that made him to go to Hades, and what good did Lazarus do that made him to go into Abraham's bosom?

🗁 Good Things the Rich Man Received

"Son, remember that you in your lifetime received your good things," says Abraham. Abraham calls the rich man a "son" (*teknon* in Greek), and the rich man calls Abraham "father." It shows that the rich man believes in God, believes in Jesus. Especially, the rich man represents a Christian who has exerted his utmost for God and has stored a lot of self-righteousness, considering the fact that he is rich.

From what Abraham says to the rich man, we can find the reason why he is tormented in Hades. Abraham does not give many reasons, but one reason is that he received his good things in his lifetime. Here, his lifetime represents the period during which he believed in Jesus. What kind of good thing did he receive? Did he used to play golf on Sunday instead of attend services? Or did he go to a dance club and drink in secret? No, not that kind.

His "good things" meant that he believed in Jesus according to his own righteousness, without following the living Jesus. This is the good thing that he received in his lifetime. Such faith leads him into Hades, because it is the faith made by his old self which should, above all things, have been destroyed on the cross.

📁 Evil Things Lazarus Received

Lazarus received evil things in his lifetime. The evil things he received represent the trials he underwent, following Jesus and denying himself, until his old self was destroyed on the cross. The things that happened during this period were evil to the eyes of his old self, his adversary, but good things to his new self.

We must meet Jesus and follow Him to the cross, not follow the trail of the rich man.

You can then believe as the living Jesus leads you, not as your old self leads. This is to believe in Him not as you please but as He pleases. And it means receiving evil things, which actually is following Jesus to the cross, in your lifetime. If you do not take evil things, you will be finally like the rich man. And when you are in torment and cry out to the Lord, He will say to you, "Son, you stopped your ears about what I had told you and believed in your own way, didn't you? You chose your good things then, so you are tormented now."

We cannot go to heaven unless we die. Likewise, in order to go to the sinless world we have to die united with Jesus on the cross. No cross, no resurrection.

📁 Tormented and Comforted

The rich man avoided the process in which his old self would be destroyed, and to complement such evasion, he worked very hard, performing self-righteous acts. However, he only succeeded in deceiving himself. And he is tormented in Hades now.

On the contrary, Lazarus is comforted. It is quite natural that he is comforted in the kingdom of God. However, also, he is comforted in the following sense. Lazarus followed Jesus to the cross, was resurrected and received the Holy Spirit. The Holy Spirit is the Comforter.

Read the following passage from the Gospel of John.

> But when the Comforter is come, whom I will send to you from the Father, even the Spirit of truth, which proceeds from the Father, he shall testify of me: _____ John 15:26

The term "Comforter" is translated from *parakletos* in Greek, which has the same essence of a word as *parakaleo* (to comfort). By receiving the Holy Spirit Lazarus is comforted in the kingdom, which is the real comfort.

A Great Gulf

Read verse 26.

> And beside all this, between us and you there is a great gulf fixed: so that they which would pass from hence to you cannot; neither can they pass to us, that would come from there. _____Luke 16:26

The rich man asks Abraham to send Lazarus to cool his tongue with water, but Abraham rejects his request for the following two reasons.

First, the rich man received his good things during his lifetime. He reaped what he sowed: He sowed tares and he reaped the same. Under this situation, he cannot reap even a single grain of wheat. It is like the light that has no darkness in it at all; reversely, the darkness cannot have a single point of light.

By nature, Lazarus' peace cannot be shared with the rich man at all. Even if the rich man is brought to Abraham's bosom at this moment, he cannot stand it due to the severe torment he feels in his person, not in the environment. In fact, that is why he chooses to stay in Hades now. To explain further this issue, think about the older son in the parable of the Lost Son in Luke 15. When the younger son returned home, the father celebrated his return. At seeing this, the older son was very angry based on his self-righteousness works saying to his father, "See, these many years do I serve you, neither transgressed I at any time your commandment: and yet you never gave me a kid..." Luke 15:29). It is torment for the older son to go in the house, so he remained outside even though his father came out and entreated him. The father's house signifies Abraham's bosom; outside of the house is Hades and the older son is the rich man. This is how the heaven and hell divides.

As such, the rich man cannot feel the relief of Abraham's bosom; that his torment is in his person, not in the environment. In order for the rich man to stay with Abraham, he should have the same heart with Abraham through Jesus.

In the text, Abraham is telling the truth even if he sounds as if he is cold-heart toward the rich man.

Second, there is a great gulf fixed between the rich man and Lazarus. It does not signify a geographical border between the kingdom and Hades, which are blocked from each other by sheer cliffs. But it means the gulf of thought between the carnal man and the spiritual man. In the previous section, "I Am the Resurrection and the Life," Jesus and Martha talk about the resurrection. Jesus talks about the resurrection of here and now, but Martha considers only the resurrection in the last days in the future. He explains it to her over and over again, but she cannot understand it, which shows the great unseen gulf between Jesus and Martha through which they cannot pass.

The rich man and Lazarus are living in the same world physically, but there is a great spiritual gulf between the two. The rich man cannot reach Lazarus even if he prays to God or begs Him.

The only solution for that the rich man is to be resurrected truly through the cross. After that, he can not only cool his tongue with a drop of water but he can also swim in the rivers of living water.

Until breathing our last, we still have an opportunity to make the resurrection of Lazarus ours.

Epilogue

Both the rich man and Lazarus represent those who call Abraham their fathers but one of them stays in Hades while the other is in the kingdom of God. Their locations are determined by what they did while believing in Jesus. The former made every effort to do good, except one thing; that is, following Jesus to the cross. Contrarily, Lazarus did only one good thing; that is, he followed Jesus, denying himself, to the cross, which is an evil thing at the same time to the eyes of the old self of Lazarus. You will know what you should do while believing in Jesus.

According to the spiritual arrangement, we, each of us, are destined to believe as the rich man at first. And when the time comes, we will believe, if chosen, as a "Lazarus" and will receive eternal life in Abraham's bosom. That is, we will start believe in Jesus as a Lazarus when the time comes; the time for us to truly repent to meet Jesus after spending a long time as a rich man under the law and so being used up. From this time on, if we follow Jesus to the end to the cross and are resurrected, we are a Lazarus. We are the "chosen" by God. But even though we meet the real Jesus, if we give up during the process of following Him to the cross for any reason whatever, we are "called but not chosen" and will die as a rich man who refused to follow the gospel even in front of Abraham. Read Matthew 22:14: "For many are called, but few are chosen."

You will surely hope for the faith of Lazarus. Meet and follow "a man Jesus" to the cross now, if you mean it. Then you will reap the resurrection of life in Abraham's bosom in your lifetime.

Let us meet there!

The Rich Man and Lazarus, Part II
– Crafty Old Self

Luke 16:27-31

Then he said, I pray you therefore, father, that you would send him to my father's house: [28]For I have five brothers; that he may testify to them, lest they also come into this place of torment. [29]Abraham said to him, They have Moses and the prophets; let them hear them. [30]And he said, No, father Abraham: but if one went to them from the dead, they will repent. [31]And he said to him, If they hear not Moses and the prophets, neither will they be persuaded, though one rose from the dead.

    Let us continue to look into the story of the Rich Man and Lazarus.

    In the previous message, I defined this rich man as the believer who has understood the gospel of Christ legalistically. However, he has not yet reached the point where he realizes that he has legalistic faith. So he does not truly repent to follow Jesus to the cross. Quite naturally, in the absence of true repentance, he would not wish to follow Jesus, but would do other good works of his own to complement his disobedience. He is the man who has not yet come to his true senses.

    We will see here his spiritual position between the law and grace and the craftiness of his old self to escape the cross. We should not be deceived by our old selves who play like this.

The Rich Man's Spiritual Position

The rich man in Hades feels sorry for his five brothers in his father's house. The rich man entreats his brothers' salvation. We are touched by his great tender heart to care about his brothers, even as he is himself in hell. But such a pretentious heart is only useful to deceive carnal believers and the people of this world.

Who are the five brothers, anyway? "Five" is symbolic of the law. The brothers of the rich man symbolize those believers under the law having same blood with him. Their father also signifies an instructor of the law known from having birthed legalistic sons. Their father represents legalistic preachers in church nowadays.

Differently from his brothers, however, the rich man stays in Hades while his brothers are living in the house. What does this mean? It relates to the matter of their recognition. The five brothers are also in Hades like the rich man but they have no idea of where they are. They, in their recognition, will not go into the Hades until they realize they are in the wrong in faith when they understand the gospel.

For example, in Scripture, the sinners are likened to the lepers. The lepers cannot feel pain even if their limbs are damaged. This is like the five brothers of the rich man. And if a leper feels pain and torment, his sense has come around, and he will want to see the doctor and live. This is the case of the believers who will be saved by Jesus. However, the rich man does not fall into this case. He feels torment, obviously, but it is not painful enough to follow the doctor—Jesus. Therefore, he tries to withstand such torment without leaning on the Savior, Jesus.

In this way, the five brothers are described as staying in a different place from that of the rich man. Refer to the following illustration for the spiritual locations of each of them.

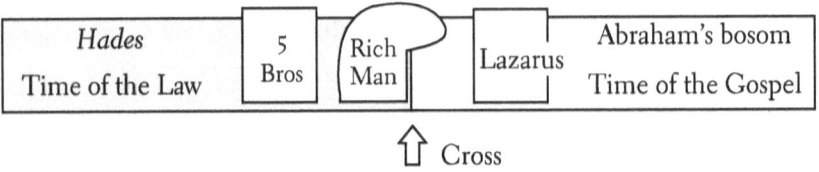

The rich man is in Hades, by realizing that his life as the believer was in great trouble, laboring and being heavy laden. This is because the gospel has revealed to him that He came forth to the resurrection of damnation (John 5:29). Even though he understood the true way to resurrection, he did not wish to follow Jesus to the cross. He understood what he should do, but his body did not want to move. This means he can somehow yet manage the torment. When he suffers further torment, he might give up and cry out to God, and truly repent to follow Jesus. I hope this true repentance would occur in his lifetime.

Compassion of the Rich Man

The rich man did not want his brothers in the house to come to the place of torment. He wished that his brothers would not have a faith like his; it actually meant that he wanted their salvation. He looks like a good man with a warm heart who is caring about his brothers, really, even in his torment. But he is not. Why?

He is in the place of torment. He is the man who really needs salvation. He should have prayed and followed Jesus to the cross first, and then he would have known what salvation is. However, he does not want that salvation, but says he is apprehensive for his brothers' salvation. The salvation that he does not want to have, but wants to give to the brothers: What kind of salvation is this? If he thinks that the salvation is so desperate to give his brothers is one he should have obtained first for himself, then what he says will make sense. He is a pure hypocrite.

The five brothers require salvation, not the useless humane compassion of the man in Hades. In fact, out of ignorance, he is going to ruin his brothers in terms of salvation. God loves the five brothers more than the rich man does. God takes care of them and already has allowed them to hear Moses and prophets as the best condition for their salvation, as Abraham said. However, the rich man wanted to break this best condition by sending them one risen from the dead. If that was better, God should already have done so. The rich man in Hades is demon-possessed and cannot see and cannot know the heart of Jesus and God, who are working for salvation.

Under this circumstance, no matter what good he does, it will hinder the salvation plan of God. He who is in Hades cannot help his brothers at all in terms of salvation. He is supposed to seek his salvation first to really help his brothers. That is what God wants. Likewise, we should be saved first, above all things, in order to be able to help save others.

Do you know why the rich man mentioned his brothers? For him, the torment was yet endurable. Therefore, he tried ease to show off that he was a man of good heart who cared about his brothers. He was a big hypocrite. He tried to get the good repute of men, not of God, even while he was in such torment.

We know some people who said they were very much impressed by the words of this book, and came to our church. However, they could not follow the Word to the cross, so in the middle of the process, they left our church. Yet, they told us that this message was the truth that all should hear and follow. Except for the cross, humans could have been born again a million times–whenever we wanted.

Subtle Complaints of the Rich Man

Let us consider verses 29-31.

Abraham said to him, They have Moses and the prophets; let them hear them. [30]And he said, No, father Abraham: but if one went to them from the dead, they will repent. [31]And he said to him, If they hear not Moses and the prophets, neither will they be persuaded, though one rose from the dead. _____ Luke 16:29-31

The rich man asked Abraham to send Lazarus, raised from death, to his brothers. It may mean that if someone rose from the dead to give witness of the heaven and hell he saw, people will believe and listen to him.

In fact, we sometimes hear someone talking about the experiences they have on a visit to the heaven: They tell us that they met the Lord there and report on the houses of the church members; the materials and sizes. They relay in real time that if a man pleases the Lord, his house will be enlarged in proportion and will be decorated with precious stones. Hearing this, many Christians repent and confirm their hope and faith about the heaven.

As said above, the witnesses of heaven and hell have great power and influence. We also think if God shows His power with miracles, unbelievers will believe. So we do not see any flaw in the request of the rich man to send Lazarus to them. Yes, definitely it will help, but only temporarily. It will not be the final solution to cause them to repent. For instance, the Jews who had seen the resurrection of the Lazarus of Bethany in John, far from believing in him, they planned to kill him (John 12:10). The repentance depends on the man himself, not on the good circumstances.

Nevertheless, in this story, Abraham speaks with the spiritual meaning of "one risen from the dead." That is, he considers "one risen from the dead" as "one whose old self is destroyed on the cross by following Jesus, and is resurrected like Lazarus." This is clear because he mentions "Moses and prophets," versus "one risen from the dead." Moses and the prophets signify the law; and "one risen from dead'" signifies the gospel. Abraham reveals the relationship between the law and gospel.

What the rich man is saying is, "My brothers have been taught by the law. However, they will react differently and repent if they are taught by the gospel, the one who rose from the dead."

This is the subtle way of the rich man expressing his complaints to God that he and his brothers were not given the gospel in the first place, so they could not repent properly.

Moreover, it seems that he has the wish to repent. Not at all. He has no intention of repenting at all. If he really wanted to humble himself and repent in front of God, he would have done so anytime, anywhere, regardless of whether he was facing Moses and prophets or the one risen from the dead. He does not really want to repent, so asks for the better circumstances which will never be sufficient in his eyes. And he is saying he wants repentance, but will die without repentance.

See here; even he is being tormented, he never repents and is hypocritical, pretending to care about his brothers and to wait for repentance. This is the works of his crafty old self, his adversary. If he loses to his adversary, he will die in sin.

Unfortunately, our thinking will not be much different from what the rich man thinks. When we meet and understand the gospel at last, we will regret our thinking, saying, "If only I had known the gospel earlier..." or "If Jesus had taught me directly, I would have already repented and been born again, and again."

We had better stop saying things like that; instead, just repent now.

Jesus comes to the man who repented after spending sufficient time under Moses and the prophets. If Jesus comes early to a man who is still under the process of the law, that man will despise Him. The gospel is not always good in man's eyes, compared to the law. The law and the gospel each have their own role in your salvation. Think about Jesus on earth. He came when the Jews had long been under the law. So God uses the current legalistic preachers in churches as they are, but for us, if we spent a goodly amount of time there, we must come out of it to receive the true resurrection.

If you desire to be the one who rose from the dead, you should fear God, love Him and obey Him with all your heart in your present condition. If you are real in your desire, God will send you one risen from the dead outright, and in your lifetime he will usher you into the kingdom where Lazarus dwells.

Epilogue

We have seen the substance of the compassion and the complaints of the rich man. These are the works of the crafty old self. The old self does so in order to escape the cross where he is supposed to be destroyed. For the old self, it would be natural to think of all kinds of deceptions in order to survive, but if he survives, you die instead. Wake up so as not to be deceived by your old self. Repent and follow Jesus to the cross.

Our faith initially begins with the faith of the five brothers and the rich man. And it is finally fulfilled in the faith of Lazarus. Lazarus signifies the man who is made free from the devil and has perfect communication with God. We need to have the faith of Lazarus, any way, in our lifetime.

Let us be wise to our old selves and be Lazarus!

SADDUCEES SAY, NO RESURRECTION!

Matthew 22:23-33

The same day came to him the Sadducees, which say that there is no resurrection, and asked him, [24]Saying, Master, Moses said, If a man die, having no children, his brother shall marry his wife, and raise up seed to his brother. [25]Now there were with us seven brothers: and the first, when he had married a wife, deceased, and, having no issue, left his wife to his brother: [26]Likewise the second also, and the third, to the seventh. [27]And last of all the woman died also. [28]Therefore in the resurrection whose wife shall she be of the seven? for they all had her. [29]Jesus answered and said to them, You do err, not knowing the scriptures, nor the power of God. [30]For in the resurrection they neither marry, nor are given in marriage, but are as the angels of God in heaven. [31]But as touching the resurrection of the dead, have you not read that which was spoken to you by God, saying, [32]I am the God of Abraham, and the God of Isaac, and the God of Jacob?   God is not the God of the dead, but of the living. [33]And when the multitude heard this, they were astonished at his doctrine.

When a man is dead, we can sometimes hear people pray that he might go to heaven where there are no sorrows and pains. That is, people pray for the dead person to end his torment in this world and resurrect into heaven. Likewise, we believe that when we die we would rise again to live with Jesus forever. In both cases, we expect to attain the good world of resurrection that comes after the death of our bodies.

However, a sorrowful spirit brings a sorrowful life. The life that such resurrection will bring is the continuation of our existing life, not a separate new and good one. It is because the physical death itself does not change the spirit, the substance of man. That is, the spirit abides in the body, and the spirit will leave the current body when we die. The current spirit will remain unchanged regardless of death. Therefore, even if we die and are resurrected without healing in the spirit, we will not see the world where there is no sorrow and pain. Nevertheless, we and the Jews think this kind of meaningless resurrection is the resurrection of the Scripture. We are mistaken at this point.

The resurrection the Scripture speaks about is the healing of our spirit through Jesus while we are alive, not the one that comes after death. Yes. God has given us the promise of resurrection so that we may have love, joy, and peace in the kingdom of God in our lifetime. Of course, when we have this resurrection while we are alive, we will be in the kingdom of God forever, even after death.

I will now describe the true meaning of the resurrection Jesus speaks about in His dialogue with the Sadducees who say that there is no resurrection.

The Meaning of Having the Wife of the Brother

The Sadducees are known as those who think there is no resurrection. We know this also through this passage in Acts: "For the Sadducees say that there is no resurrection, neither angel, nor spirit: but the Pharisees confess both" (Acts 23:8). The Sadducees deny the resurrection after men are dead. Differently from them, the Pharisees say there is resurrection. But in fact, both the Sadducees and the Pharisees have the same concept of the resurrection which refers to the life after death. Regarding the same nature of resurrection, one says there is none, and the other says there is. However, as said, the Scripture does not speak about such a meaningless resurrection as that which they argue about. The Scripture says the healing of the spirit in the present time is our resurrection, which Jesus teaches at the end of the text.

Anyway, the Sadducees did not believe in the resurrection because of many contradictions that might happen if they accept it. But as I explain, their question is based on their misunderstanding about the resurrection.

The Sadducees asked questions about the resurrection because they found conflicts with the levirate law handed down by Moses.

📁 Levirate

According to the law of Moses, when one of several married brothers dies having no children, a brother of the deceased will take the widow as his wife and attempt to have a son with her in his deceased brother's name (Deuteronomy 25:5-6). This was their practice in order to not let the name of the deceased brother fade out. The Sadducees asked Jesus about a hypothetical case in which seven brothers all had the wife, and all died without a child. They wondered which brother she would call husband in the afterlife, since she had married them all. We are very much anxious about it too. This anxiety shows that we have much the same mindset as the Sadducees.

It is not God's prime purpose in establishing the levirate law that Israelites should literally marry in that way. However, through levirate marriage, God wishes them to understand the spiritual marriage between God and His people. That is, Jesus is the bridegroom and we are brides. Jesus' coming to us has to be in order. The shadow, which is the law, comes first, and then comes the reality, which is Jesus.

The levirate law reveals to us the relationship between the law and grace. The law and grace both are of God, so they are brothers. We, the believers, are the women who are supposed to give birth to a child by receiving the word of Jesus, in order to be saved.

The law, which comes first, will not and cannot produce a child to us and the law dies. Here, "dies" means our true repentance whereby we, the believers, realize that we are unable, under the law, to birth a child with a dead mate. At that moment the other brother, the living one, or grace, should come in us to give us a child. When we have a child, the eternal life, we will be saved. This is what the levirate regulation reveals.

In fact, Jesus is in a difficult situation, because the Sadducees gave Him a non-sense question, which, nevertheless, was based on ignorance. However, Jesus takes this opportunity to explain the spiritual revelation in answer to such questions.

They Neither Marry, Nor Are Given in Marriage

Read the following verses.

> Jesus answered and said to them, You do err, not knowing the scriptures, nor the power of God. [30]For in the resurrection they neither marry, nor are given in marriage, but are as the angels of God in heaven. _____ Matthew 22:29-30

Jesus points out two errors they have made in response to their question: First, they are mistaken about the Scripture, and second, they are wrong about the power of God. I will mention their mistakes about the Scriptures first, then their mistakes regarding the power of God.

Now, regarding the mistakes about the Scripture, what did the Sadducees mistake? They erred in the following points: They did not catch the spiritual meaning of the levirate law as explained above, not to mention the resurrection. They only knew the literal interpretation of the levirate law and resurrection.

We who have the same misunderstanding as the Sadducees might think, "When we die, we will neither marry, nor are given in marriage, but are as the angels. We will have no gender." We are disappointed at the thought of not being able to have a physical sex life. However, we would be comforted by someone's saying, "Nevertheless, there would be full of other indescribable joys."

Basically, this kind of ludicrous thinking has the same background of the question of Sadducees; that is, "Therefore in the resurrection whose wife shall she be of the seven? For they all had her." In fact, they represent us in the Scripture. They are us.

Of course, we may be curious about what marriage will be like in heaven, but the Scripture is not meant for that. Basically, we should remember that Scripture and Jesus' sayings are *not* meant to solve our curiosities of the world, but to reveal the truth and to heal our spirits for salvation.

All Acts Are "Marry and Are Given in Marriage"

Jesus says, "For in the resurrection they neither marry, nor are given in marriage, but are as the angels of God in heaven."

What Jesus means is that "at the spiritual resurrection we will understand the true meaning of the resurrection and the levirate law, and will stop believing that Jesus is confined within the literal meaning of them."

The levirate law was given to the Israelites to reveal the truth of spiritual salvation. However, being blind, they could not understand the spiritual meaning of the said law. They believed in God by exercising this law literally; they were doing "(in literal sense) marry or are given in marriage" in response to the law of levirate. Therefore, when Jesus says, "The children of this world marry and are given in marriage" (Luke 20:34), it means they, the believers under the law, read "marriage" in the Scripture as "literal marriage" and implemented it.

Therefore, whatever they do in relation to the marriage of the Scripture, they are doing the act of "marry and are given in marriage." Actually, their act of questioning "whose wife shall she be?" itself is "they marry and are given in marriage."

I will explain further. They have legalistic eyes. When it comes to the word "food" in the Scripture, they will interpret it as, literally, the food to eat. Likewise, the "wine" as the wine to drink. In this way, they are in the world of literal meanings of "marry, eat and drink" in response to the Scripture. They are the children of this world who remain sinful and are condemned.

Read the following passage.

And as it was in the days of Noah, so shall it be also in the days of the Son of man. ²⁷They did eat, they drank, they married wives, they were given in marriage, until the day that Noah entered into the ark, and the flood came, and destroyed them all. ²⁸Likewise also as it was in the days of Lot; they did eat, they drank, they bought, they sold, they planted, they built; ²⁹But the same day that Lot went out of Sodom it rained fire and brimstone from heaven, and destroyed them all. ³⁰Even thus shall it be in the day when the Son of man is revealed. _____ Luke 17:26-30

What did they who were to be judged do when the flood came in the days of Noah? They ate, drank, married wives, and were given in marriage. Also, what were the Sodomites of the flesh doing before their destruction? They ate, drank, bought, sold, planted, and built (Matthew 24:37-39).

It is not that they were condemned because they physically did the above actions. We all have to eat and drink to survive. So nothing could be wrong with these actions.

However, these actions, such as eating, drinking, marrying, and building, in the Scripture are mentioned in relation to our salvation. So, their spiritual meaning will be eating of God's Word, drinking of Jesus' blood, marriage with Christ and building the kingdom of God in us. Then, what if we interpret them all as the things that are related to this material world literally and act accordingly? We will naturally die in sin, failing to be saved from the sinful world, because we neglected the correct meaning of Scripture.

This was the status of the people at the time of Noah and Lot, like the Sadducees here. If you also now read the Bible literally, it proves that you are a dead person.

📂 In the Resurrection

When we meet "a man Jesus," He will teach us how to read the Bible as He did to Sadducees as in above text. And at the time of resurrection after going through our own cross united with Jesus, we will stop reading levirate law as the method of literal marriage. Naturally, we will not be doing physical "marry or are given in marriage" with reference to the levirate law.

Jesus says "in the resurrection they neither marry, nor are given in marriage." Jesus is explaining the relationship between the law and grace during salvation by way of the levirate law.

📂 Angels in Heaven

Regarding the angels, the "angels of God in heaven" does not mean spiritual beings like the traditional angels. Here, the angels are those who are saved, resurrected and born again, being one with God through Jesus. They are the people of God who are in perfect obedience to Him, but they were previously devil-possessed, disobeying God. The angels are the born-again and those who are resurrected.

Regarding "in heaven," when we are born again, God comes into our hearts. In this instance, we, each of us, becomes the heaven where God abides, and at the same time becomes an angel. The born-again me is the angel and the heaven.

Resurrection – the Power of God

Read verses 31-32.

> But as touching the resurrection of the dead, have you not read that which was spoken to you by God, saying, ^{32}I am the God of Abraham, and the God of Isaac, and the God of Jacob? God is not the God of the dead, but of the living. _____ Matthew 22:31-32

After explaining their mistaken interpretation of Scripture, Jesus proceeds to explain how the Sadducees do not know the power of God.

The power of God, Jesus says, does not mean physical power which generates thunderstorms and earthquakes or does various miracles to heal the sick and to raise the dead. That will make all His creatures terrified and have them worship Him, which gods in other religions might do. However, the power of the real God is that which makes His creatures live through the sacrifice of Himself, the only begotten, on the cross. Only the real God will do this.

The power of God is to give life to us through Jesus on the cross and His resurrection thereafter. This, in one word, is the resurrection. The power of God is the resurrection.

God of Abraham–Isaac–Jacob

Touching on the resurrection, Jesus mentions the God of Abraham, Isaac, and Jacob. What relation do they have with the resurrection? Some people say that, to our eyes, Abraham, Isaac, and Jacob are dead, but in God's eyes they are resurrected and are living currently in heaven with God. However, this type of interpretation comes from the misunderstanding of the resurrection, which, they think, refers only to the life after death. However, the true resurrection should occur in our lifetime.

Jesus mentions the God of Abraham, Isaac, and Jacob because it is the resurrection process. When the dead man meets and follows the God of Abraham, the God of Isaac, and the God of Jacob progressively, he will become a resurrected living spirit. And now he is living.

I will explain how that is. Isaac and Jacob are the son and grandson of Abraham. These three generations figuratively refer to the stages of the progressive resurrection of Abraham, the figure of the believer. During this process, God will treat Abraham according to his level of growth; i.e., Abraham–Isaac–Jacob. And to the eyes of Abraham, God will look different at each of the three stages. It is one God, but three different Gods by each stage will appear to the eyes Abraham as he grows. We discussed this triune God in Part One of this book. The triune God by itself means to say the God who saves, or resurrects, men through Jesus Christ.

In our case, if we go through in the lead of God, the three growing stages of Abraham–Isaac–Jacob, at the stage of Jacob, we will be grown up (born again), saved and resurrected. This is why Jesus mentions the God of Abraham–Isaac–Jacob in relation to the resurrection.

Now we will see the characteristics of the God of Abraham–Isaac–

Jacob respectively.

Consider this passage from Romans.

> Moreover whom he did predestinate, them he also called: and whom he called, them he also justified: and whom he justified, them he also glorified. _____ Romans 8:30

Here above, the God of Abraham, the God of Isaac, and the God of Jacob represent God who calls us, justifies us, and glorifies us.

The God of Abraham Calls.

God called Abraham out of Ur of the Chaldees (Genesis 12:1) so that He might lead him into the land of Canaan. This signifies that God called us out of this sinful world so that He might lead us into the kingdom of God. According to providence of calling, we came to church, believed in Jesus, and joined the church activities. Up until now, we are meeting the God of Abraham.

When we have fully used up this level of faith, like the prodigal son in the far country, we will meet the God of Isaac, who corresponds to Jesus, at the next stage. Judging from the fact that we are reading this book at the moment, we are almost there.

The God of Isaac Justifies.

Even though Abraham left Ur, he made many mistakes in believing God, but God made him a man who offered Isaac, his only son, to God in the land of Moriah. The offering of Isaac was received by God. Thus, Abraham was justified (James 2:21). The God who made this development in the resurrection to Abraham is the God of Isaac.

The God of Isaac is Jesus. When we meet Jesus He will take us to the cross of Golgotha, which is represented here by Moriah. During this period, our old self will be destroyed together with Jesus on the cross. By this, He is offered as our sacrifice to God. If we offer Jesus to God in this manner, we will be justified, like Abraham who offered Isaac. As we can see, our offering of Jesus to God was made possible only by Jesus Himself, the God of Isaac.

The God of Jacob Glorifies.

When Abraham offered Isaac, Abraham did receive him back (Hebrews 11:19). This is the figure of the resurrection. Thus, the God of Jacob will come to work in our lives. Jacob walked with God all throughout his life. He is the father of the Israelites and his name is representative of all believers. God has glorified him. Such glory of Jacob is manifested through the life of Joseph in Genesis. Jacob is a type of man who is resurrected from the dead, having the Holy Spirit in him.

We will be meeting the God of Jacob when we offer Jesus on the cross and receive Him back as the Holy Spirit. By the Holy Spirit in us, we are glorified forever. The Holy Spirit is the God of Jacob.

A man will be resurrected when he has passed through the stages of the God of Abraham–Isaac–Jacob. Through those stages, God calls us, justifies us, and glorifies us. He makes us live by delivering up Jesus to the cross and having Him resurrected in us during the above process. This is the power of God and the resurrection of the dead. For this reason, Jesus mentioned the God of Abraham, the God of Isaac, and the God of Jacob while speaking about the power of God to resurrect us.

Both Jesus and the Sadducees use the same word, resurrection, but they are on a different page.

🗁 God is Not the God of the Dead, But of the Living

When Jesus said to the Sadducees that they mistook the power of God, He does not mean to say that God had the power to handle the case of one woman and seven husbands after their deaths. The Sadducees had no understanding of the resurrection through which God makes us live, but only stuck to the carnal resurrection.

The dead do not know God even though they read the Scripture. Also, God cannot communicate with the dead, nor can the dead with God, because they cannot hear God at all. Thus, God is not, and cannot, be the God of the dead, but of the living. Apparently, they are the ones who are dead, while Jesus is alive. Jesus says to the Sadducees, "You are the dead. That's why you raise such a question of this world, not hearing what God wants through the Scripture."

In order for the Sadducees to be the living, they have to meet the God of Abraham–Isaac–Jacob stage by stage and will be resurrected into the world of the living. Then God will be theirs too, as He is Jesus'.

Are you reading the Scriptures as Jesus reads, or like the Sadducees?

They Were Astonished

Read verse 33.

> And when the multitude heard this, they were astonished at his doctrine.   _____ Matthew 22:33

The Jews have been diligently searching the Scriptures throughout history, but all their knowledge is useful only to create a dead God. And when they come to hear carefully what Jesus says, they will be amazed by the gospel that reveals the truth.

This will be the same to us. We have been diligent in believing in Jesus for a long time, based on our interpretation of the Scriptures. However, if you meet "a man Jesus," you will also be shocked to know that you have read the Scripture literally up to now in the same manner as the Sadducees.

Be astonished, and seek the correct way of believing before it is too late.

By Any Means I Might Attain Unto the Resurrection

Finally, I wish to share one more truth about the resurrection of the afterlife. A lot of us still wish to believe that the resurrection will occur after life on earth is over. Such belief might be substantiated by the saying of Paul, "By any means I might attain unto the resurrection of the dead" (Philippians 3:11). When we read this verse, not knowing the resurrection and being born again are same, we think as follows:

"Paul, who is already born again, also wishes to attain unto the resurrection of the dead. There surely will be the resurrection of the dead after death, and Paul also eagerly wanted to be included in such a resurrection."

We are mistaken. Paul is already resurrected by being born again, and the resurrection that he wanted to attain is not his, but that of the dead, the church members. Paul struggled to take others to the resurrection, as he was led to it by Jesus. He is now doing what Jesus did.

When you are resurrected, you will be trying, naturally, for the rest of your life, to attain the resurrection of the others, the dead.

And this is the only way you can love your neighbor as yourself.

Epilogue

We can draw two conclusions from the question the Sadducees asked Jesus.

First, we read the Scriptures legalistically, like the Sadducees, at the initial stage of belief. And later we will find the hidden spiritual meaning through Jesus, if we are blessed to meet Him. Nevertheless, if we are satisfied with keeping the literal commandments of the Scriptures, we will remain to eat, drink, marry wives, and be given in marriage, like children of this world who are to be condemned. We should not stay under the law, but welcome grace.

Second, the resurrection is the power of God by which He gives us the Holy Spirit, the eternal life. And we can receive the Holy Spirit only if we follow the God of Abraham–Isaac–Jacob, the triune God.

Do not be so disappointed for not knowing the spiritual meaning of the Scriptures at first hand. It is the providence of God that we face the law, the legalistic meaning, first. If you understand and follow what is said here, then you are ready to meet the God of Isaac who will resurrect you.

After the resurrection, you will have perfect communication with God, and you will live to attain the resurrection of the others. That is the way for you to love your neighbors as yourself as Jesus did.

Have such beautiful life on account of Jesus!

Finishing the Book...

We have to have communication with God, but by the devil in me, that communication is perverted at all times, even up to this moment. When we meet "a man Jesus" we will be able to see the devil in us, our old selves. From that time on, there will be fights between Jesus and the me who is deceived by the devil. If we really repent and fear God at this point, we will follow Jesus to the cross, denying ourselves. If not, we will be on devil's side, refusing to follow Jesus, unwittingly, and forsake Him. In this case, we will die in sin.

Whether we wish to admit it or not, we must realize that we believed in Jesus with the devil in us. Therefore, the faith that we currently have can never be correct, but is perverted and legalistic. The time has come for believers to fulfill our existing legalistic faith by meeting "a man Jesus." Then we can receive all the good blessings that are promised in Jesus.

Paul the apostle says:

"I speak the truth in Christ–I am not lying, my conscience confirms it in the Holy Spirit–I have great sorrow and unceasing anguish in my heart. For I could wish that I myself were cursed and cut off from Christ for the sake of my brothers, those of my own race, the people of Israel. Theirs is the adoption as sons; theirs the divine glory, the covenants, the receiving of the law, the temple worship and the promises. Theirs are the patriarchs, and from them is traced the human ancestry of Christ, who is God over all, forever praised! Amen."
_____ Romans 9:1-5 NIV

All you readers may have seriously believed in Jesus for a very long time. As one of them, I believed in Him in the same condition. However, now, as the one who has met Jesus in my life, and as the one who became one with the Christ, I strongly desire to preach and share this Jesus to my brothers and sisters in Christ worldwide.

It is important to preach Jesus to the people who do know Him at any level; but more importantly, I am heartbroken about the brothers and sisters who are wandering at the gate of the truth.

I wish all of you in the Lord to meet "a man Jesus" as testified to in the correct meaning of the Scriptures, and eventually have the adoption, glory, and all the promises in Christ realized in you.

Grace and peace to you all.

Amen.

Published Titles:

Fresh Eyes to Read the Bible I: *Biblical Steps for Growing in Faith*
   This book presents the steps for growing in faith by considering the arrangement of the Bible's books. You will gain a very different but true perspective, to issues like Inheritance of Adam's Sin,' Parable of the Prodigal Son, End Times, Law and Grace, and so forth.
   ISBN: 978-89-953885-4-9

Fresh Eyes to Read the Bible I: *With Added Illustrations*
   Over 30 illustrations are added to *Fresh Eyes to Read the Bible I*. While the content remains unchanged, the illustrations are intended to enhance the reader's understanding of the unseen truth explained in the book. The illustrations would be beneficial, so this edition is recommended over the original edition above.
   ISBN: 978-89-953885-7-0

Fresh Eyes to Read the Bible II: *The Real Jesus*
   This Book lets the readers know that the true spiritual meaning of Scripture are quite different from the morals and ethics of the world, and will reveal the real Jesus, who we should meet here and now for our salvation.
   ISBN: 978-89-953885-5-6

Fresh Eyes to Read the Bible III: *Good, Evil, and the Resurrection*
   Scripture, if we read it correctly, introduces us to Jesus, a man whom we should meet for salvation. Jesus is not mere understanding or knowledge about Him in our brain. This book testifies about "a man Jesus" freshly by exploring the hidden meaning of the Scripture.
   It covers such subjects as communication with God, tithes and offerings, the origin of evil; the devil/Satan/demons, and the Word and resurrection correctly.
   ISBN: 978-89-953885-6-3

Simple Truth: *Illustrated Introductory Guide to Bible Truth*
   This book speaks about the underlying truth to understand Scripture correctly, with illustrations. It answers questions like, "Who are we?" "How are we born into this world?" "What should we live for?" by exploring the hidden meaning of the Scripture.
   This book can serve also as an introductory guide to the *Fresh Eyes to Read the Bible I, II & III*.
   ISBN: 978-89-953885-8-7

Forthcoming Titles:

Anchor of the Soul
    This book will introduce the living Jesus here and now whom we are missing unwittingly. Also this book explains the Lord's Prayer in depth with a fresh reading.

ADDITIONAL ORDERS

To order additional copies of this title, please contact one of the following distributors: Ingram, Spring Arbor, Amazon.com, Barnes & Noble or visit our web site at www.haggaibooks.com or www.fass.kr.

www.ingramcontent.com/pod-product-compliance
Lightning Source LLC
Chambersburg PA
CBHW021801220426
43662CB00006B/139